THE JAPANESE AMERICAN EXPERIENCE: CHANGE AND CONTINUITY

THE JAPANESE AMERICAN EXPERIENCE: CHANGE AND CONTINUITY

MINORU YANAGIHASHI

LIBERTY HILL PUBLISHING

Liberty Hill Publishing
2301 Lucien Way #415
Maitland, FL 32751
407.339.4217
www.libertyhillpublishing.com

Due to the changing nature of the Internet, if there are any web addresses, links, or URLs included in this manuscript, these may have been altered and may no longer be accessible. The views and opinions shared in this book belong solely to the author and do not necessarily reflect those of the publisher. The publisher therefore disclaims responsibility for the views or opinions expressed within the work.

Unless otherwise indicated, Scripture quotations taken from New Life Version (NLV). Copyright © 1969 by Christian Literature International.

Paperback ISBN-13: 978-1-66285-318-0
Ebook ISBN-13: 978-1-66285-319-7

DEDICATION:

To Yukiko "Susie" Propst (1926-2015), maker of Japanese dolls and supporter of Japanese cultural development

CONTENTS

PREFACE

The book has its genesis through two presentations sponsored by the Southern Arizona Japanese Cultural Coalition. The first, "Japanese Americans in Hawai'i," was given on November 3, 2016, and featured a slideshow and panel discussion. The second, "Japanese American Internment Camps in Arizona," was given on April 11, 2018, and was a slide presentation. A paper was written for each event, and these two unpublished papers became the basis for the subject matter of the book.

I am a Nisei (second-generation Japanese American), born and raised in Honolulu, Hawai'i. My perspective derives from living through World War II and experiencing Hawai'i becoming the fiftieth state. The principal focus is on my Nisei generation, with emphasis on the Hawai'i Nisei because of my background and interest.

"Nisei" is a Japanese word, but it is also a word adopted into the English language. The term refers to children of Japanese immigrants in countries in North America and South America. In this book, the focus is only on the second-generation Japanese Americans.

Yet when most people use the word "Nisei," they're talking about a specific time frame, starting with Japanese Americans of the 1920s; then to those who entered the mainstream prior to, during, and after World War II; and finally those who were part of the Japanese community up until the end of the twentieth century.[1]

---

[1] My use of the term "Nisei" applies only to those whose ancestors came from Japan in the early twentieth century up to 1924 when immigration was stopped. A small number of Japanese have settled in America since World War II and their children, although Nisei, are not the subject of this book. Therefore, my definition of Nisei is limited to those born in the early decades of the twentieth century up to the beginning of the war. Those Nisei born in the postwar era are not included in my definition.

It is these Nisei who have been accorded a recognition not given to any other second-generation immigrant group. There is no singling-out of the second generation of Chinese, Korean, Filipino, or any other ethnic group. Although the story of the Nisei has been adequately covered, their experience had to be fully linked with the past and its legacy for future generations explored. The Nisei generation, as defined in this book, are in their eighties and nineties and will soon pass from the scene. However, printed materials, recorded interviews, letters, and memorabilia remain to tell their stories. All aspects of their experiences need to be shared.

The Nisei are the children of the Issei (first-generation), the emigrants who left Japan for Hawai'i and the mainland (continental) United States. By being born in the United States or its territories, the Nisei are American citizens, a path to citizenship provided by the Fourteenth Amendment of the US Constitution. The Issei, on the other hand, were aliens and ineligible for citizenship, could not vote or hold public office, and, until the 1950s, were prohibited by various state alien land laws from owning property. However, it was at this time they were finally accorded the right to become citizens by the McCarran-Walter Act of 1952. The Issei quietly accepted their role in the lower strata of American society, but the Nisei were unwilling to accept a subordinate role.

What happens when these emigrants decide to settle in their adopted country? This question becomes increasingly complex with the second-generation. There are certain terms used frequently in discussions about cultural change or its continuity: acculturation, assimilation, Americanization, and ethnic identity.[2] Here we are concerned with how these words are used to specifically describe how the Japanese responded to change.

The words acculturation and assimilation are sometimes used interchangeably, but they are distinctly different processes. Acculturation and assimilation occur when two cultures come into sustained contact. In acculturation where the American culture was dominant, the minority Japanese accepted and adapted American middle-class norms and culture. The

---

[2] See Eileen H. Tamura, *Americanization, Acculturation, and Ethnic Identity: The Nisei Generation in Hawai'i* (Urbana, IL: University of Illinois Press, 1994).

early Japanese in Hawai'i were considered temporary workers and weren't expected to be integrated, but once they settled, acculturation picked up. The Japanese language was spoken less, western clothes were worn, and certain customs weren't practiced. Still, they were able to retain their language, values, food, and family traditions. Japanese clothing was worn at home and at special occasions, Japanese food was the daily fare, and traditional cultural events and celebrations were observed.

Assimilation, on the other hand, is the process where the Japanese are absorbed into the dominant American culture. They not only take on American cultural traits, but the structure of their community is affected by changes occurring in economic and social relationships: for example, living and working in suburbia, joining service clubs, and being part of the increasing number of intermarriages. Sometimes, the term Americanization is used in place of assimilation, having gained prominence during World War I and been in use ever since. The proponents of Americanization insist the Japanese Americans speak English, eliminate vestiges of Japanese culture, become Christian, and profess their loyalty to the United States. The goal of assimilation and Americanization is cultural homogeneity and uniformity. But in the case of the Japanese Americans, total assimilation or Americanization was difficult to attain for the Japanese held on to their culture, albeit in modified form.

Finally, ethnic identity is how an individual associates, identifies, and has psychological attachment to an ethnic group. Even with all the changes, a Japanese American can have a sense of attachment to traditional Japanese cultural markers. Ethnic identity is important for members of a minority group and for the younger generations, as it gives them a sense of belonging and identification. Acculturation and assimilation are processes, while ethnic identity is what emerges with individuals identifying and taking on traditional cultural traits.

One generation makes a big difference. The assimilation of the Nisei took place gradually as they were being Americanized to a large degree. The story of the Nisei begins in the 1920s when they came of age and extends into the second decade of the twenty-first century. It took nearly a century of continuous struggle to achieve any semblance of complete assimilation. The brunt of the hardships, prejudices, and persecutions was borne by the pioneering Issei. Because of these painful experiences, the Issei and Nisei, especially the Issei, were reluctant to share their stories, so little was known of their experiences for several decades. They preferred not to be reminded of their bitter pasts—the harsh treatment they had suffered at the hands of Americans. It took the Sansei (third-generation Japanese Americans), with firm support from the younger Nisei, to point out the blatant racism and discrimination endured by the Issei and Nisei and to move to correct the injustices.

As the stories were told and researched, it soon became apparent that the accomplishments of the Nisei were remarkable. They had left lasting legacies for future generations. To paraphrase Tom Brokaw, in terms of ethnic assimilation, the Nisei were "the greatest generation."[3]

Interest in the Japanese Americans has been part and parcel of the growing interest in Japan, its people, and culture. As a result of World War II, a sizable number of Americans were trained in the Japanese language and many served in the American occupation of Japan. Some Americans developed a keen interest in Japan and decided to study and research Japanese history, society, and culture. Consequently, works on Japan expanded widely to where there was heighten interest.

But more to the point, a growing interest in the *Nikkei* (all persons of Japanese descent) arose from a change in the political and social climate in America.[4] The civil rights movement of the 1960s resulted in ethnic groups, including Chicanos, Puerto Ricans, Native Americans, Pacific Islanders, and Asian Americans expressing their grievances and demanding their rights. Each ethnic group was proud of its culture and heritage. Pressure

---

[3] The title of the book by Tom Brokaw. It is about the generation that, like the Nisei, experienced the hardship of the Great Depression and fought and lived through World War II. Tom Brokaw, *The Greatest Generation* (New York: Random House, 1998).

[4] In this book, *Nikkei* (person of Japanese ancestry) is used interchangeably with "Japanese." For *Nikkei* living in the United States, the term "Japanese Americans" refers to the second and succeeding generations, who were born in the United States. The Japanese living in the continental United States are refer to as mainland Nisei or mainland Japanese and those in Hawai'i are Hawai'i Nisei or Hawai'i Japanese. The acronym AJA, which stands for Americans of Japanese Ancestry, is not used.

was placed to establish ethnic studies in colleges and universities, and the department of Asian American Studies was founded on several campuses.

It didn't take long for the Sansei to become cognizant of their Japanese heritage and to want to learn more about their "roots." They wanted to know why and how their ancestors came to America and how they overcame prejudice and persecution, particularly how they endured the confinement in concentration camps and the infringement and denial of their civil rights during World War II. Out of these concerns arose a movement led largely by the Sansei to seek redress for the injustices.

About the same time, *Nikkei* began to share their stories about the internment. Several *Nikkei*-conceived projects were initiated, including the recording of oral history, collection of camp poetry and photographs, and the exhibition of internees' art works. Although many *Nikkei* had already died without telling their stories, sufficient data was collected, and, with the publication in recent years of several internment camp accounts, a comprehensive picture of internment life emerged.

Chapters 1-4 cover the beginning of immigration, providing a snapshot of the acculturation and assimilation processes, principally in Hawai'i, and how the Nisei settled down and held on to their traditions. The story of the *Nikkei* starts in Hawai'i with their first arrival. Hawai'i served as a stepping-stone for those Japanese emigrants moving on to the West Coast. It is only later, starting in the 1900s, that emigrants went directly from Japan to the mainland. Therefore, Hawai'i is where the early emigrants had their first massive contact with a foreign culture, and what generally transpired in Hawai'i also occurred on the mainland. Nevertheless, there were differences in the reactions faced by the Japanese emigrants on the mainland when compared with what the Hawai'i Japanese experienced. As a result, the assimilation of Hawai'i Japanese did differ in some degree to what occurred on the mainland. With these contrasts in mind, the beginning chapters cover the assimilation of the Hawai'i Japanese and ends with their wartime experience.

What the mainland Japanese endured during World War II was distinctly different, so chapters 5-7 are devoted to the internment camp experience occurring at this time. Of the ten internment camps, the two camps in Arizona are examined. These two camps serve as an archetype of all the camps, for they were all located in a similar environment—desolate, isolated, and dusty desert sites—the only exception being two camps in swampy and humid Arkansas. Moreover, the housing is the same military barrack-type construction, and all camp policies came from the War Relocation Authority or WRA. Internees' accounts of the Arizona camps are strikingly similar to those held in other camps. Of course, there are variations in individual experiences but overall, the similarities are remarkable. Therefore, what happened in the Arizona internment camps, generally speaking, happened in the other camps.

The final three chapters cover the decades after World War II, with the resettlement of the internees and the movement to correct the injustices. However, the major theme is the continuity of Japanese culture—how cultural traditions and values are maintained or modified during assimilation. An associated challenge is that of ethnic identity—what it is to be a Japanese American. There is a shift in gear to that of observer-participant, as two local organizations in Arizona are examined for their role in cultural development. Japanese families and these two organizations perpetuated and transmitted traditional practices, even though in toned-down fashion.

This writing is my personal view of the Nisei generation. There are books on the history of the Nisei and sociological studies. Rather than doing a comprehensive examination, a daunting task to be sure, I have taken three big slices of the Nisei narrative —from the early migration up to World War II in Hawai'i; the internment camps in Arizona; and the postwar developments in Hawai'i and on the mainland. Hawai'i and Arizona are disparate milieus—but afford broader perspectives of the Nisei experience. The aim is to show clearly what transpired in Hawai'i and on the mainland. It is my hope the reader will be able to understand and appreciate the struggles and accomplishments of the Nisei.

Since this book is for the general reader, a few comments on the use of Japanese and Hawaiian words are necessary. Japanese and Hawaiian words are italicized except for place names, personal names, and words that have been accepted into the English language and are listed in Merriam-Webster's Collegiate Dictionary, Eleventh Edition. Such words as Nisei, Issei, origami, judo, haole, and lei are not italicized. Singular and plural are not distinguished in Japanese and Hawaiian, so the English plural "s" is not used. Nisei could mean a single Nisei or several Nisei. However, for Hawaiian words treated as English words, such as haole and lei, common usage allows the plural "s" to be used. The diacritical mark known as 'okina (glottal stop) is shown as ('); it is used because its omission could change the meaning of the Hawaiian word. The macron, a diacritical mark placed above a vowel as an aid to proper pronunciation by indicating a stressed and elongated vowel, has been omitted from Japanese and Hawaiian words. A glossary of Japanese and Hawaiian words is provided at the back of the book.

ACKNOWLEDGMENTS

Over the years, I gathered information from individuals through informal and formal interviews, casual conversations and discussions, and from their writings. Several individuals were participants in the events described but some had passed away. The contributors cannot be thanked individually, but mention needs to be made of a recent contribution. I am indebted to Austin K. Yamada for sharing his father's letter and for providing additional information about the conditions at Poston.

It was not meant to be this way, but my family offered their assistance in putting together the book. My son Mark helped with the images and with computer questions. My daughter Lisa read the entire first draft and made numerous corrections, enhancing the readability of the text. My partner Evelyn provided inputs and patiently endured the book's long gestation. To all, a profound *mahalo* (thanks).

PART ONE

IMMIGRATION AND ASSIMILATION

CHAPTER ONE

THE BEGINNING (1868–1924)

On May 17, 1868, *Scioto*, a passenger ship, departed Yokohama with 148 contract laborers, of which six were women. They were indentured workers who had signed contracts to work on the sugarcane plantations in Hawai'i for three years. Sugarcane grows in a tropical or subtropical climate and requires an extensive tract of land, while its cultivation and harvesting requires a large labor force. It is strenuous, labor-intensive work. Sugar, known as "white gold," was the crop that required the importation of laborers to the Hawaiian Islands and to the Americas. In fact, slavery was introduced to the Americas in the 1600s to work on producing sugar, and this was considerably before the introduction of commercialized cotton and tobacco. The strong demand for sugar propelled the shameful use of slave and indentured labor. But there is a clear difference between the complete subjugation of the slaves and the voluntary servitude of the indentured workers; in reality, however, both toiled under similar conditions. Critics have characterized the indentured laborers in Hawai'i as "virtual slaves" because their lives were severely restricted and controlled.

They were called *Gannenmono* (first-year people) in Japanese, for they arrived in Honolulu on June 19, 1868, the first year of Emperor Meiji's reign. In those days, it took about one month to travel from Japan to Hawai'i. The laborers were quartered in the lower steerage of the ship, and the crowded decks were hot, noisy, and smelly. Why would anyone want to take such

3

an arduous trip, traveling over four thousand miles to a land with strange people, custom, and language? What were the reasons for this exodus?

The emigrants left for economic reasons. Facing poverty and overall poor economic conditions, many were willing to take the risk; probably a more compelling motivation was the hope of finding a better life. Even if the economic conditions weren't too onerous, the dream, or the possibility of a better existence, drove these emigrants forward. They were willing to risk it all for an ideal. If the dream is big enough, overcoming obstacles is possible. Even today, the dream of a better life drives people from countries in Central America and Africa to migrate. Moreover, the escape from violence and even death has been a major reason to migrate. But the emigrants from Japan were not trying to escape persecution or violence—for them, it was purely for economic reasons and the possibility of a better life.

Eugene Van Reed, a Dutch American merchant, was the Kingdom of Hawai'i's consul in Japan. He acted as a recruiting agent for the kingdom and offered laborers a pay of four dollars per month, with ship passage, food, and housing provided by the sugar plantations. Reed made it sound glamorous and enticing and was able to find workers in the Tokyo and Yokohama areas.[5]

Unfortunately, these urban dwellers had no farming skills and were unaccustomed to living in a rural setting. Soon after arriving in Hawai'i, they found the plantation work strenuous and living conditions intolerable. A misunderstanding about their pay and other complaints arose, and finally about fifty men and four women gave up and returned to Japan. Another forty men decided to move to the mainland and only fifty were left in Hawai'i. The first attempt to bring indentured laborers had ended in failure. No efforts were made to bring contract workers from Japan for another seventeen years.

---

[5] Information on the early Japanese emigrants in Hawai'i presented in this chapter came from the following sources: Yukiko Kimura, *Issei: Japanese Immigrants in Hawai'i* (Honolulu: University of Hawai'i Press, 1988); Paul R. Spickard, *Japanese Americans: The Formation and Transformations of an Ethnic Group* (New York: Twayne Publishers, 1996); Dennis M. Ogawa, *Kodomo No Tame Ni (For the Sake of the Children): The Japanese American Experience in Hawai'i* (Honolulu: University of Hawai'i Press, 1978); Gary Y. Okihiro, *Cane Fires: The Anti-Japanese Movement in Hawai'i, 1865-1945* (Philadelphia: Temple University Press, 1991).

For its part, the Japanese government had its own self-interest in mind when it initially allowed for migration. The government hoped the remittance from workers abroad would help the national treasury by earning foreign exchange. This would help reduce the foreign debts incurred in the drive to modernize Japan. The Japanese government was displeased when the initial effort failed and believed the Japanese laborers had been mistreated. Consequently, the Japanese government stopped further emigration to Hawai'i, but in reality, the Japanese government was not overly concerned about the welfare of the workers; rather the Meiji leaders were anxious about how Japan was seen throughout the world and concerned about the prestige of the nation. They had learned how the Chinese laborers were mistreated, and how this reflected back to the weakness of the Chinese government. Japan didn't want the same thing happening to its workers, for it would reflect badly on Japan. One of the chief concerns of Meiji foreign policy, which became an obsession with the leadership, was the projection of Japan as a modern and great power that was to be treated with respect.

The failure of the first attempt didn't bode well for the sugar plantations. The plantations had expanded, and there was a need for more laborers—it was a desperate situation. The Native Hawaiians were of no help, as they were not inclined toward heavy labor in the fields, and preferred working for themselves and not for money, thereby subsisting off the land. Moreover, a large portion of the Hawaiian population was decimated by smallpox, measles, and venereal diseases brought by foreigners.

Among Asians, the Chinese were the first to arrive in the 1850s, and they were also the first to leave the plantations when their contracts ended in the 1870s. Many of them saved enough money to return to China, but others remained in Hawai'i and opened small businesses—such as grocery stores, bakeries, tailor shops, and restaurants. Others became farmers, growing taro or rice. A large contingent moved to the mainland and this had dire consequences, causing virulent, anti-Chinese racism to erupt especially in California. The whites blamed the Chinese for taking jobs away, lowering wages, and accused them of resisting assimilation and forming

Chinese enclaves. As a result of pressures from the white communities, Congress passed the Chinese Exclusion Act of 1882, effectively barring further Chinese immigration for more than sixty years.

No longer able to hire Chinese laborers, the plantations began to look again to Japan for workers. They established contacts in the southwestern prefectures of Japan, especially in Hiroshima, Yamaguchi, Kumamoto, Fukuoka, and Wakayama. When King David Kalakaua was on his state visit to Japan in 1881, he met with Emperor Meiji, and a labor agreement was proposed. King Kalakaua was interested in aligning with Japan as a foil against increasing white domination in Hawai'i. He proposed a marriage between his niece, the Princess Ka'iulani, and Prince Yamashina, but it was unsuccessful. Prince Yamashina was in the collateral branch of the imperial family, therefore, he was not in a direct line of descent. The Japanese government was cautious about protecting its image, and it took another four years before the Meiji government finally decided to lift its ban on immigration to Hawai'i in 1885.

On February 8, 1885, the steamship, *City of Tokio*, arrived in Honolulu with 945 *Kanyaku Imin* (government-sponsored indentured laborers). There were 199 women onboard, and this was significant because it differed from the Chinese example of exclusively male groupings. They had signed three-year contracts with wages of nine dollars per month, in addition to food and lodging. Historians consider this the beginning of Japanese immigration to Hawai'i, for it was the initiation of sustained immigration, formally recognized by a treaty between the Kingdom of Hawai'i and Japan—the Hawaiian-Japanese Labor Convention of 1886. The Japanese government was careful in its approach, protecting its interest by stipulating the inclusion of Japanese interpreters and physicians for the Japanese laborers. The treaty was negotiated by Robert Walker Irwin, an American businessman who was appointed by King Kalakaua to be the Hawaiian Minister to Japan. Irwin had a shipping business and decided to reside permanently in Japan. He was also the first American to legally wed a Japanese woman, Iki Irwin. Irwin's six biracial children, highly unusual at the time, faced continual racial prejudice.

Irwin developed a close relationship with Kaoru Inoue, Minister of Foreign Affairs, a senior statesman of the Meiji government, and this friendship helped in the successful negotiation. He followed through by accompanying the first group to Hawai'i; four months later, a second group of 983 government contract laborers arrived in Honolulu. The treaty itself was formally signed on January 28, 1886 and lasted until June 1894. By that time, 29,339 government contract laborers had arrived in twenty-six boatloads. With the end of the treaty, government-sponsored immigration was immediately replaced by private immigration. The companies taking over the role played by government in immigration was known as *imingaisha* (private emigration companies), and they handled immigration from 1894 until it was ended with the signing of the Gentlemen's Agreement of 1907. It is estimated about fifty-seven thousand Japanese arrived in Hawai'i during this period of private immigration.

In contrast to the *Gannenmono*, the *Kanyaku Imin* weren't city folks but were farmers from the southwestern prefectures who were accustomed to working in the fields. They were ambitious and dreamed of making enough money to return to Japan wealthy, respected, and ready to enjoy the good life. The practice of working temporarily away from one's native village or town is known as "sojourn" in English, while the individual is known as a "sojourner." In Japanese, it is called *dekasegi* and the worker *dekaseginin*. The practice of *dekasegi* was common in rural Japan in late nineteenth century, the early stages of industrialization, as many peasants temporarily left their villages to work in rapidly expanding towns and cities. Although the emigrants were like sojourners and intended to return to Japan, many of them found it difficult to save enough money to pay the transportation cost. They simply didn't have the money and had to forgo their dream of returning.

In the ensuing fifteen years from the arrival of the *City of Tokio* to the turn of the century, over 85,400 laborers, mostly single men, came to Hawai'i and the mainland. Although some returned to Japan, the majority, around sixty-one thousand, remained in Hawai'i.[6] This is a huge number, given the total population of Hawai'i was around 154,000 at that time. These men were frustrated at not being able to fulfill their dreams of returning to Japan, but soon they realized Hawai'i was their permanent home and afforded them a better life than what they could hope for in Japan. They didn't lack ambition, and they were better prepared, having a higher level of schooling than that of any immigrant group. The Meiji government had imposed a compulsory public education system in 1872. As a result, the Japanese immigrants had a relatively high level of literacy, a level not seen in any other ethnic groups.

By 1900, approximately 40 percent of the total population of Hawai'i were Japanese, and they were the main labor force on the plantations. What caused this massive stream of Japanese workers, who were mostly farmers, to leave their country for a distant land? Again, the root cause was economics and the desire for a better life. The time was opportune to migrate, as the rural areas of Japan were suffering severe depression due to the implementation of the deflationary fiscal policy of Finance Minister Masayoshi Matsukata beginning in 1881. The agrarian sector was hit hardest by the combination of falling agricultural prices and increased taxation.

Until the late 1880s, taxes on farm production accounted for over 70 percent of the total national income. Between 1883 and 1890, nearly 368,000 farmers lost their farms for failure to pay taxes, and many lost their holdings through mortgage foreclosures.[7] Japan was modernizing rapidly, and the burden of the Meiji government's modernization program was placed on the backs of the farmers. To escape poverty, many were ready to migrate, and the Japanese government began to look at immigration as a safety valve to relieve the pressure of economic discontent.

Besides the large number of emigrants from the southwestern prefectures, workers were recruited from Okinawa as well. It was a logical place

---

[6] Paul R. Spickard, *Japanese Americans: The Formation and Transformations of an Ethnic Group* (New York: Twayne Publishers, 1996), 162-63.

[7] Steven J. Ericson, "Matsukata Fiscal Policy," in *Kodansha Encyclopedia of Japan*, vol. 5 (Tokyo: Kodansha, 1983), 133-34.

to look for laborers. The tropical climate of Okinawa is similar to Hawai'i, and the workers were already familiar with working in the field in warm climate. Moreover, the economic conditions were just as bad, if not worst, than that of mainland Japan. Many peasants lost their land because of the heavy tax burden; in several cases, it was twice that of a comparable prefecture in Japan proper. Consequently, peasant riots occurred in the 1880s against tax practices. Overall, the standards of living in Okinawa was lower than in mainland Japan, and it was getting worse. Okinawan officials finally sought relief through overseas emigration, and the first group of twenty-six Okinawans arrived in Hawai'i on January 8, 1900. By mid-1920s, some 26,500 had emigrated. Of these, 10,119 went to Hawai'i and the rest to Brazil and Peru.[8]

The heavy demand for sugar, particularly from the West Coast, made sugar production a profitable business. The plantations expanded rapidly, necessitating the importation of thousands of workers. This system of plantations resulted, in part, from the Great Mahele (division of land) that took place in 1848 during the reign of Kamehameha III (1825-54). The Hawaiians had no concept of private property rights—no private land ownership existed at the time. Under pressure from the foreigners, the king divided the land in Hawai'i among the monarchy, government (chiefs and governing officials), and common people, but the commoners had to put in their property claims. Sadly, many did not and they lost their opportunity to own land. A couple of years later, foreigners were allowed land ownership, and the white businessmen took advantage of the situation and bought about two-thirds of government lands, while also taking over the unclaimed land. It didn't take long for the foreigners to own large tracts of land they could use for commercial purposes. This was the beginning of the plantation system.

---

[8] Robert K. Sakai and Mitsugu Sakihara, "Okinawa," in *Kodansha Encyclopedia of Japan*, vol. 6 (Tokyo: Kodansha, 1983), 87.

Plantation workers cutting sugarcane.
Courtesy of Densho.

The white businessmen and plantation owners led the movement to overthrow the Hawaiian monarchy in 1893. They systematically subordinated the Native Hawaiians and took over control of the economy and the government. Five years later, they supported the move to have the islands annexed by the United States, making Hawai'i a US territory. The plantation owners wanted to be under American rule so Hawaiian sugar wouldn't be subject to tariffs. Furthermore, a pretext given for the annexation was the supposed threat of Japanese domination of the islands, as evidenced by the large Japanese population. Annexation, it was argued, would prevent a takeover by the Japanese, but the push to be part of the United States had some unintended consequences. In conjunction with annexation, Congress passed the Organic Act of 1900, which invalidated all contract labor, thereby inadvertently ending indenture labor and freeing Japanese workers from their contracts.

When Hawai'i became a US territory, it came under the US Constitution. Congress considered indentured contracts to be akin to slavery, and, hence, in violation of the Fourteenth Amendment of the Constitution. Accordingly, Japanese workers were free to move out of the plantation, and those with enough money saved began to return to Japan. But over forty thousand decided to move to the West Coast where economic opportunities were better. These emigrants moving from Hawai'i to the mainland were known as "transmigrants."

The influx of transmigrants from Hawai'i to the West Coast caused anti-Japanese sentiments to erupt, similar to what the Chinese experienced in the 1880s. Whites with nativist views resented the Japanese because they looked different, spoke a different language, had strange customs, and tended to live in separate communities. Labor unions and elected officials led the anti-Japanese movement. According to their xenophobic arguments, the Japanese were threatening their economic position and lowering their standard of living, being called "unassimilable." Moreover, Japan's military success, especially its victory in the Russo-Japanese War of 1904-05, gave rise to fear of a "yellow peril"—a racial metaphor that falsely represents East Asians as a political or military threat to the Western world. The Japanese were going to "invade" the West Coast, as rumors and false information about the Japanese were spread by the Japan Exclusion League, a nativist organization.

Racism became an international issue. In 1906, the San Francisco school board segregated Japanese students in the public schools, causing an international crisis. This action branded Japanese Americans as undesirable, and the Japanese government, being sensitive to racial discrimination, vehemently objected and said it was an affront to the national honor of Japan. President Theodore Roosevelt intervened and persuaded the school board to rescind its segregation policy. In return, Roosevelt promised to halt Japanese emigration. He issued an executive order in 1907, ending transmigration of Japanese aliens from Hawai'i to the mainland and negotiated the Gentlemen's Agreement of 1907, which effectively limited further immigration from Japan. United States promised not to enact discriminatory legislation against the Japanese. In return, the Japanese government pledged to stop the flow of laborers to the United States, allowing only merchants, ministers, tourists, and students to visit. Only those Japanese emigrants already admitted to the United States were allowed to bring their spouses, children, and close relatives.[9] Therefore, Japanese plantation workers were no longer able to leave for work on the West Coast as the Japanese government tightened its immigration policy, stopping the flow of male workers from Japan.

Early on, the emigrants who came to Hawai'i were overwhelmingly men; the ratio of men to women was seven to one. Of those who were married, only a few wives went along while most stayed in Japan, expecting their husbands to return after their sojourn. The Meiji government's decision to allow women to migrate resulted in immigrant societies that were different from the exclusively male societies of the Chinese and Filipino immigrants. The ratio of men to women was gradually lowered to five to one, for it was assumed by the Japanese government that inclusion of more women would result in stable communities of Japanese laborers.

Japanese women workers. Courtesy of Densho.

---

[9] Greg Robinson, *A Tragedy of Democracy: Japanese Confinement in North America* (New York: Columbia University Press, 2009), 13-14.

Japanese worker with stripped canes.
Courtesy of Densho.

The Organic Act of 1900, by abolishing the contract labor system, made it possible for Japanese men to marry Japanese women. In those days, interracial marriages were unthinkable. Seven years later, the Gentlemen's Agreement opened the way to bring in wives, children, and near relatives. Therefore, the desire to start families began to spread among the men. From the standpoint of the plantation owners, it made sense to have families, for it would lead to permanent settlement and improve productivity and morale. With the encouragement of the owners, a movement was started to bring over wives, children, and close relatives: thus, many families were formed by *yobiyose* (summoned emigrants). Emigrants had to pay their own passage expenses but were under no contract and could choose whatever occupation they wanted. This period, from 1908 to 1924, is referred to as *yobiyose* jidai (summoned emigrants period), which significantly increased the Japanese population in Hawai'i and on the mainland. It is estimated that between sixty to seventy thousand Japanese arrived at this time, and many Japanese families can trace their beginning to this period of *yobiyose*.

As a youngster, my father came to Hawai'i with his parents because of such summoning, arriving in Honolulu on August 31, 1908, while my mother, as a child, came on similar summoning with her family on September 3, 1905. My paternal grandfather came over as a skilled worker; he was a tinsmith, an occupation that no longer exists. Tinsmith worked and repaired things made of sheet metal, items such as kitchen sinks, counters, basins, vents, and tubs. Gradually, tinsmith work transitioned into plumbing because many of the finished products were for the kitchen and bathroom. When my father took over grandfather's business, the letterhead proudly announced the business as "sanitary plumber and tinsmith," but it was mostly plumbing with tinsmith as a sideline. Many immigrants coming over in the *yobiyose* phase had some skills and avoided plantation and other agricultural labor.

To recapitulate, changes in the emigration pattern had an impact on the number and characteristics of the emigrants arriving in Hawai'i and on the mainland. In the first phase, from 1885 to 1894, there were 8,325 government-sponsored emigrants, of which 81 percent were men and 19 percent were women. The next phase had an increase in the number of women, but the majority were still men; this migration, dating from 1894 to 1907, was handled by private companies. The third and final phase included family members and relatives, and several women. It began in 1908 and ended in 1924 with the cessation of all Asian immigration to the United States. These emigrants were no longer contract laborers but many had skills, and they came on their own initiative.

In the *yobiyose jidai* phase, there was an unusual group called *shashin hanayome* (picture brides). Although the ratio of men to women had narrowed, there was still a shortage of women. Japanese men working in Hawai'i or on the mainland wishing to get married needed to return to Japan to find a bride through the traditional practice of *miai* (meeting to discuss an arranged marriage). But few had saved enough money for the trip, so a way had to be found whereby marriage could take place without the physical presence of the groom. The solution was to use a *nakodo* (go-between) to facilitate the negotiation between the families without input from the prospective bride and groom. Information about the families would be exchanged as well as photographs of the bridal couple. In those days, a traditional arranged marriage with the use of *nakodo* was common but the use of photographs was a new innovation.

Marriage was based on the collective decision of the families and was a union of two families. It wasn't for the individuals concerned and love wasn't a factor.[10] Once the respective families agreed to the marriage arrangement, the bride's name was entered into the husband's family registry, and the marriage was considered official in Japan. The bride was eligible for a passport and could travel to Hawai'i or the mainland to meet her husband. However, this type of marriage was illegal in the United States. When the picture brides arrived in Honolulu, mass wedding ceremonies had to be held at the dockside or in nearby hotels to make the marriages legal. It made for a chaotic scene.

Why did the women become picture brides? Why did they get married to someone living in a distant foreign country, based on limited information and photographs? One reason was economics. Many came from poor families who had hopes for financial prosperity so they could send remittances back home to help their households. Since the marriages were arranged, the brides felt they couldn't go against the wishes of their families. There was the pressure to fulfill family obligations, and this sense of obligation was powerful in Japanese society.

---

[10] Arranged marriages continue in Japan, although it has significantly decreased. Today, the wishes of the couple are respected.

15

Arrival of picture brides.
Courtesy of Densho.

Photographs can be deceiving, for what you see is often not what you get. As the ship arrived, the scene at the dockside was filled with confused men and women, armed with photographs, frantically trying to find their mates. It was, in most cases, a traumatic and disappointing experience.

My grandmother-in-law was a picture bride. She received several photographs of a handsome man regally sitting on a horse, attired in a nice business suit and looking quite wealthy. She was shocked when she met her husband at the dockside. He was shorter than her and he looked much older, with a wrinkled, sun-burnt face. She later found the horse and the suit were borrowed, and he was definitely not wealthy! A few ladies were so shaken, they went back to the ship and returned to Japan. But the majority resolutely stuck it out. Further disappointment was in store when the brides saw their living quarters. The shacks were not what they were accustomed to in Japan. Nevertheless, most of the women stayed with their husbands, even though some were later abused. The Japanese behavioral norm of *gaman* (bear or endure) enabled the women to persevere and made the unbearable at least bearable. Women, for example, learned to patiently tolerate the inconveniences of the moment in order to keep the family together. *Gaman* fitted in with the traditional role of the subservient women and was a rationale, a psychological mechanism allowing individuals to stoically endure the suffering, downplay the pain, and move on.

A total of 14,276 picture brides arrived in Hawai'i from 1907 to 1923 and, during a comparable period, over 10,000 made it to the West Coast. The arrival of picture brides ended with the passage of the Immigration Act of 1924. The complexion of the Japanese population changed dramatically with the narrowing of the ratio of men to women. Before the Gentlemen's Agreement of 1907, the percentage of Japanese women admitted into Hawai'i, compared to Japanese men, was 13.3 percent, but after the Gentlemen's Agreement, the percentage of women admitted increased to 58.4 percent. There were nearly five Japanese men for every Japanese woman in 1900, but by 1920, the ratio of Japanese men to women dropped to about 1.6 to 1.

Women were more than housewives, working together with men in the sugarcane fields. The women did most of what the men did: working on irrigation, weeding, stripping leaves off cane stalk, and loading the cut canes to be taken to the mills. The men wore *ahina* (denim cloth) jackets and pants to protect against scratches by the serrated edges of the sugarcane stalks and insect bites. Bandannas were used to protect against the sun. The women copied the men's clothing and wore long sleeve *palaka* (light weight denim) jackets with a checkered blue and white pattern and *hakama* (trousers) made of denim. They wore large straw hats, with kerchiefs extending to the top of the hat for protection against the sun. For women, field work was in addition to the chores of cooking, washing, and taking care of the children.

With the formation of stable families, the Japanese population in Hawai'i grew dramatically. About 180,000 Japanese arrived in Hawai'i between 1885 and 1924. Although over 20 percent (36,000 plus) left for the mainland or returned to Japan, high birth and low mortality rates made for a sudden increase in the Japanese population. By the 1920s, 43 percent of the total population of Hawai'i were *Nikkei*. They became the largest ethnic group in Hawai'i, and this was the peak of the Japanese population in the prewar period.

Such spectacular population growth drew adverse reaction—anti-Japanese and nativist sentiments erupted. In Hawai'i, the West Coast, and throughout the United States, there was a real fear of a Japanese take over in certain areas. Partly in reaction, Congress passed the Immigration Act of 1924, effectively ending all immigration of Asians into the United States. No longer could Japanese nationals be admitted, thus ending the immigration of the Japanese. The era of Japanese immigration and population growth ended abruptly.

CHAPTER TWO

SETTLEMENT AND ASSIMILATION (1924–1941)

T he Immigration Act of 1924, which ended the migration of Japanese to Hawai'i and the mainland, is sometimes mistakenly called the Japanese Exclusion Act of 1924. The Immigration Act of 1924 didn't specifically name the Japanese but barred all aliens not eligible for citizenship from migrating to the United States. Since the Japanese migrant workers were aliens, the entry of new Issei was denied and with no Issei arriving, the emergence of the Nisei became important. The Nisei steadily made up a larger portion of the Japanese population. In 1900, the Nisei comprised 8 percent of the *Nikkei* population; it was 25 percent by 1910; by 1920, it reached 45 percent. Therefore, the 1920s is the beginning of the Nisei generation. From this time on, the number of Nisei was of paramount importance; any noticeable rise in the overall Japanese population was due to the birth rate, not migration. Moreover, the Nisei were increasingly a major part of the workforce and were potential voters.

Prior to 1920, the increase in the Japanese population was rather dramatic, but after 1920 it stabilized. According to the census of 1920, the *Nikkei* population in Hawai'i and on the mainland was 220,122; it increased to 277,940 in 1930, and to 284,731 in 1940, an average increase of 3,230 per year. In 1920, the Japanese were concentrated in Hawai'i (109,274)

19

and the West Coast (93,490), with California having the largest number (71,952), followed by Washington (17,387), and Oregon (4,151).[11]

Besides the stabilization of the *Nikkei* population, the census figures showed another important feature—the difference in the spatial distribution of the Japanese. The Hawai'i Japanese were concentrated because of the islands' limited space, but the mainland Japanese were widely scattered, extending from Washington near the Canadian border to areas in California close to the Mexican border. This spatial distribution affected the processes of acculturation and assimilation.

Geographical factors played a role in the employment opportunities. Initially, the Issei in Hawai'i were plantation laborers, but after the contract system was abolished, many *Nikkei* left the plantations and moved to Honolulu and other towns as others moved to the mainland. Once outside the confines of the plantations, Issei went into domestic and personal services jobs, such as maids, waitresses, waiters, and gardeners. Others became fishermen or farmers and a few opened their own small-scale businesses. Even though they pursued these various occupations, the Hawai'i Japanese were never far apart from each other.

On the mainland, the economic opportunities were greater but were widely dispersed. After transmigration from Hawai'i ended, Japanese went directly from Japan to Angel Island in San Francisco Bay, which was the principal immigration station on the West Coast, comparable to New York's Ellis Island on the East Coast. It is estimated about one hundred thousand Japanese came through Angel Island. The Japanese workers' jobs were scattered; some worked in lumbering in Washington and Oregon and others in the canneries of Washington and California. Those working on the railroad or in mining had to go further into the interior, some going as far as Colorado.

The workers were young, single men who were mobile and could go to distant and remote places, engaging in various types of work. By the 1920s, many of the men had married and settled down, beginning to raise families.

---

[11] Spickard, *Japanese Americans*, 162.

In the western states, agricultural land was abundant, but California Alien Land Law prohibited land ownership by aliens. The Issei got around this law by placing land ownership under the name of their children, who were American citizens. Therefore, many were able to acquire land and became owners and managers of truck farms.

PLANTATION AND LABOR RELATIONS

The uniqueness of the plantation system made the situation in Hawai'i quite different. In the early 1900s, there were over seventy sugarcane plantations. It was a multiracial environment with the Japanese being the largest group, comprising 80 percent of the workforce. The plantation owners segregated the racial groups into separate living quarters, which differed from plantation to plantation. It began with dilapidated shacks, which were replaced by row houses or long bunkhouses, serving as communal sleeping quarters with partitioned sections for families. Everyone slept on the wood floor or on bunk beds. At night, no talking was allowed after lights were turned off. They couldn't leave the plantation without permission. For diversion and relief from the oppressive surroundings, workers resorted to alcohol, drugs, and gambling. Some laborers took more drastic steps by deserting from work, but they were usually captured and punished.

In their respective camps, the Japanese, Chinese, Koreans, and Filipinos were allowed to use their native language, to socialize among themselves, and to have their native foods. For the Japanese, meals meant a simple diet of rice as the staple, with protein derived from dried and broiled fish and from *tofu* (soybean curd) and *aburage* (fried tofu). It was mostly a vegetarian diet, heavily made up of *tsukemono* (pickled vegetables) and *daikon* (Japanese radish)—food that required little refrigeration. Therefore, within each ethnic camp, the workers were allowed to have their familiar diet. But by having closed ethnic camps, the plantation owners hindered assimilation and instead unwittingly fostered ethnic solidarity. The Japanese camp developed as a close-knit unit, wherein the Japanese were allowed to promote and maintain their values, culture, and customs.

At the same time, the Japanese had to work with other racial groups and had to communicate with them. Consequently, a unique working dialect was developed. When foreigners first came to Hawai'i, pidgin Hawaiian was developed for communication between English-speaking foreigners and Native Hawaiians. As different emigrant groups arrived, pidgin English developed—a hybrid language with a mixture of English, Hawaiian, Japanese, and other languages, and with a simplified grammar and reduced vocabulary. It evolved into a language of the local people, what linguists call Hawai'i Creole English; a lingua franca enabling the Japanese to communicate with other groups. By bringing people together, it helped the assimilation process but at the same time, the segregated quarters slowed acculturation and allowed the ethnic camps to maintain their distinctive cultures. The twin processes of assimilation and continuity were at work in the camps.

Plantation agriculture had its workforce organized along lines of racial hierarchy. The managers and administrative staff were haole (Caucasian). On the field, the top official was the *luna* (overseer or foreman), who was usually a haole, often a Portuguese ("Portagee" in pidgin).[12] The plantation heads not only wanted Caucasians as managers and supervisors but strove to balance the labor force with white workers. For the owners, too many Asian laborers meant the possibility of trouble. Therefore, European workers were hired, but most of the European workers, such as Scots, Spaniards, and Russians, worked for only a short duration and usually left for the mainland. The Portuguese were the exception, most coming with their families and settling in Hawai'i.

They blended in nicely, hence in 1878, the Kingdom of Hawai'i and the plantation owners sought to hire more Portuguese and succeeded in recruiting an additional thirteen thousand Portuguese from the Portugal-owned islands of Azores and Madeira. When the owners selected a Portuguese as *luna*, it was obviously based on race, for the Portuguese had

---

12 *Luna* and haole are Hawaiian words. Haole means Caucasian or white person. In this book, it refers specifically to European Americans. Portuguese, Puerto Ricans, and Spaniards are Caucasian but are often not considered haole because they were brought in to work on the plantations.

little background in agricultural work. In fact, they came from a seafaring background and were seamen or fishermen.

The Asian laborers—Japanese, Chinese, Koreans, and, at the bottom, the Filipinos, the last emigrant group to arrive—had little possibility of advancement. Their activities were closely monitored. They were paid low wages semi-monthly, and their purchases were limited to what was offered by the company store. This type of paternalism is described by Merle Travis's popular song "Sixteen Tons" with the familiar refrain—"I owe my soul to the company store."[13] The workers were totally dependent on the company store. Such dependence made the workers a mere "number." Each worker was given a *bango* (Japanese word for number), which was a number on a small metal tag worn around the neck. The *bango* was used because the *luna* couldn't pronounce or remember Japanese names.[14]

The work in the sugarcane field was backbreaking. Workers were up at 4:00 a.m. and in the field by 6:00 a.m., working ten hours a day, six days a week. The *luna* kept a firm grip on them and, at times, were abusive, riding around on horses with whips in hand. Housing was of poor quality and medical care was deficient. There are few recorded testimonies and documentation about the dire conditions of the plantations, but one important source is the *holehole bushi* (immigrant workers' songs). *Hole* in Hawaiian means to strip the dry leaves, as in sugarcane leaves being stripped off the stalk. The men usually cut the cane, and the women stripped the dry leaves. *Bushi* is Japanese for "melody" or "tune."

The *holehole bushi* used the melody of Japanese folk songs and the lyrics came from the immigrants. The plantation owners allowed the Japanese workers to sing while working, for it lessened the tedious nature of the work and helped increase productivity. These songs describe the immigrants' hopes, dreams, trials, and disappointments, and the pathos expressed are quite touching. According to Dr. Franklin Odo, retired professor of the

---

[13] The lyrics by Travis is in numerous recordings but the most famous is by Tennessee Ernie Ford. Musixmatch. com.

[14] The *bango* was important to get paid. The pidgin English expression *huli bango* (no work, no pay) literally means to turn in your ID number so you'll get paid. *Huli* in Hawaiian means to "turn over."

University of Hawai'i at Manoa and former director of the Smithsonian Asian Pacific American Center, *holehole bushi* "reveal nuances of life and love, labor and lust among Japanese immigrants in relatively unvarnished and gritty detail."[15] Especially poignant were the songs sung by the women workers.

Two contract periods have gone by.
We are still here.
Destined to become fertilizer
For sugarcane.

My husband cuts the cane stalks.
And I strip their leaves.
With sweat and tears we both work
For our means.

Shall I go to America?
Or shall I go home to Japan?
I'm lost in thoughts
Here in Hawai'i.

If I work at *holehole,*
All I'll earn is thirty-five cents.
If I sleep with a Chinaman,
I'll make one dollar![16]

The *holehole bushi* was saved from extinction by Nisei musician and teacher, Harry Minoru Urata. He preserved and taught the songs to students and, most importantly, he interviewed Issei and recorded the songs.

---

[15] Franklin S. Odo. *Voices from the Canefields: Folksongs from Japanese Immigrant Workers in Hawai'i* (New York: Oxford University Press, 2013), xi.

[16] Tamura, *Americanization*, 14.

As a result, we are able to feel and understand the pathos, emotions, and reactions of early immigrant workers.

In the period from the 1920s up to World War II, the Hawai'i Japanese played an insignificant and subordinate role. The Issei couldn't vote, hold office, or work for the government, and the Nisei were too young to be involved with politics. During this period, a few well-established haole families, some dating back to the early missionaries, dominated the political and socioeconomic arenas of Hawai'i. These haole business elites were euphemistically called the "Big Five," a haole oligarchy comprised of five corporations—Alexander and Baldwin, C. Brewer & Co., Castle and Cooke (Dole), Theo. H. Davies & Co., and American Factors (Amfac). They originated from the sugar industry but expanded into the pineapple industry, banking, insurance, utilities, shipping, warehousing, and transportation. This consortium controlled the prewar economy and was the "movers and shakers" of Hawaiian society.

Only in labor relations were the Hawai'i Japanese able to have significant impact. At first, Japanese workers reacted to harsh conditions by resorting to individual action, engaging in arson or assaulting the *luna*. A more common tactic was work slowdown, but it was by their collective actions that the Japanese workers seriously affected the sugar industry. They were the dominant ethnic labor group in the agricultural industries from the early 1900s to the 1930s, so their collective actions had consequences. In the resulting bitter struggles, the Japanese in Hawai'i helped to alleviate the brutal working conditions by direct confrontations—resorting to labor strikes.

With the enactment of the Organic Act of 1900, contract labor became illegal, and this opened the way for workers to formally protest against plantation management. At the beginning, work stoppages or strikes were limited because the workers lacked leverage to push their demands for higher wages and better working conditions. But as the protest widened, there were other issues besides wages and working conditions. The work stoppage at the Olaa Sugar Plantation on the Big Island illustrated one of the abuses suffered by the laborers.

On June 25, 1905, about one thousand Japanese workers walked out when a Japanese worker died after taking medication prescribed by the company doctor, who was found to be incompetent. The Japanese laborers demanded the dismissal of the doctor and a Japanese company interpreter, who was accused of siding with the company, but the doctor and the interpreter remained employed so the walkout was for naught.

There were three major strikes in the pre-World War II period—the sugar strikes of 1909, 1920, and 1924. Each strike involved thousands of plantation workers, but the biggest was the 1924 strike when thirteen thousand Filipino sugar laborers walked out for eight months. All three strikes were unsuccessful; the companies usually got their way and strikers lost their jobs, but some concessions were granted. The strikes of 1909 and 1920 are of particular interest because the Japanese led the way, playing an important role in organizing and implementing the strikes.

The 1909 strike took place on the island of O'ahu. Approximately seven thousand Japanese laborers in all the plantations left the fields. The strike was undertaken to improve working conditions and to correct disparities in the pay scale. After three months, the strike ended in failure and all the leaders were arrested. They were pardoned by the acting governor after spending some time in jail. Success was impossible because only the Japanese went on strike—the other ethnic groups continued working. The owners had cleverly segregated the workers by ethnicity, with each group having their own camp. In this way, the ethnic groups were in competition with each other, and the threat of the groups coalescing and joining together in protest was avoided.

The owners pushed back and labeled the Japanese as "agitators" and viewed them as a threat to their control. The owners lost $2 million, and the strike evoked strong anti-Japanese sentiments. After the strike, the plantation owners imported large numbers of Filipinos laborers to offset the Japanese. The territorial government, dominated by the haoles, supported the owners, and the following year, the haole elites in the legislature retaliated by pushing for the elimination of Japanese language schools. It was their way of suppressing the Japanese.

Although the strike was a failure, it was the first step in the use of confrontational approaches. It did end the wage differential based on race and led to improvements in working conditions and housing. Overall, it didn't lead immediately to broad reforms, but it could be argued the groundwork was laid.

The sugar strike of 1920 started on O'ahu and was a multiracial strike led by two unions, the Filipino Labor Union and the Federation of Japanese Labor. It initially began with two thousand Filipinos going on strike, but four days later, the Japanese joined the strike and became the predominant factor—numbering four thousand—and when family members are included, the total number of participants was thirteen thousand. The strike covered the four major islands and lasted seven months. The strikers demanded reduced working hours, maternity leave, and overtime pay, but wage increase was the principal issue. World War I had caused an inflation in Hawai'i, with prices rising continually while wages stayed the same, thus creating an intolerable situation.

The strike was costly for the Japanese community. Even with the help of the union, many families became destitute and over twelve thousand were evicted from their plantation homes. The pathetic sight of thousands of homeless strikers and their families, with the elderly hobbling and children crying, all trekking from the plantations to Honolulu was etched into the minds of the Japanese community for many years. Adding to the misery, about 1,500 strikers were stricken with the Spanish flu, a global influenza pandemic. The strike took its toll on the plantation consortium; the Hawaiian Sugar Planters' Association (HSPA) lost $12 million in potential income.

Most observers said the strike was a failure because the strikers eventually capitulated. The territorial government arrested the Japanese strike leaders and brought them to trial for conspiring to dynamite the house of a plantation official. All fifteen defendants were found guilty, and the haole elites' distrust of the Japanese was deepened by the strike. They lobbied Congress to change the Chinese Exclusion Act of 1882, wanting to end the dependence on Japanese emigrant labor by bringing in the Chinese workers. It was unsuccessful but led eventually to the Immigration Act of 1924, which turned out to be a drastic move by ending all Asian immigration. In retrospect, the strike was somewhat successful, leading to a 50 percent pay raise, better bonus system, improved medical services, housing, sanitation, water system, and more recreational facilities. But the results were not immediate, and it took several years before the workers benefited. A majority of workers returned to the plantations, but about 2,100 workers found other jobs.[17]

In the strikes of 1909 and 1920, the haole oligarchy was able to break the strikes and win the confrontations, but eventually the strikers were able to gain better working conditions, improved housing and sanitation, and even the wages and bonuses were adjusted and increased. More importantly, workers showed they were no longer willing to remain submissive and patient; they could now organize to protest and take action. And they could leave the plantation if the opportunity presented itself; they were no longer tied to a contract.

Labor relation activities, painful as there were, are part of the process by which the Hawai'i Japanese were assimilated into the larger society. The Issei, for the most part, were preoccupied with maintaining their Japanese tradition, customs, and values. They worried their children would lose their Japanese identity in the multicultural environment of Hawai'i. As previously discussed, the segregated policy of the plantation and its compactness helped the Japanese to perpetuate their traditions and customs. During continuing assimilation, there were other institutions and organizations that aided the Japanese in maintaining their traditions, thereby providing community solidarity. These organizations and institutions are discussed in the following chapter.

---

[17] Tamura, 216.

CHAPTER THREE

JAPANESE COMMUNITY

From the beginning of immigration and throughout the prewar period, community organizations and institutions were essential in drawing together the Issei and Nisei. They provided social services, means of communication, and protection against discrimination. The Japanese tended to immediately form social, occupational, business, and education groups, and it didn't take much effort to mobilize them to defend and promote their common interests. The following five major organizations or institutions stood out for their role in the social, political, and religious lives of the Japanese. These entities facilitated the maintenance and continuity of the culture, traditions, and values, making it possible for the Japanese to exist as an ethnic community. While adapting to the pressure of the larger society, they sought to perpetuate the Japanese way, thus ensuring the continuation of the Japanese community.

JAPANESE LANGUAGE SCHOOLS

Outside of the family, language schools are the most important institutions for teaching, integrating, and disseminating an ethnic group's tradition and values—this is true for all immigrating ethnic groups. The Japanese language schools serve as the core of the Japanese community. They teach not only language skills but ensure the continuation of traditional cultural activities.

The Japanese language school I attended was the Hawai'i Chuo Gakuen (Central Institute of Hawai'i). It was the second Japanese language school established in Hawai'i, the first school was founded in Kula, Maui in 1895. The Chuo Gakuen was founded on April 6, 1896 by Reverend Takie Okumura who became one of the most influential Japanese community leader of his time. It was a neighborhood school and was close enough I could walk barefooted in twenty-minutes. Elementary school children wore no shoes, and this was true for both the Japanese and English language schools. Young children going barefooted was a financial necessity in many ethnic families and became a customary practice. Besides, in the Hawaiian culture, going barefoot was an accepted practice. Like the ancient Hawaiians, the young people found going barefoot to be comfortable and practical. But the war brought many changes, and students began wearing shoes to the English language elementary schools. The most disruptive effect of the war, however, was the permanent closing of the Hawai'i Chuo Gakuen while I was in the fourth grade.

Takie Okumura.
Courtesy of Hawai'i Public Radio.

School was extremely traditional where status and hierarchy were strictly observed and practiced. Teachers were highly respected, and we learned how to bow to them and to never talk back. Heavy in regimentation, school started by lining up in the schoolyard in formation by class, with the top student at the front. Announcements were read by the principal, and we then marched to the classroom. Already some changes were made because of the possibility of war and pressure from the outside community. At the front of the classroom, the picture of the *Showa-Tenno* (Emperor Hirohito) was replaced by that of George Washington. Otherwise, school went on as usual. The standard instructional method was by rote. Examinations were an essential part of the educational system, and there was constant pressure to excel. I still have a certificate for passing an examination—imagine, receiving a certificate for just passing an exam.

During the day, we attended the English language school and later in the afternoon attended the Japanese language school for one or two hours. There were also weekend sessions. Attendance at Japanese language school was mandatory in Japanese families. We were told education was of prime importance and to study hard, for it was the key to success in life—it determined your status in society. Nevertheless, some boys resented going to Japanese school and had to be forced. They hated the strict rules and, most importantly, they wanted the free time to play with non-Japanese youngsters. It was confusing at times, attending the Japanese school right after the English public school. The public school was informal and relaxed, but the Japanese school was strict and disciplined. It was necessary to quickly shift one's thinking and behavior. Most Nisei preferred and were more interested in the English language school than the Japanese school. But parents stressed the importance of both schools and made sacrifices so their children could receive the best education.

My father was educated in Japan and learned English by attending private and public English language schools in Honolulu, becoming bilingual. Mother, on the other hand, only spoke Japanese and had little formal education. She wrote to me when I was away in simple *kana* (Japanese syllabary) and seldom used *kanji* (Chinese character). When reading the Japanese newspaper, she

31

relied on the *furigana*, tiny *kana* placed alongside *kanji*, which indicated the pronunciation of the *kanji*.[18] It meant she didn't know the Chinese character and needed the *furigana* to understand the meaning. Even though her education was limited, she always stressed the importance of attending the public school and the Japanese language school; playing hooky was never an option. Books were an important part of the learning environment, and I was surrounded by books. I devoured the *Lincoln Library of Essential Information*, a one volume general reference book. There was an encyclopedic set, books on Egyptian archaeology, and so forth. I don't think my father read these books. In any case, education was emphasized in Japanese homes, and reading was an important component.

The Issei worried about their children becoming so Americanized they would lose their cultural heritage and the ability to communicate in the native tongue. It was a real concern, as they observed their children adopting the ways of the dominant American culture. Even though the Japanese language schools served as the bulwark against the tide of Americanization, many parents worried about assimilation and decided to send their American-born children to Japan for all or part of their education. These young students were called *Kibei*, which literally means "return to America"; hence they were Japanese Americans who returned after being educated in Japan. It was a prevalent practice and reached its peak in the early 1920s, then it steadily dwindled. In all, about fifty thousand Nisei (25 percent) were sent back to Japan as children, and of these, almost ten thousand returned to the United States and are, therefore, *Kibei*.

Kibei usually stayed with their grandparents or other relatives while in Japan. They were considered "outsiders" and never fully accepted into Japanese society. They came back expecting to be respected for their Japanese education and to be given honored positions in the Japanese communities. Instead, the opposite occurred, and they were despised for being pro-Japan and not fitting in with the American way of life. They were often targeted

---

[18] Japanese newspapers in Honolulu used the prewar orthography of printing the *kanji* with the *furigana*, and this practice was followed for several years in the postwar period. Meanwhile in Japan, the language had undergone major changes, especially the simplification of the Chinese characters, and *furigana* was seldom used. But the local Japanese papers continued its use as a reading aid for the Issei.

as being "disloyal." But ironically, because they were fluent in Japanese and English, and were knowledgeable about both cultures, they were sought after by the US Army and many served with distinction in the Pacific War.

The extraordinary increase in the number of Japanese language schools was viewed with alarm by many Americans. In 1910, there were 140 Japanese schools in Hawai'i with about seven thousand students; by 1933, there were 190 schools with 43,606 students. A concerted opposition against the Japanese schools developed, especially during World War I when a wave of patriotism swept over the nation. Anti-Japanese sentiments continued unabated for the rest of the prewar decades. Americanizers, those that wanted to instill American middle-class values, criticized the curriculum offerings of the language schools. Unfortunately, some of the course offerings had overtones of militaristic and nationalistic sentiments, and opponents were quick to point out the anti-American nature of these courses. Two stood out: *kendo* (Japanese fencing), which was taught and practiced in middle and high schools; and *shushin* (moral training), which was taught in primary and middle schools. One day, I saw my older brother with his black *kendo* outfit with mask and protective paddings. He looked like a warrior, and I was impressed.

Shushin was especially controversial because of its emphasis on Confucian filial piety, wherein the individual is subordinate to the family, thus discouraging individualism, and where loyalty to the emperor is emphasized. Opponents believed the teaching of mikado (emperor of Japan) worship and loyalty to the homeland was un-American. In order to exert control, the Territorial Legislature enacted the Irwin Bill in November 1920, which required the Japanese language schoolteacher to have a permit from the Department of Public Instruction and to pledge not to contradict American ideals or institutions. Moreover, in 1922, the legislature took further control by regulating enrollment and textbooks. Kindergartners and first and second graders were prohibited from attending language school, and the subject matter of textbooks was closely examined. The next step was an attempt to altogether eliminate the language schools. The legislature passed the Clark Bill in 1923, which imposed a one-dollar tax per student each year. This tax affected enrollment, making it difficult for the schools to continue and many closed. The Japanese community fought back and after seven years of litigation, the US Supreme Court, on February 21, 1927, declared the school control laws were unconstitutional and allowed the schools to continue.[19]

KENJINKAI

Emigrants migrating to a new country tend to associate with people of similar background and from the same hometown or locale. For Japanese emigrants, it was natural to seek out those from the same hometown, but this usually meant a small number of individuals; hence they began to relate to those from a larger territorial unit, the *ken* (prefecture). The emigrants referred to themselves as *Hiroshima-Jin* (person from Hiroshima Prefecture) or *Kumamoto-Jin* (person from Kumamoto Prefecture), rather than *Nihon-Jin* (Japanese). It is the same as colonists calling themselves Virginians rather than Americans in the early days of Colonial America. Japan as a nation-state was a relatively new concept. The Tokugawa government—a form of centralized feudalism—ended in 1868 with the establishment of the Meiji government. Since the Meiji government was new, many emigrants didn't immediately think of themselves as citizens of Japan but instinctively thought about themselves as belonging to a specific prefecture.

Chie Nakane, a Japanese social anthropologist, uses two theoretical concepts to explain the group consciousness of Japanese: "attribute" and "frame." Attribute is being a member of a definite group, holding a situational position, usually acquired by birth or by achievement. Examples would be worker/executive or student/professor. On the other hand, frame is being a member of a locality, an institution, or an organization. Examples would be a member of X prefecture or Y company. Group consciousness of the Japanese depends considerably on frame. The Japanese give precedence to association over type of occupation. For example, instead of saying, "I'm

---

[19] Ogawa, *Kodomo*, 146.

a professor," the Japanese is likely to say, "I belong to Z university" or "I'm from X prefecture." Initially, the listener prefers to hear about the university than his or her position as professor.[20]

In group identification, a frame such as the prefecture is of prime importance; the attribute of the individual is a secondary concern. What matters isn't whether a man or woman holds or doesn't hold a PhD but rather from which university he or she graduated. Nakane says, "The criterion by which Japanese classify individuals socially tends to be that of particular institution, rather than of universal attributes."[21] It is such group consciousness that promotes the strength of an association. This explains why a concept such as "prefecture" (a frame) can be a powerful group identification.

The *kenjinkai* (prefectural associations) were organized quickly by the Issei, each association representing a specific *ken*. My parents belonged to the Hiroshima *kenjinkai*, the largest *kenjinkai* on O'ahu. Approximately one-fourth of Japanese immigrants in Hawai'i were from Hiroshima. It was through the *kenjinkai's* informal network that information about local community activities flowed. In the early years, they served as benevolent support organizations, helping emigrants with their personal problems, furnishing relief and social services, and providing the means for individuals to come together to socialize. Emigrants found it comforting to associate with people from the same place. The older Nisei continued the *kenjinkai* activities until the early post-World War II period, but the *kenjinkai* slowly lessened its role of providing services with the passing of the Issei and the older Nisei.

The annual *kenjinkai* picnic is an example of an activity open to everyone from the same prefecture. This socializing event provides a sense of community solidarity. Every year, the Hiroshima *kenjinkai* held a gathering at Ala Moana Park near Waikiki, which featured lots of food and games. Each family brought their own *bento* (lunch box), while the *kenjinkai* provided beverages and extras. I remember the games because each child won a prize by just participating, so I usually came home with a bundle of prizes. For

---

[20] Chie Nakane, *Japanese Society* (Berkeley: University of California Press, 1970), 1-2.

[21] Nakane, *Japanese Society*, 3.

the adults, it was a time to catch up on gossip and have a good time social-izing. In the beginning, the annual picnic drew huge crowds. With the passing of years, attendance slowly declined. Nevertheless, it was still effec-tive for its social gathering functions. *Kenjinkai* operates today in Hawai'i and on the mainland, but only for organizing picnics, dinners, and other social events.

The *kenjinkai* of the various prefectures came together to promote com-munity-wide activities. The celebration of *Tenchosetsu* (emperor's birthday) was an important cultural event for the Japanese immigrants and the most controversial because Japanese workers refused to work on that day. The emperor was a symbol of the Japanese heritage, and the Issei were proud of their heritage. At first, the plantations resisted, but by the mid-1890s owners conceded and allowed the Japanese to take a day off and celebrate with picnic, dancing, music, and with *sumo* (wrestling) and *kendo* (fencing) matches. When serious social and political issues arose, the *kenjinkai* became a mobilizing agent for the entire Japanese community. In the case of the language school crisis of the early 1920s, an issue of profound impor-tance to the community, the *kenjinkai* fought for the retention of the schools. The white elites wanted the schools closed because they were considered an obstacle to the Americanization of the Japanese and a threat to white dominance in Hawai'i.

A notable example of mobilization and support was the infamous case in 1928 of a nineteen-year-old Nisei, Myles Fukunaga. He kidnapped and murdered George Gill Jamieson, a ten-year-old son of a prominent banker with the Hawaiian Trust Company. The company had pressured the impov-erished Fukunaga family of six siblings to pay their overdue rent of twenty dollars and had threatened eviction. Fukunaga was the eldest child, and he was frustrated he couldn't help his family and resented the financial pressure put on his family. He decided to take revenge by kidnapping the Jamieson boy and demanding a $10,000 ransom to help his parents return to Japan and escape the poverty in Hawai'i.

Fukunaga went to the school where Jamieson was enrolled, dressed as a hospital orderly, and called the boy out of class and told him his mother had been injured in a car accident. He took the boy away in a taxi to a hideout. There he inexplicably bludgeoned to death the kidnapped victim and sent a ransom note to Jamieson's parents, demanding a ransom for their son's safe return. Later, Fukunaga phoned the father and, concealing his face, met with the father at a designated place but he only received $4,000. He promised to return the boy and quickly fled. A few days later, Fukunaga was apprehended, and he readily admitted his guilt and even asked to be hanged. Before this crime, he had tried to commit suicide. Obviously, he suffered from a mental disorder but pleas for a psychiatric examination were denied, and his sanity was never properly assessed. There was an angry outburst over the crime, and the Territorial Guard had to be called to prevent a threatened lynching.

The *kenjinkai* came together and fought for Fukunaga's honor and the integrity of the Japanese community. It held several meetings, and the meeting halls were jam-packed with anxious members. Leaders of the *kenjinkai* and other community leaders collected signatures for petitions and asked for executive clemency on the grounds of insanity. They argued Fukunaga was mild-mannered and well-educated, and his sudden aberrant behavior was due to insanity. A verdict of insanity would relieve the Japanese community of collective responsibility, but the petitions were denied. Fukunaga was quickly tried and convicted, all within two weeks, and was sentenced to be executed. Appeals were made to the US Supreme Court, but all attempts failed and Fukunaga was hanged on November 19, 1929. The execution was hurriedly carried out for vengeance's sake. The haoles viewed the kidnap-murder as a Japanese threat to their control in Hawai'i. The quick execution also opened an ugly racial divide, worsening the relationship between Japanese and Caucasians.

A few days after the hanging, about six thousand Japanese gathered on the grounds of Chuo Gakuin. The *Hawai'i Hochi*, the Japanese language paper that staunchly defended Fukunaga, organized the mass protest. As a whole, the Japanese community had ambivalent feelings. On one hand, they were sympathetic toward the Fukunaga family, for Fukunaga was devoted to his family and did it for the sake of his parents; on the other hand, they felt disgust or *haji* (shame) because the incident reflected badly on the community. In any case, the Japanese community was fearful of haole reprisal and came together in self-defense.[22]

Another incident occurred three years later that impacted Japanese-haole relations and caused great concern among *kenjinkai* leaders. This was the infamous Massie Affair. It involved two dramatic trials: one for rape in 1931 and the other for murder in 1932. Five "local boys" allegedly raped Thalia Massie, the twenty-year-old wife of a naval officer, Thomas Massie. Two of the accused, Joseph Kahahawai and Ben Ahakuelo, were Hawaiians; Horace Ida and David Takai were Nisei; and Henry Chen was a Chinese Hawaiian. This group of boys couldn't be called Hawaiians or Japanese or even Asian, so the term "local" was coined by the media, and it has been in vogue ever since to differentiate the non-whites from the haoles. The five local boys were indicted and tried for rape, but due to changing testimonies by key witnesses and conflicting evidence, the jury deadlocked and a mistrial was declared. The outcry was immediate—the Honolulu papers believed the suspects were guilty, while the Navy pressed for justice and the white business community wanted prompt convictions.

Thalia Massie's mother was incensed and sought vengeance. Meanwhile, Ida was beaten by a group of sailors. Soon after, Thalia's mother, with the help of Lt. Massie and two sailors, kidnapped Kahahawai and killed him. Into this horrendous scene stepped in Clarence Darrow, the famous lawyer. He signed on to be the defense lawyer for the Massies, perhaps to add further notoriety to his illustrious but fading career. Darrow termed the murder a "honor killing."[23] A second trial began in 1932 against Massie's mother and the other three accomplices. The jury returned a guilty verdict

---

[22] For a definitive book on the Fukunaga case, see Jonathan Y. Okamura, *Race to Death in 1920s Hawai'i: Injustice and Revenge in the Fukunaga Case* (Urbana, IL: University of Illinois Press, 2019). The case was made into a drama play, "A Walking Shadow," written and directed by Taurie KInoshita. It was first performed on October 2018. My wife, Evelyn, is related to the Fukunaga family. She says the family never talked about the case. It was a matter of *haji*. The concept of *haji*, or loss of face, is not only pervasive in Japanese culture and in family affairs but is common in other Asian American societies. Among the Chinese, it is called *mianzi* and *chaemyun* among Koreans.

[23] Darrow is known for his defense role in the famous Scopes' "monkey trial" of 1925. "Honor killing" is a term used by the Mafia to justify the killing of an offender who had damaged the name of the victim's family.

convicting all four defendants of manslaughter, but Territorial Governor Lawrence Judd commuted the ten-year sentence imposed on all the defendants and they only served an hour in custody under the sheriff.

It was a shocking outcome. The governor made his decision under heavy political pressure. There was an uproar nationally; the federal executive branch became involved, and Congress held emergency hearings. There were talks of suspending civilian rule by imposing martial law, while tensions grew with the possibility of race riots. Almost all politicians and media in Hawai'i and throughout the United States supported the Massies. However, non-whites in Hawai'i were convinced the convicted haoles had gotten away with murder, and they resented the haoles being favored by a dual system of justice.[24]

The Massie Affair had several ramifications. First, the territorial governor commissioned the Pinkerton Detective Agency to investigate the Massie Affair. In their report, Pinkerton concluded the rape never took place, and the guilty verdict on the murder of Kahahawai was correct. Second, the Massie case divided Hawai'i along racial line—it was "locals" versus haoles—and colored racial relations until World War II. It caused whites to fear the Japanese, coming as it did on the heels of the Japanese leadership in the labor strikes and the agitation resulting from the Fukunaga case. Since two of the accused "local boys" were Nisei, *kenjinkai* and other Japanese community leaders came to the defense of the accused. The Japanese newspaper, *Hawai'i Hochi*, editorialized strongly in support of the five boys as the Japanese community, as a whole, stood firmly against the haole supporters of the Massie. Third, it affected the political scene—the complexion of Hawaiian politics changed. In the election of 1932, Democrats flipped a few white-dominated Republican seats. Finally, the Massie Affair showed that in times of turmoil, when fear prevails, racism can erupt, and the rule of law ignored. Often it is the alarm over immigrants or foreigners, which leads to extreme measures such as concentration camps and other forms of

---

[24] Several books are available on the Massie Affair. Recent publications include: David Stannard, *Honor Killing: How the Infamous "Massie Affair" Transformed Hawai'i* (New York: Viking Press, 2005); John P. Rosa, *Local Story: The Massie-Kahahawai Case and the Culture of History* (Honolulu: University of Hawai'i Press, 2014).

severe restrictions, resulting in the denial of constitutional rights. Indeed, within a decade, massive racial fears would arise and lead to the wholesale incarceration of fellow citizens and the denial of their fundamental rights and liberties.

TANOMOSHI

One of the problems facing emigrants is the need for funds to start a business, or cover the myriad of financial contingencies that suddenly occur. For the emigrants, the existing financial establishments are strange and remote. The banks seem to be a foreboding place—the transactions, huge amounts of paperwork, legal language—all seem to be too difficult. Besides, emigrants often don't qualify for a loan because they are aliens and don't have collateral. To overcome these financial obstacles, Japanese emigrants formed their own lending source, the *tanomoshi* (mutual financing group). The name derives from the Japanese word *tanomu*, which means "request." It is a common practice in overseas ethnic communities to have their own mutual financing groups. The Chinese have their mutual financing association called *hui*, while the Koreans have their *kye*. The emigrants find it comfortable to work with an arrangement based on mutual trust and dependency.

Tanomoshi had its antecedent in the traditional *ie* (extended household or family), the primary unit of social organization in rural Japan. Traditional *ie* is primarily a residential group comprised of kin relations but can include non-kin members, forming an extended family. In rural areas, it is a form of social group consciousness that becomes a managing body, a corporate residential group.[25] It is this type of human relationship that *tanomoshi* represents, a group of people joined together based on trust and a sense of obligation. But over the years, as *tanomoshi* expanded in Hawai'i, it went beyond close friends and began to accept acquaintances. Closer scrutiny of potential members became necessary with the development of

---

[25] Nakane, *Japanese Society*, 4-5.

loose relationships. The level of trust is different between the tight bond with close friends and the tenuous and potentially corruptible relationship with acquaintances. Eventually, there were cases where individuals suffered financial losses and friendships were affected when *tanomoshi* broke up. The Japanese Merchants Association of Honolulu warned Japanese residents they could lose their money in these mutual financial aids clubs.

There were several types of *tanomoshi*, differing in how contributions were made to the pool and how they were distributed. The most common form of *tanomoshi* was for ten to twenty friends to pool their money together, with each contributing a sum at a regular interval: for example, a monthly payment. Each member would have access to the accumulated fund on a rotating basis, the order determined by lottery. Therefore, everyone had the opportunity to take the loan. It was possible to receive the pot earlier by bidding a higher interest payment. The winning bidder would then have to pay each member the amount of interest he bid.

The procedure was simple. No signatures or documents were needed, as it was a verbal agreement, requiring mutual trust and a sense of obligation and dependency. Social pressure prevented members from defaulting. Therefore, these mutual financing groups became a common means of economic assistance for the Issei and for the early Nisei. The *tanomoshi* was a key to opening new businesses, for business ventures would find it difficult to start or even survive without the pooled money. Some viewed it as an investment, joining several *tanomoshi* and making money from the high interest. Meetings were held on a monthly basis, and the meetings itself served as a social gathering for the members. *Tanomoshi* not only served as a means of financial transactions, but it promoted camaraderie and gave the members a sense of belonging to a close-knit group.

The younger Nisei found little use for such a traditional grouping and with the passing of the Issei, the pattern of obligations and interdependencies lessened. The Nisei preferred dealing with banks and eschewed financial dependence based on interpersonal relationships. From the beginning, *tanomoshi* was more important in Hawai'i and other overseas Japanese communities than it was in Japan proper because of the emigrants' greater need and the immediate dependence on mutual relationships. But by the beginning of World War II, this need and dependency diminished, and *tanomoshi* became basically an organization of the past.

RELIGIOUS ORGANIZATIONS—CHRISTIAN

It was the Christian missionaries and followers who were the first to try to convert the Japanese plantation laborers. Christianity was already pervasive in Hawai'i, being introduced and propagated by Congregationalist missionaries from New England in the 1820s. Protestant missionaries had labored for over sixty years prior to the arrival of the Japanese workers, so the Japanese found Christianity firmly established. Missionaries, however, found it challenging to convert the Japanese who were either passive or resisted the foreign religion. The cultural barriers were huge because Buddhist and Confucian ideals were entrenched in the thinking of the Japanese.

Among Christian leaders working with the Japanese laborers, the most effective and relatable were Christian evangelists of Japanese ancestry. Hence, there was an urgent need to bring in native Japanese ministers. In response to the need, Kanichi Miyama, a Methodist Episcopal minister, was sent to Hawai'i and arrived in Honolulu in 1887. He was able to reach out to the Japanese workers, move them away from immoral vices, and restore orderly life, something the Caucasian ministers weren't able to do. Miyama founded the Honolulu Japanese Christian Church, the first Japanese church in the islands. Especially significant was his conversion of Taro Ando, the Japanese Consul General, to Christianity. Consul General Ando was instrumental in helping to spread the gospel message to the immigrants.[26] Miyama and Ando founded the Japanese Mutual Aid Association, which later became the Japanese Benevolent Society. The Japanese community received social service from this organization.

---

[26] Ogawa, *Kodomo*, 46-47.

Evangelist Miyama left after a couple of years when he was called back to San Francisco by the California Conference of the Methodist Episcopal Church. The church he founded in Honolulu was reorganized as a Congregational church in 1892 and began to look for a new pastor. Reverend Orramel Gulick, who was born in Hawai'i and had just returned to Hawai'i from mission work in Japan, persuaded a young Japanese minister, Reverend Takei Okumura, to come to Hawai'i. Okumura turned out to be an energetic, bold, and visionary leader. After arriving, in addition to being pastor of the Honolulu Japanese Christian Church, he immediately involved himself in all sorts of community activities. Early on, he advanced the education of the Japanese by establishing the first Japanese language school in Honolulu, the aforementioned Hawai'i Chuo Gakuen (Central Institute of Hawai'i). The Japanese children were speaking English and pidgin but were losing their Japanese language, so a language school was urgently needed. He founded a dormitory for students, the Okumura Boys and Girls Home, and the religious lives of these students were impacted because they were required to attend church. Later, he was instrumental in bringing about the Japanese YMCA. In 1903, he left the Honolulu Japanese Christian Church because he wanted to start a new church. The following year, Okumura founded the Makiki Christian Church. He wanted the church building to resemble a Japanese castle, and in 1924, when the church building was completed, it did indeed look like a Japanese castle. Because of its distinctive architecture, the church is a Honolulu landmark.

Reverend Okumura was concerned about the heavy drinking, gambling, prostitution, and other vices in the Japanese community. Japanese men resorted to alcohol, women, and gambling to escape from the onerous working conditions. Initially, Rev. Okumura depended on Japanese traditional values and culture to correct the social abuses of plantation life and to address the economic and social needs of the Japanese. But he changed his approach and, starting in 1921, he promoted an educational program among plantation workers using American values and mores. He worked to Americanize the Issei, believing the Japanese should follow the American lifestyle. His goal was to blend Japanese and American elements, bringing together the two cultures and their values. He wrote, "I do not say that we should be Americanized in everything good and bad. On the contrary, I have been urging every youth to pick the good things of America and assimilate them, and thus become desirable elements in our community."[27]

Christianity, he believed, would work better in such an environment. Okumura wanted the Japanese to remain on the plantation, to be accepted into Hawaiian social structure, and he wanted to avoid confrontation with the haoles. He opposed labor strikes because the haoles would be antagonized but by siding with the owners, he antagonized many Japanese workers. For Rev. Okumura, Christianity became a way for the Japanese to integrate into Hawaiian community and to become American. While he did turn many of the immigrants away from their sinful vices, most Japanese immigrants stubbornly clung to their old ways of thinking.

Of all the Protestant denominations, the Congregationalist had the greatest impact on the Japanese, for the early missionaries were predominately Congregationalist and stemmed from the Puritan tradition of New England. The Honolulu Japanese Christian Church and the Makiki Christian Church were the leading Japanese Congregational churches in Honolulu, up to World War II. However, the Honolulu Japanese Christian Church changed its name to Nu'uanu Congregational Church in 1942 in deference to wartime concern about being identified with Japan. Although both the Nu'uanu and Makiki Congregational churches began as predominantly Japanese churches, they have become multiracial churches and are now part of the Hawai'i Conference of the United Church of Christ.

Another church that was for the most part Japanese and Congregational was the Kalihi Union Church (KUC). Horace Wright Chamberlain, a descendent of a missionary family, acquired property in Kalihi, which at that time was outside the city of Honolulu and used it to establish the church. When I became a Christian, while attending the University of Hawai'i, I

---

[27] Ogawa, 139.

began going to KUC and by that time, it too had become a multiracial church. In 1991, KUC became a member of the Evangelical Church of America.[28]

Although many Japanese are members of various Protestant churches, there are a few ethnic churches serving mainly those of Japanese ancestry. One example is the Oriental Mission Society (OMS) Holiness churches, which were meant to reach out to the Japanese people. In 1929, a few lay people formed the Wai'alae Holiness Church; it was a mission church of the Japanese Holiness Church movement in Japan. Two years later, the Wahiawa Holiness Church was founded and the following year, in 1932, the Honolulu Holiness Church was established. At that time, a split occurred, and those churches broke away from the Holiness Church group in Japan and became members of the OMS Holiness Church of North America. The Holiness churches were distinctive in having two language ministries—the Japanese language ministry for the Issei and the English language ministry for the Nisei—thereby serving both generations. When the war began, all Holiness churches were closed and even after the war, both the Wai'alae and Wahiawa Holiness churches remained closed but the Honolulu Holiness Church emerged in 1945. Later it changed its name to Honolulu Christian Church (1982), recognizing that if it wanted to grow, it had to become multiracial. It was joined in the postwar period by two other conference churches; although predominantly Japanese, they too appealed multiracially. On the mainland, the conference, which had been the only denomination founded by and focused toward Japanese and Japanese Americans, found that it too had to expand its membership to other ethnicities.

RELIGIOUS ORGANIZATIONS—BUDDHIST

For most emigrants, religion was intertwined with their culture; it was part of their heritage. Most of them were nominal Buddhists, and religion didn't play a significant part in their lives. When they arrived in Hawai'i,

---

[28] Evelyn and I became members of KUC and were one of the first couples to be married at the new church sanctuary. Evelyn's parents were members of Honolulu Holiness Church, where her father attended the Issei Japanese service and her mother attended the Nisei English service.

there were no Buddhist temples or priests, so whatever Buddhist practices or customs they observed, they did out of habit or instinctively.

From the beginning, Buddhist adherents were concerned about Christianity intruding gradually into the lives of the plantation workers. Lacking Buddhist priests to teach and propagate the faith, the Buddhist followers petitioned the Honpa Hongwanji headquarters in Japan of the Jodo Shinshu sect to send priests to Hawai'i. This sect of Buddhism became the largest in Hawai'i, with the first Buddhist priest, Soryu Kagahi, arriving in 1889. He found the emigrants seriously deficient in their faith and engaging in many vices. Yet he was able to establish a Buddhist temple in Hilo, on the Big Island, before he returned to Japan. He was followed by several priests, and they found it took considerable effort to make Buddhism relevant to the needs of the emigrants. The beginning phase was difficult because the emigrants had not followed Buddhist practices and customs consistently for several years. They were slow in responding and lacked enthusiasm toward the religion. Moreover, the multicultural environment made the work very challenging. The plantation owners, did its part, by donating land and helping to build temples. The owners had their own interest in mind, for they thought any religion would help the emigrants in their family life and would provide stability, discipline, and motivation, thereby making for a productive and satisfied labor force.

Since the eighth century, Buddhist thoughts, arts, and customs had profoundly impacted Japanese culture. Buddhism permeated the culture, and its temples became propagators of the Japanese culture. With Buddhist temples nearby, it was natural for Issei and Nisei in Hawai'i to profess to be Buddhist because Buddhism was taken to be part of their culture. In contrast, mainland Japanese were less likely to identify with Buddhism because they were scattered, further removed from Buddhist temples, and surrounded by a predominantly Christian environment. Not surprisingly, mainland Japanese tended to be Christian rather than Buddhist, and this was particularly true in Washington and Oregon, where there were only a small number of Buddhist temples.

The emigrants were willing to follow religious customs but often did this without deep-seated religious conviction. Buddhism didn't make the demand that its followers forsake all other gods, as in Christianity, but allowed for coexistence with Shintoism and Confucianism. Filial piety, with its emphasis on loyalty to the family and interpersonal relationships, is an essential part of Japanese culture and is derived from Confucianism. Japanese were inclined to take in values and customs from Confucianism, Shintoism, and Buddhism in syncretic fashion, but when it came to Christianity, it was different; it demanded absolute belief and devotion.

Buddhism came closest to Christianity by providing solace to the Issei in its concern with individual salvation and what happens after death. On a personal level, Buddhism did help to relieve loneliness and provide comfort for the old Issei. Buddhist priests performed needed services, wrote letters, settled family problems, acted as go-between in marriages, and handled disputes between management and workers. Buddhist adherents were active participants in such traditional celebrations as *bon* festival (honoring the dead), *mochitsuki* (rice pounding), *setsubun* (last day of winter), and *Hanamatsuri* (Flower Festival). These celebrations recalled the customs of the villages back home and renewed the emigrants' bond to his or her community. In addition, life cycle events were extremely important in bringing together the community. Marriages were held in Shinto shrines, whereas funerals were held in Buddhist temples.[29]

A major event in the life cycle of the Japanese is the funeral. Funerals illustrate the importance of Buddhist customs and traditions. Except for Christian funerals, nearly all Japanese funerals are conducted Buddhist-style. The ritual is detailed and prescribed funeral etiquette must be followed to avoid embarrassment. Although the Japanese in Hawai'i and on the mainland have made modifications and omitted certain practices, the traditional funeral format is generally adhered to. A Buddhist funeral is a two-day event. *Tsuya*, a wake service, is held at night before the *soshiki*, the funeral service. At the *tsuya*, friends and relatives offer their condolences to the grieving family

---

[29] Shinto is the indigenous religion of Japan. It emphasizes ritual purity and considers death an impurity. For these reasons, it doesn't deal with funerals, but Shinto customs have influenced Buddhist funeral practices.

and say their goodbyes to the dead. The priest recites a Buddhist sutra in a brief ceremony. The next day at the *soshiki*, the priest chants a sutra and participants burn incense for the soul of the deceased. Since the ritual can be complicated, it is best to follow what others are doing. It is difficult to understand what the priest is chanting, and I suspect most of the attendees have no idea what is being chanted. *Koden* (bereavement money in an envelope) is presented to the bereaved at the *tsuya* or *soshiki*. The amount given varies with the closeness of the relationship with the deceased.

Issei usually gave money as gifts at funerals, weddings, and other occasions: it is a pattern of social relationship based on *giri* (reciprocal obligation). One is obliged to give a gift and a return is expected. Since the value of the gift can be calculated, it fit in with the Issei's liking for an orderly and predictable society. My father showed me his record book listing donors' name and dollar amount of *koden*, wedding, and other monetary gifts. He predicted the exact amount of money I would receive for my wedding from his friends. If a donor didn't give the expected amount, it would upset him. Issei didn't appreciate surprises; they demanded predictable behavior. For Nisei used to the American way of thinking, such a strict sense of obligation was onerous; a far cry from the free-wheeling, individualistic style of Americans.

After the *tsuya* and *soshiki* ceremonies, food and drinks are served. As it turns out, it is often a reunion for people who haven't seen each other for a while; a time to catch up on what others are doing. It brings together friends and relatives and is an important part of the life cycle of the Japanese. The Hawai'i Japanese had a unique way of recording such get-togethers. After the funeral ceremony, everyone would line up outside in a straight row with the casket in the center, and a panoramic shot would be taken. Many old funeral photos had to be unrolled to be seen.

Buddhism was considered old-fashioned and un-American by many Nisei. Since the young Nisei had a limited command of the Japanese language, Buddhist priests found it difficult to impart Japanese values, change ways of thinking, and teach the tenets of Buddhism. A breakthrough was needed, and the answer was found—it was to make Buddhism appealing to the Nisei by "Americanizing" its institutional practices. Probably the most outstanding proponent of changing Buddhism to be in accord with American values and practices was Bishop Yemyo Imamura, head of the Honolulu Honpa Hongwanji Mission. He arrived in 1902 and immediately started to adapt Buddhism to the American way. Buddhist "temples" became Buddhist "churches," priests became reverends, Sunday worship services were initiated, and there were even Buddhist "Sunday schools." An English department was established at the Honpa Hongwanji Mission. Buddhist temples became a socializing institution, providing activities for young children and teenagers. The Young Men's Buddhist Association (YMBA) and Young Women's Buddhist Association (YWBA) were created, which followed the lines of the Christian YMCA and YWCA. The *bon'odori* (festival dance) became an entertainment and socializing event with times to dance, enjoy special food, and meet friends.[30]

To summarize, for many Japanese emigrants, religion was stated or nominal. Buddhism and Shintoism were considered part of the culture, and one participated in their rituals, celebrations, and other events to fulfill socializing needs rather than fulfilling religious beliefs. Christianity was considered an "outside" religion and wasn't intertwined with Japanese culture; nevertheless, attempts were made to accommodate Christianity to Japanese customs and values. The emigrants' personal lives were mixed in with religious observances—Buddhist and Shinto altars in the homes, Christian or Shinto marriages, Buddhist or Christian funerals, Buddhist or Shinto festivals—all were part of the religious rites of passage. Religion helped individuals be an integral part of a larger community.

JAPANESE LANGUAGE NEWSPAPERS

The Japanese language press was an essential component of the Japanese community. It was particularly important for the Issei because it was the channel through which flowed printed information about events in Japan and of the local Japanese community. Besides news, the emigrant newspaper

---

[30] *Bon'odori* is held annually in mid-July to mid-August. Originally, it was to celebrate the arrival and departure of the ancestor spirits, but it is now completely secularized.

covered cultural events and had the usual announcements and advertisements. My parents subscribed in the prewar days to the *Nippu Jiji* and, at times, to the *Hawai'i Hochi*. Interestingly, they paid particular attention to the obituary section.

The first Japanese newspaper in Hawai'i appeared in 1892 and was the *Nippon Shuho* or *Japanese Weekly*. By the first decade of the twentieth century, Honolulu had two Japanese newspapers: the *Hawai'i Shimpo*, which had the largest circulation, and the *Nippu Jiji*. But it didn't take long for the *Nippu Jiji*, which had supported the workers in the labor strikes, to overtake the *Shimpo*, which had backed the plantation owners. The *Nippu Jiji* continued to expand its circulation and prior to World War II had the largest Japanese language newspaper circulation in Hawai'i, and exceeded that of any mainland Japanese newspaper.

Newspaper publishing was difficult in Hawai'i, and a couple of newspapers had already folded when the *Hawai'i Hochi* was founded by Frederick Kinzaburo Makino in 1912.[31] Makino was a determined individual and wasn't about to be deterred by any obstacle. He began as a community activist and started his newspaper as a platform to promote his ideas and follow up on his beliefs.

**Frederick Kinzaburo Makino.
Courtesy of Densho.**

---

[31] The papers that folded were *Hawai'i Nichinichi Shimbun* and *Nippon Shuho*.

Makino was born in Japan, where his Japanese mother reared him by herself when his father, an English merchant, died suddenly when Makino was a child. He took his mother's name. Although Makino grew up in the Japanese tradition and went to Japanese schools, he also attended an English language school and became fluent in English. Makino moved to Hawai'i in 1899 to be with his brother, who had a small store. He worked as a plantation laborer, then moved to Honolulu and opened a drug store in 1901.

Makino became interested in the labor movement and helped found the Zokyu Kisei Kai (Higher Wages Association) during the 1909 strike, along with Yasutaro Soga, the editor and owner of *Nippu Jiji*, Motoyuki Negoro, and Yokichi Tasaka. These four leaders were tried, found guilty, and imprisoned for several months for leading the strike. But soon, a serious split developed between Makino and Soga. At first, both agreed on organized resistance and criticized the Hawai'i Sugar Planters' Association over the treatment of the workers. But Soga began to move away from confrontation to a more accommodating posture toward the white elites and wanted harmony rather than the confrontational protests and legal actions. In this way, his position was similar to that of Rev. Okumura of Makiki Christian Church and those of another advocate of conciliation, Senichi Ueno, the Japanese Consul General.

Makino and Soga became bitter rivals, and their papers became platforms for voicing their respective views. They debated various issues, including the Japanese language school controversy, the O'ahu sugar strike of 1920, the fight for citizenship rights of Japanese veterans of World War I, the Fukunaga murder case, and the Massie case.[32] On all these issues, Makino was much more outspoken and was noted for his aggressive editorials. He attacked the abuses of the haole oligarchy and wasn't shy about taking a strong position on community issues. Makino fought for a retrial for Fukunaga, whereas Soga opposed a new trial and was unsympathetic

---

[32] Tom Brislin, "Weep into Silence/Cries of Rage: Bitter Divisions in Hawai'i's Japanese Press," *Journalism and Mass Communication Monographs* 147 (December 1995): 1-29. Discover Nikkei, *Fred Kinzaburo Makino: A Biography—His Contributions to Society Through the Hawai'i Hochi*, Pts. 1 & 2 (Honolulu: Hawai'i Hochi, November 29, 2010). www.discovernikkei.org/en/journal/2010/11/29/fred.kinzaburo-makino/.

about the sentencing, believing justice had to be served. Soga, although milder in his editorials, could also be totally unyielding.

What emerged was two contrasting approaches in dealing with the haole leaders. In his writings, Makino, like a gadfly, employed the confrontational approach to fight for the rights and freedom of the Japanese. He did achieve successes in the labor disputes and in the Japanese language school crisis. But the conciliatory approach of Soga and Okumura was also of importance in successfully mitigating the haole reaction, thereby helping in the assimilation of the Japanese. Both approaches, the *Hochi's* confrontational style and the *Jiji's* conciliatory style, helped to level the playing field, thus beginning the process of ending white domination.

The *Hochi* and *Jiji* had an English language section to reach out to the Nisei, most of whom couldn't read Japanese. Eight days after the Pearl Harbor attack, the Japanese language papers were forced to close. But a month later, the military governor—Hawai'i was under martial law—having no way to communicate with the Issei, had to rescind the initial order and allowed the papers to operate under his directives. The papers were forced to change their names; the *Hochi* became the *Hawai'i Herald* on October 23, 1942, and the *Nippu Jiji* became the *Hawai'i Times* on November 2, 1942. During the war, both papers promoted American patriotism and loyalty. In retrospect, they played important roles during the war, expressing pride in their heritage and at the same time Americanizing the Japanese, thus furthering assimilation. With the passing of the Issei and the older Nisei, circulation dwindled, and the *Hawai'i Times* was forced to close in 1985.[33]

The prewar press did more than cover the news and announcements; it actively promoted and participated in community events. It had an enormous influence on the molding of public opinion by providing a public forum, guiding and stimulating discussions, and taking positions on social and political issues. The Japanese community was totally dependent on

---

[33] Noriko Asato, *Teaching Mikadoism: The Attack on Japanese Language Schools in Hawai'i, California, and Washington, 1919-1927* (Honolulu: University of Hawai'i Press, 2006). Helen Geracimos, *Shaping History: The Role of Newspapers in Hawai'i* (Honolulu: University of Hawai'i Press, 1996).

the press for much of the information about the community. However, the war changed the role of the Japanese press, and it was no longer the primary source of information. There were now many other sources, and the Japanese press could no longer play a leading role in determining or influencing public opinion. The tenor, for example, of the *Hochi* changed, and it no longer took strong positions on social issues. The Japanese papers never recovered their prewar dominance. The *Herald* reverted to its original name of *Hochi* in 1952, and in 1962 a Japanese businessman bought the paper. In 1969, a sister paper, published in English, took the name *Hawai'i Herald*. Although discontinued after four years, it was brought back in 1980 and continues today alongside the *Hochi*. Circulation has dropped over the years, but the *Hochi* remains as the only Japanese language paper in the islands.

The press had a paradoxical impact on acculturation. On the one hand, it preserved and strengthened ties with Japan, thereby contributing to the solidarity of the Japanese community and hindering acculturation. This aspect of the press appealed to the Issei. On the other hand, the press helped its readers to adjust to the American lifestyle and encouraged integration with the larger Hawaiian community, thereby furthering acculturation. The press coverage of social issues and the adjustment problems faced by Japanese Americans were of interest to the Nisei.

EVE OF THE WAR

As the 1930s concluded, the Japanese population in Hawai'i stabilized at 158,000 (37,000 Issei and 121,000 Nisei and Sansei); it was 37 percent of the total population of Hawai'i (423,000). The *Nikkei* comprised the major part of the workforce, an indispensable component of the Hawaiian economy. Through the efforts of the labor movement, led principally by the Japanese, working conditions of the laborers had improved with higher wages and better working conditions. There were no major strikes after 1924.

The national press depicted Hawai'i as an idyllic place. On the surface, the so-called "paradise of the Pacific" seemed serene, but for Hawai'i Nisei, changes in the working and living environment, and in their life style, attitude, and behavior, were all indications of the serious challenges they would soon be facing.

The large Japanese population continued to vex the haole leadership, as they feared the Japanese would gain control of the community. To prevent this from happening, they moved to limit the study and use of the Japanese language by closing the Japanese language schools. The Japanese language was considered a hindrance to Americanization, but they had a broader concern—to limit the pervasive use of pidgin English by all ethnic groups. The goal of the haole elites was to have English as the only standard language. Since about one-third of the population was Japanese, and the Japanese used pidgin extensively, it was in many respects an anti-Japanese movement.

Pidgin English is the popular name for the local spoken language, what linguists call Hawai'i Creole English. Pidgin is a dialect and not a formal language. It is a vernacular used in casual conversation at the beach, playground, or at home, and usually not used in the classroom or at work. Pidgin is an additional spoken language that has complicated in-home conversations. I used Japanese when speaking to my mother and Japanese or English with my father. English or pidgin was used with my brothers and sisters, and it was always English and/or pidgin with friends and acquaintances. After living on the mainland for several years, I found it took two days to make the adjustment and switch to pidgin when visiting in Hawai'i. For many Nisei growing up in an ethnically diverse environment, standard English wasn't comfortable to use, and with their limited Japanese, it was natural for pidgin to become their casual language.

The haole elites countered the use of pidgin by establishing "English Standard" (ES) public schools in Honolulu. It began in 1924 with Lincoln Elementary School and then was followed by Robert Louis Stevenson Intermediate School and Roosevelt High School. Admission to the ES schools was based on passing an oral entrance examination in English. Immediately, a racial and class divide was created in education between haoles and non-haoles. Students admitted were predominately haoles from middle class families, who already had command of English—haoles from affluent families went to Punahou, a private school. Part-Hawaiian and Asian students with command of the English language were admitted to the ES schools but only a few Japanese qualified. But this prewar ES system rapidly lost its distinctiveness after World War II, when the enrollment of non-haoles vastly increased, as their use of English improved; they were soon the majority. In 1961, the ES system was abolished. It was deemed "undemocratic."

Another development the Americanizers didn't want to see was a Japanese enclave. There was no Little Tokyo or Japantown in Honolulu. The Japanese population was scattered throughout the city but still clustered around certain districts, namely 'A'ala, Kaka'ako, Makiki, Mo'ili'ili, Liliha, Palama, and Kalihi. I lived, at that time, in the 'A'ala district, which came closest to being a Japantown. There was the 'A'ala Market, which covered an entire city block. It was noted for its variety of seafood and exotic food products. The 'A'ala Rengo ('A'ala Alliance), a shopping complex with retailers and vendors, carried various Japanese sundries. There were eight hotels, and four Japanese temples, and churches.

But the establishments that interested me were the three Japanese movie theaters—Nippon Theater, Kokusai Theater, and the beautiful Toyo Theater. Toyo Theater opened in 1936, and at the front was a walkway bridge over a large koi pond. The Toyo had a distinct Japanese architectural style, whereas the Kokusai was modern. The Nippon was old and had no style at all. These neighborhood ethnic theaters played an important part in my early social life. I viewed many samurai movies called *chambara* (sword-fighting films), the Japanese equivalent of the cowboy movies. My favorite hero was Tange Sazen. He appeared in a totally white outfit, had a cut over one eye, and fought with only one good arm. A typical action scene would have him surrounded by a dozen men, and he would cut them down, one by one, until only half were left and the remnant would run for their lives. Tange Sazen would then sheathe his sword and stroll nonchalantly down the street toward the sunset. The sword fights were carefully choreographed. There was no blood, and each victim, when slashed, would slowly pirouette and fall to the ground. It was beautiful, like a ballet. The morning matinees were cheap, and the theaters were ideal, air-conditioned gathering spots.

However, the war changed the complexion of the entire district. The Japanese movie theaters continued to operate but showed English movies. Toyo became 'A'ala Theater but reverted back to Toyo after the war. Business and religious establishments were forced to close, and the Japanese residents moved to other parts of the city. Slum housing sprouted and buildings began to deteriorate. By the 1960s, homes and buildings were demolished under an urban redevelopment program, and the neighborhood was transformed.

From our discussion, we have seen how Japanese culture and tradition were promoted and maintained by the Japanese language schools, the *kenjinkai*, Japanese language newspapers, Buddhist temples and Christian churches, and even by the practice of *tanomoshi*. There were some in the multicultural Hawaiian society who were not pleased to see the flourishing of Japanese culture. The haole leaders didn't want Japanese culture to thrive; instead they promoted Americanization to keep the Japanese Americans in their place so they would not be a threat to their rule. These advocates of Americanization wanted the Japanese to discard their culture and become Christians. Some *Nikkei* leaders, including Okumura and Soga, were willing to cooperate and not hinder Americanization. But they viewed Americanization differently as a process enabling the Japanese Americans to be socially mobile and allowing them to achieve middle class status while keeping their culture. It was more acculturation than assimilation. The haole elites, however, didn't trust accommodating the Japanese; they feared possibly losing control and being dominated by the Japanese.

If Americanization meant upward mobility, and this was what the Nisei wanted, how can they move out of the lower strata of society? The immediate answer was to move off the plantation where the Japanese workers were not respected, lacked freedom, and had no chance for advancement. Once the contract labor system was voided, the Japanese workers were able to move out of the plantations. The *Nikkei* had ambivalent feelings about leaving the plantations. They would have more direct contact with

Caucasians and other ethnic groups, which would help assimilation and increase their opportunities but it would also expose them to discrimination. The key to success in the outside world was educational and occupational achievements. Although the *Nikkei* had achieved higher education levels than other ethnic groups, they didn't have the requisite educational background to have highly skilled jobs, managerial positions, and to enter the professions. There were Japanese small business owners of grocery stores, bookstores, drugstores, and other mom-and-pop shops, but most self-employed Japanese were in farming, fishing, coffee growing, and specialized food outlets, such as *tofu* shops. The majority of Japanese Americans were employees in the service sectors. Some were in domestic and personal services, such as maids and gardeners, or worked in trades, sales, and clerical occupations.

The number of professionals slowly increased but was small, given the size of the population. There were in Hawai'i, for example, about a dozen Japanese dentists in 1940. My dentist was Dr. Riuichi Ipponsugi. His office was within walking distance and was an upstairs office with a long stairway and had no receptionist. In those days, if you wanted a Japanese dentist, you didn't have much choice. Dr. Ipponsugi's dental practice was interrupted when he was interned in a detention camp in New Mexico for the duration of the war.

What about the status of women in the workforce? The younger women were expected to help family finances by taking on jobs. Their employment opportunities were limited to office and retail positions or working in the pineapple and fish canneries. Liz, my oldest sister, wanted to go to college but in many Japanese families, college was not an option for women and girls were expected to stay home and help with the family. Liz did manage to enroll in a business school and learned shorthand, a necessary skill to be a secretary. She found a job with a movie distribution company and later with the army's Criminal Investigation Department at Fort Shafter. Two other sisters, Dale and Diane, followed Liz's footsteps and went to business school and became office workers in the postwar period. But in most cases, women were in unskilled jobs. Upward mobility for women was limited to the professions of teaching and nursing. Overall, there was no dramatic breakthrough in the socioeconomic realm. The glass or bamboo ceiling was rather low but barely penetrated.

Attitudes defined the role of women within the family and, as we have seen, in the workplaces. In a traditional Japanese patriarchy family, men played the dominant role and were the breadwinners. Nisei women found, however, that out of economic necessity, they had to not only do most of the family chores but had to hold down outside jobs. In many Japanese families, multiple income was required to cover the cost of living. And this was necessary even after marriage, for incomes from both spouses were needed to meet expenses. My sisters had to work until they retired.

I remember an incident at family dinner after my father and brothers had retired from the dining area. I got up and started to help with the dishes. My grandmother sternly said, "Stop helping with the dishes. Men should never help in the kitchen. It is the role of women." My mother didn't say a word. Over the years, she never objected to my helping in the kitchen—she was Americanized enough to recognize the old way of thinking was unacceptable. At that moment my sisters' eyes rolled and I could tell from their facial expression that they were saying to themselves, "Here we go again with this old-fashioned thinking!" It showed how disparate were the attitudes of the older from the younger generation. Such outmoded views disappeared over time, and women's position within and outside the family improved.

The attitudes held by Japanese not only determined individual behavior within the family but also affected their relationship with other ethnic groups. How did the Japanese view themselves and other racial groups? The Japanese immigrants came from a stratified and hierarchical society. They were status-conscious and had a superiority complex in their attitude toward other ethnic groups. They tended to look down on the Native Hawaiians, considering them to be happy-go-lucky and unambitious, and had disdain for the Koreans and Filipinos who came after them. This sense of superiority over other ethnic group bolstered the Japanese self-esteem as they themselves faced discrimination. The Japanese even carried discriminatory feelings against segments of their own people. These were people engaged in despised occupations or lived in certain urban ghettos, or were from distant islands of Japan.

Japanese pride themselves on their homogeneity and see themselves as a pure race, as the myth of racial purity distorts their view of certain groups. In feudal times, an outcaste group known as *burakumin* (hamlet people), or by the pejorative term *eta*, suffered severe social prejudice for being a "contaminated" group. They originated accidentally from several sources—defeated foes or those whose work was considered "unclean," such as people working in tanneries, butcheries, or cemeteries. Even when they moved out of these "dirty" occupations, they were still stigmatized as "dirty," and discrimination continued for generations. *Burakumin* are physically and culturally and in all other ways like any ordinary Japanese, and you couldn't tell by their appearance but a telltale clue was their residence—they live in certain city ghettos. The few *burakumin* in Hawai'i tried to pass in society but were found out, usually when the family records were examined in preparation for marriage. Even today, Japanese are reluctant to associate with *burakumin* and are careful to avoid intermarriage with them.

In Hawai'i, the *Naichi* (insiders) Japanese, those from the four main islands of Japan proper, discriminated against those from Okinawa, an island in the Ryukyu Archipelago. The Okinawans first arrived fifteen years after the first emigrants from Japan proper. A smaller number migrated to the mainland, so this discrimination was only a problem in Hawai'i, where the percentage of Okinawans in the Japanese population was significantly large. Up to 1924, about 16,500 Okinawans had migrated to Hawai'i. By the 1960s, there were approximately thirty thousand people of Okinawa lineage in Hawai'i. They made up about 20 percent of the Japanese Hawaiian population. They are ethnically Japanese, but there are some differences in language and culture, thus forming a subculture. Because of Okinawa being close to China, its culture shows heavy Chinese influence. The language spoken is considered a Japanese dialect, with many differences in word pronunciation.

When I was growing up in Hawai'i, I heard the *Naichi* Japanese talking disparagingly about the Okinawans. Okinawans were considered inferior because they were from a distant island. Its culture is distinctive enough to be differentiated. *Naichi* Japanese held stereotypical views of the Okinawans, seeing them as being hairy, having large eyes, being shorter in stature, and being darker in complexion. They were referred to as *yaban* (savage), or as clumsy and stupid, or more often as dirty and smelly. At my parents' house, a metal pail hung from the kitchen window and the garbage was dumped into it. An Okinawan man would come on schedule to collect the "pig-slop," which was used as feed at the piggeries owned by Okinawans in the Kalihi-uka district. Since the work at the piggeries was dirty and smelly, and pig-raising was considered lowly, the Okinawans were looked down on, similar to the treatment given to the *burakumin*. It wasn't until the Okinawans achieved success in their business ventures during and after World War II that the attitude of *Naichi* Japanese slowly changed and stereotyping stopped. Gradually, there was less differentiation between *Naichi* and Okinawan.

CHAPTER FOUR

PEARL HARBOR AND ITS AFTERMATH

I t was a typical Sunday morning, December 7, 1941, with blue skies and small patches of white clouds. I was a nine-year-old playing in the yard when I noticed black puffs of smoke in the sky but thought nothing of them. The military occasionally conducted practice with antiaircraft batteries shooting at targets towed by a distant plane. My brother, who was playing baseball, ran home yelling, "War! The Japanese are attacking!" It was the start of World War II for America, a war that was already going on in Asia and Europe and, for Japan, it was the beginning of *Taiheiyo-senso* (Pacific War).

The Pearl Harbor attack was a complete surprise, but for those following US-Japan relations, it wasn't totally unexpected. Relations between the two countries had deteriorated since the early 1900s. Japan was victorious in the Sino-Japanese War (1894-95), in the Russo-Japanese War (1904-05), and had emerged as a major power in East Asia. Japanese militarism, virile nationalism, and expansionist policies caused Americans to fear a possible conflict with Japan. Homer Lea, in his book, *The Valor of Ignorance*, published in 1909, predicted a war with Japan in the Pacific.

Japanese leaders felt Japan wasn't treated as a great power, an equal with the Western powers, and they felt especially slighted during the Versailles Peace Conference (1919), the Washington Naval Conference of 1922, and the London Naval Conference of 1930. The Japanese militarists resented the weak and timid civilian leadership and decided to act. The Japanese

61

Imperial Army took control and moved into Manchuria in 1931 and in 1937 invaded North China, thereby beginning a protracted war with China. The United States vehemently opposed Japanese expansionism but was unwilling to take military action. After the fall of France, Japan occupied French Indochina; consequently, United States finally acted and applied economic sanctions. Japanese assets in America were frozen in July 1941 and, more importantly, one week later, an oil embargo was put in place, effectively cutting off 88 percent of Japan's oil import. Japan had only an oil reserve of three years, so the embargo was a threat to its security.

The Japanese military and political leaders faced a dilemma: Submit to American demands and withdraw from Indochina and China; or continue to advance into Southeast Asia, seizing the strategic resources of rubber, tin, and oil. The Japanese Imperial Army preferred to focus northward to China and the Soviet Union, but its position was weaken by the stalemate in North China and by its defeat in the Nomonhan conflict with the Soviet Union in 1939. The Japanese Imperial Navy chose to focus southward to Southeast Asia and out into the Pacific Ocean. In either case, the Japanese leaders felt they couldn't give up what they had won. At that moment, the Japanese fleet needed oil and the admirals won out. Japan decided to advance southward, which meant conflict with the United States was inevitable.

By the 1940s, relations had worsened to a degree where both sides began to prepare militarily. American military planners began to prepare for a possible attack, even an invasion by Japan. The navy strengthened the base at Pearl Harbor by redeploying its fleet from California while the army held maneuvers. When rumors spread that the civilian Japanese might sabotage the planes at the airbases on O'ahu, the army ordered the planes to be clustered together, in a row, so they could be easily guarded. Unfortunately, it provided a better target for the Japanese pilots during the Pearl Harbor attack.

The large *Nikkei* population presented a problem for the military and haole civilian leaders. It was assumed the Japanese might side with Japan, and if an invasion occurred, they might commit sabotage. Administration officials in Washington, DC, including President Roosevelt, questioned the loyalty of the Japanese Americans.[34] The government began to take precautionary steps against possible subversive actions by the *Nikkei*. The Federal Bureau of Investigation (FBI), headed by Robert L. Shivers, with the aid of army and navy intelligence, and with the help of local informants, compiled a list of Japanese community leaders and individuals having links with and sympathy for the Japanese government; this was an arrest list to be used in case of war.

Shivers was sent to Hawaii in 1939 to assess the loyalty of the Japanese population and to ensure the internal security of the islands. He met with Nisei through advisory groups and came to the conclusion the overwhelming majority of *Nikkei* were loyal, and there was little possibility of subversion. Therefore, he believed there was no need to remove and confine the Japanese Americans.

As rumors and innuendoes flowed through the community, Japanese Americans were filled with fear and anxiety about the spreading suspicion. A patriotic rally sponsored by the O'ahu Citizens Committee for Home Defense was held at McKinley High School and was chaired by Dr. Shunzo Sakamaki. Dr. Sakamaki, a Nisei, was a Japanese history professor and later my mentor at the University of Hawai'i at Manoa. The rally, held on June 13, 1941, was attended by a large crowd of about two thousand. Colonel M. W. Marston, speaking for the commanding general, promised to protect the Japanese Americans if they would demonstrate their loyalty. The fear in the Japanese community was somewhat alleviated by this assurance.

However, concerns over Japanese American disloyalty caused the government to conduct several investigations. Two reports were particularly pertinent—the report by Kenneth Ringle of the Office of Naval Intelligence and the report by Curtis B. Munson, a special agent of the White House. They both concluded the Japanese Americans were not a security threat and the vast majority were loyal to the United States. But President Roosevelt and other administration officials chose to ignore or dismiss these reports. Racial bias played a role in government officials assuming

---

[34] Robinson, *Tragedy*, 33.

Japanese Americans to be potentially dangerous, even though there were no credible evidence of espionage. Articles by such writers as Albert Horlings fueled a false and distorted image of the Japanese Americans. Horlings argued it was a big gamble to trust the loyalty of the Japanese Americans. "To a remarkable degree Hawai'i's Japanese are untouched by American ways; all their pride of race, family, and religion binds them to Japan," he wrote. He advocated for the complete removal of Japanese Americans to the mainland.[35]

When the bombs started falling that Sunday in December, the loyalty question would soon become critical, but at that moment, we were stunned by the attack. Why would Japan jeopardize the safety of the local Japanese? Why are they bombing us? A profound sense of *hagi* hung over us.

While no Japanese bombs fell on Honolulu, there were civilian casualties within the city. The casualties were caused by US antiaircraft shells failing to explode in the air due to faulty fuses or fuses incorrectly timed in the confusion of the moment. Enemy planes were supposed to be brought down by the exploding shells or flak. Instead of bursting in the air, the shells fell to the ground and exploded.

Luckily that Sunday, I wasn't involved with the special class at the Japanese language school, the Hawai'i Chuo Gakuen. A shell exploded in the schoolyard and sent shrapnels into the auditorium where children were gathered for a Sunday morning class. A seven-year-old girl was killed, and a boy had his hand nearly severed by a shrapnel. He was taken to a hospital, and doctors had to amputate his hand and part of his forearm. Another shell landed at the corner of King and McCully streets, killing a three-month-old baby, her mother, and aunt and set fire to their house. One shell fell on a noodle restaurant, killing three and wounding four, and a shell fell near Piikoi Street, killing one woman. In all, about thirty-nine shells fell in the city, and forty-nine civilians died and thirty-five were wounded.

The shell that fell near Piikoi Street has an interesting story. Evelyn, my wife, lived at that time at Piikoi Street near South Beretania Street,

---

[35] Albert Horlings' article appeared in *The Nations* (July 25, 1942) and is reprinted in Ogawa, *Kodomo*, 304-9.

where her parents had a grocery store with living quarters in the rear. On that Sunday morning, she was playing in the store and, tempted by chocolate-covered graham crackers, proceeded to take a few. Evelyn had been warned several times by her parents that taking crackers, cookies, and candies will eat into the profit of the store and *"bachi ga ataru"* (you'll be punished). Suddenly there was a loud bang. Soon a neighbor ran by yelling, "War! War!" She didn't know what was going on, but later when the meaning of war was explained, she looked at her chocolate-smeared hand and remembered her parents' admonition—*"bachi ga ataru."* Suddenly she realized and cried, "I started the war. I started the war!" She felt guilty, for the shell that fell nearby had killed her girlfriend's mother. For you history buffs, now you know how World War II began!

It didn't take long for the war to seriously affect the lives of those you know. A tragic event occurred out at sea. My neighbors, the Kidos, lost their father and son. They were fishermen returning from their trip when an American P-40 fighter plane strafed the boat, killing both father and son. In the confusion and stress of the Pearl Harbor attack, incidents of civilians being killed or wounded were never publicized, and even among friends and acquaintances, we never talked about them. It was wartime and such incidents weren't discussed. Censorship prevented the public expression of grief and anger. Today, the blurring and the dismissing of details are called the "fogs of war," and the casualties and sufferings inflicted on noncombatants are referred to as "collateral damages." Perhaps it makes it easier to accept the loss by viewing the event this way.

The Japanese in Hawai'i weren't massively evacuated to concentration camps, whereas the Japanese living on the West Coast were forcefully relocated with loss of property and other assets. The Japanese population in Hawai'i was too large; it would have been logistically impossible to move the Japanese en masse. Moreover, the economy would have been drastically affected, for the Japanese made up a major part of the workforce. Also, the Japanese were so intermingled with the larger community that it would have been difficult, if not impossible, to separate all of them. And finally, prominent community leaders, and even the head of the FBI, played a role in advising on the treatment of Japanese and on the question of loyalty. Shigeo Yoshida, Nisei educator, and Hung Wai Ching, Chinese American YMCA executive, both of whom had influence in haole and Japanese circles, were instrumental in persuading the authorities to forgo mass evacuation. However, it is not to say that authorities didn't think about relocating the Japanese Americans. As previously discussed, writers such as Albert Horlings had argued for mass removal of the Japanese Americans in Hawai'i. After inspecting the damage done at Pearl Harbor, Secretary of the Navy Frank Knox submitted a report accusing the Japanese Americans of espionage and recommending their removal from O'ahu. Actual removal was planned, with one proposal to move the Japanese to Moloka'i, the island next to O'ahu, which had no military installations. But cooler heads prevailed and the plan was quickly dropped. President Roosevelt reacted by approving a plan to remove fifteen thousand Japanese Americans from Hawai'i, but it was never carried out. It would have been disastrous for the Hawaiian economy.

Apart from plans to remove en masse Japanese Americans, individual actions were taken that abruptly changed lives. *Nikkei* lost their jobs, businesses, and other means of livelihood. Nisei students were dismissed from universities. Francis Sueo Sugiyama, a Hawai'i Nisei dental student at the University of Southern California (USC), was suddenly expelled. He was able to obtain a permit to relocate to Chicago and after much struggle, was admitted to the University of Maryland dental school, where he graduated two years later. Another Hawai'i Nisei dental student, John Masao Fujioka, was sent to an assembly center, the initial phase of internment. In all, 120 Nisei students had their education disrupted. After the war, further indignities followed when the president of USC refused to readmit the students, and denied their access to their transcripts and the ability to transfer credits to other schools.[36]

---

[36] Details provided by Carolyn Sugiyama Classen. USC posthumously awarded her father an honorary degree. Carolyn received the degree on behalf of her father in a special ceremony on April 1, 2022. The university apologized and honored the expelled Nisei students by bestowing thirty-three posthumous honorary degrees.

SAND ISLAND INTERNMENT CAMP

Something immediately had to be done after the Pearl Harbor attack, and it began with the removal of a select number of *Nikkei*. On December 8, 1941, FBI agents in Hawai'i began rounding up 493 Japanese residents, mostly Issei but included a few Nisei. The FBI used a previously complied list, the Custodial Detention List, of individuals who were prominent in the Japanese community or had strong ties with Japan. On the list were teachers and administrators of Japanese language schools, journalists, Buddhist and Shinto priests, residents who worked for the consulate, and businessmen with ties to Japan.

Mr. E. Matsunaga, a relative of my wife, Evelyn, returned from a business trip to Japan and was immediately arrested. He was held at the Sand Island Internment Camp before been sent to a mainland camp. Since he was the sole provider for a family of three children, the family needed help so Evelyn's parents took them in. When he returned after the war, he was a broken man and never recovered from the traumatic ordeal. Families were not informed about the whereabouts of their loved ones. It was only after several weeks that the families were notified and could communicate with them. Only the head of the family was arrested and taken away, which meant the break-up of the family for the duration of the war.

Most of the islanders who were arrested were detained at Sand Island, a small island at the entrance of Honolulu Harbor. It was a former quarantine station that was hurriedly renovated and made into a transfer and holding camp. The relatively small five-acre camp was enclosed with barbed wire and had guard towers. Canvas tents were used to house the internees. It was officially designated as the Sand Island Internment Camp and was administered by the army from December 1941 to the beginning of March 1943.

Sand Island Internment Camp.
Courtesy of Nisei Veterans Legacy.

The camp did serve its purpose as a transit center. A roundup of about six hundred *Nikkei* from the other islands began in February 1942, and they were temporarily detained on Sand Island. They were then transferred, along with detainees from Honolulu and surrounding areas of O'ahu, to mainland relocation camps. The move began on February 17, 1942 with the first shipload of 170 *Nikkei* from O'ahu. A second ship transported 144 *Nikkei* from the other islands to the mainland. Eight other ships were used to gradually transfer the remaining detainees. A total of about 1,450 *Nikkei* passed through on the way to the mainland camps. However, there were a few, about 149 Japanese Americans, who were transferred to the newly established Honouliuli Internment Camp on the western side of O'ahu.

Initially, conditions at the Sand Island Camp were harsh, but the facilities were renovated and camp life improved. From the government's point of view, the camp wasn't ideally located because it was at the entrance of a busy harbor and presented a security problem. Therefore, the decision was made to close the camp as soon as possible. With the opening of Honouliuli, the Sand Island Camp could be closed and it was officially shut down on March 1, 1943, after fifteen months of operation.[37]

---

[37] See the following for information on the Sand Island Internment Camp: Tetsuden Kashima, *Judgment Without Trial: Japanese American Internment During World War II* (Seattle: University of Washington Press, 2004); Yasutaro Soga (Keiho), *Life Behind Barbed Wire: The World War II Internment Memoirs of a Hawai'i Issei* (Honolulu: University of Hawai'i Press, 2008); Jeffrey F. Burton and Mary M. Farrell, *World War II Japanese American Internment Sites in Hawai'i* (Tucson, AZ: Trans-Sierran Archaeological Research, 2007).

HONOULIULI INTERNMENT CAMP

A staff worker at the Japanese Cultural Center of Hawai'i (JCCH), while going through old photographs, noticed the remains of an aqua-duct, a man-made channel constructed to convey water from one location to another. An investigation of the site began and the Honouliuli camp was rediscovered in 2003. The site was hidden from view by thick over-growth of weeds, bushes, and trees. Long ignored and forgotten, Honouliuli Internment Camp is now a National Historic Site under the National Park Service. It is in the Honouliuli Gulch, on the northwest side of O'ahu, near Waipahu at the base of the Wai'anae Mountains. Operated by the US Army, it was the largest detention facility in Hawai'i during the war, covering 160 acres and surrounded by barbed wire fence with guard towers. The camp, which officially opened in March 1943, consisted of about 150 buildings and 170 tarpaulin tents.

Honouliuli Internment Camp.
Courtesy of Densho.

At its peak, the camp held 320 Japanese inmates, most of whom were Nisei. Honouliuli was also a prisoner of war (POW) camp. It held more than four thousand POW, mainly Okinawans and Koreans conscripted by the Japanese army as laborers and captured in the Pacific theater of operations. In addition, there were a smaller number of European prisoners, mostly Germans and Italians. The *Nikkei* were housed mainly in the wooden barracks, which were separated from the POW quarters; no interaction was allowed with the captured POW.

The facilities were reasonable with latrines, hot showers, kitchens, mess halls, and later a recreation field was added. The biggest complaints were the heat and sheer boredom. The Japanese detainees referred to the camp as *jigoku dani* (hell valley) because of the oppressive heat of the gulch. There was no ocean breeze, and the gulch captured the heat and placed a lid on it. To relieve boredom, internees did landscaping, gardening, and woodcraft, but the best morale booster were the family visits, which were allowed two Sundays a month.

At the beginning, Honouliuli was basically a Japanese internment camp, but with only 320 internees, the camp was small when compared to the mainland camps, which numbered in the thousands. The population of the camp gradually changed. Starting in 1943, the Nisei were released on parole and returned to their families or transferred to mainland camps. Meanwhile, an increasing number of POWs were brought in, turning it into a POW camp. The camp was closed with the end of the war on September 1945, and only twenty-one *Nikkei* remained; none were Nisei, leaving only Issei and *Kibei*.[38]

The Honouliuli camp slowly and literally faded into oblivion. Tucked away in a desolate gulch, not even the local populace was aware of its existence. Growing up in Hawai'i, I had no idea there was such a camp. Nobody talked about it—this was the primary reason why the camp was forgotten. The internees didn't want to share their stories because the experience was

---

[38] Information on Honouliuli is found in the same sources as that of the Sand Island Internment Camp. See also Susan Morrison and Peter Knerr, "Forgotten Internees," *Honolulu Magazine* (November, 1990); Suzanne Falgout and Linda Nishigaya, eds, "Breaking the Silence: Lessons of Democracy and Social Justice from the World War II Honouliuli Internment and POW Camp in Hawai'i," *Social Process in Hawai'i*, 45 (2014).

painful to recall, a response typically expressed by Hawai'i and mainland internees. In addition, the Japanese way was to internalize suffering by resorting to traditional behavioral norms—*shikata ga nai* (it can't be helped) and *gaman* (endure or bear). These attitudinal traits were relied upon by the Issei and some of the older Nisei. According to these norms, fate has dealt you a hand, so do the best with what you have and don't complain—just persevere and quietly grin and bear it. But by not sharing their experiences, their stories were almost lost. Fortunately, JCCH has compiled testimonies and memoirs of the internees, and they have been published.[39] Now, JCCH handles the dissemination of information and the conducting of restrictive tours until it is ready to be opened to the public.

WARTIME LOYALTY AND SERVICE

As the relationship with Japan worsened in the 1920s, US military leaders made war plans that included the imposition of martial law in Hawai'i to stem the possibility of sabotage or espionage by the local Japanese. Already, the loyalty of the Japanese was being questioned. Declaring a state of martial law is a drastic action wherein the civilian government and judicial system are temporarily placed under military rule. There must be an imminent threat to the nation's security. These contingency plans had to have the tacit approval of administration officials in Washington, DC.

A few hours after the Pearl Harbor attack, General Walter Short, commanding general of the Hawai'i Department of the US Army, pressured Joseph B. Poindexter, territorial governor of Hawai'i, to immediately declare martial law. Governor Poindexter called President Roosevelt and with his approval declared martial law on December 8, 1941. Governor Poindexter thought it would last about thirty days, but he was sadly mistaken. Instead, martial law lasted for thirty-five months until October 24, 1944. It was the longest period in US history for a large civilian population

---

[39] The following are publications of the JCCH pertaining to Honouliuli: *Life Behind Barbed Wire: The World War II Internment Memoir of a Hawai'i Issei* (2008); *Family Torn Apart: The Internment Story of the Otokichi Muin Ozaki Family* (2012); Haisho Tenten, *An Internment Odyssey* (2017); and Claire Sato and Violet Harada, *A Resilient Spirit: The Voice of Hawai'i's Internees* (2018).

to be under military rule. Most legal experts say it should have ended much earlier, surely after the Japanese navy's defeat at the Battle of Midway on June 4-6, 1942. The threat of a Japanese invasion had vanished, and martial law could have been lifted—but it wasn't.

Martial law provided the legal underpinning for the internment of Japanese Americans. It is ironic that in Hawai'i, where the threat of a Japanese invasion was imminent and martial law was declared, only a few *Nikkei* were removed. However, on the mainland where there was no threat of an invasion and martial law wasn't declared, there was a massive removal of *Nikkei*. This contradiction was noted by Justice Frank Murphy in his dissent in *Korematsu v. United States.*

> This exclusion of all persons of Japanese ancestry, both alien and non-alien, from the Pacific Coast area on a plea of military necessity in the absence of martial law ought not to be approved. Such exclusion goes over the very brink of constitutional power and falls into the ugly abyss of racism.[40]

With the territorial government and the courts under military control, constitutional rights, including *habeas corpus* petition, were suspended. The military took over a few private properties. The Waikiki hotels were only for military personnel. All these entities came under the authority of the army's commanding general, who became the military governor of Hawai'i. General Short was the first military governor but he was soon replaced by Lieutenant General Delos C. Emmons.[41]

The military government issued 181 general orders. Orders pertaining to the entire population were as followed:

---

[40] Eric K. Yamamoto et al., *Race, Rights and Reparation: Law and the Japanese American Internment* (New York: Aspen Publishers, 2001), 145.

[41] General Walter Short and Admiral Husband Kimmel were relieved of their duties and blamed for the ill-preparedness of the US Armed Forces.

+ curfew
+ blackout of all windows
+ censorship of mail, news media, and other means of communication
+ fingerprinting of all over seven years of age
+ requirement of an identification card at all times
+ suspension of foreign language broadcasts

In addition, the rationing of gasoline and the monitoring of food and liquor sales affected everyone. Wages were frozen and, interestingly, even the currency was controlled. There was fear the Japanese could invade and possibly seize American currency and use it in other parts of the world. The regular currency was called in and destroyed and was replaced with emergency banknotes overprinted with "Hawai'i" in bold, capital letters on the backside. If the Japanese invaded and took over the islands, the US Government would declare the overprinted notes as counterfeit and render them useless. Since there was no invasion, it turned out to be a wasted effort. Today, the overprinted notes are highly sought-after collector's items.

There were orders specifically meant for the *Nikkei*. All Japanese language schools were closed, and the two Japanese language newspapers were suspended. *Nikkei* were restricted on their travel and excluded from certain areas near military installations. They were not allowed to change their residence or occupation without permission, nor were they allowed to assemble in groups of more than ten persons. Furthermore, they had to turn in weapons, explosives, and ammunition.[42] Aliens were ordered to turn in flashlights, portable radios, and cameras, which could be used to help the invaders.

My father had a samurai sword, a family heirloom, but he didn't turn it in, instead discreetly getting rid of it. In Japanese families, anything the authorities might consider contraband or indicating loyalty to Japan was destroyed or otherwise discarded. There was a beautiful model of the

---

[42] Robinson, *Tragedy of Democracy*, 63-66. For detailed analyses of martial law in Hawai'i, see Anthony J. Garner, *Hawai'i Under Army Rule* (Stanford: Stanford University Press, 1955).

Japanese ocean liner *Tatsuta Maru* in our living room. As a teenager, I used to admire it and always wondered why my father never got rid of it, knowing it could be used as a troopship and thereby be tainted with Japan's war effort. As it turned out, *Tatsuta Maru* was used as a repatriation ship carrying diplomats and other civilians at the beginning of the war. She was torpedoed and sunk by a US submarine on February 8, 1943, while serving as a troopship.

The military orders were most stringent against the *Nikkei*, but all citizens of Hawai'i suffered curtailment of their civil rights and liberties. An onerous act of the military was the replacement of civilian courts by military provost courts. The military courts tried about fifty-five thousand civilian cases, with traffic violations, curfew, blackout violations, and absenteeism making up most of the cases. Some of the punishments were harsh. Absenteeism from work was punishable by fine up to $200 or imprisonment up to two months. Hundreds of workers were fined or jailed.

There were a few legal challenges to the continued use of martial law, but none of the cases dealt with Japanese Americans. The *Nikkei* didn't seek any legal redress against the military. In *Duncan v. Kahanamoku* (1946), the Supreme Court ruled the suspension of civilian courts was not justified by law. Obviously, the military held on to power long after necessity had ceased. The excuse given by the military commanders was that the large Japanese population in Hawai'i posed an ongoing threat to national security. Today, we see it as a racially motivated excuse to perpetuate military rule.

Clearly, one of the objectives of martial law was to keep in check the *Nikkei* in Hawai'i. There was a serious misconception about their loyalty and propensity to be involved in subversive activities. Many whites viewed Japanese Americans with suspicion and thought they were unassimilable. Actually almost all Nisei, except for a few *Kibei*, were unequivocally loyal to the United States. They were thoroughly Americanized and wholeheartedly accepted American values and beliefs. The Issei, on the other hand, although loyal to the United States because of their children's citizenship and because they had resided in the United States for a long time, nevertheless had emotional and nostalgic attachment to the mother country. It was difficult for them to renounce their loyalty to Japan. Moreover, America had denied them citizenship, so why shouldn't they have some affection for Japan?

My parents had family ties in Japan but remained loyal to the United States, for they had two sons in the US Army and had made Hawai'i their home. Grandmother, however, held on to her allegiance to the emperor and her love for Japan. Occasionally, she would get together with other elderly Issei and gossip and talk about the war. She strongly believed Japan would win the war. The group was known as *katta-gumi* or *kachi-gumi* (win the war group). She was visibly crushed when the war ended and finally had to accept reality.

Therefore, there were a small number of Issei and *Kibei* who were disloyal, but the attitudes of these individuals didn't mean the whole group should be condemned and have discriminating actions taken against them. But actions were taken and over two thousand *Nikkei* from Hawai'i were interned—of this number one third were Nisei, mostly *Kibei*. For the record, none of the *Nikkei* engaged in sabotage, espionage, or any other subversive activities.

How could the questioning of the Japanese Americans' loyalty be overcome? Verbal persuasion wasn't enough. Concrete action had to be taken to change attitudes—to sweep aside the fears and prejudices. The men of Japanese ancestry had the answer by volunteering to serve their country, but initially, their services were not fully accepted. At the time of the Pearl Harbor attack, Nisei soldiers in the Hawai'i Territorial Guard (HTG) helped to protect military bases and to maintain public safety. Soon complaints arose about the use of these Nisei. The Nisei were suddenly discharged from the HTG, and those from the 298th and 299th Infantry Battalions, stationed at Schofield Barracks on O'ahu, were relieved of their weapons and confined to quarter. The units were turned into labor battalions.

Nisei soldiers of the Hawai'i Territorial Guard (HTG).
Courtesy of Nisei Veterans Legacy.

NISEI IN MILITARY SERVICE

The role played by community leaders Shigeo Yoshida and Hung Wai Ching and by FBI head, Robert Shivers, in persuading the authorities to drop their plans to evacuate the Hawai'i *Nikkei* was previously noted. They were also instrumental in persuading the government and military leader to allow Nisei to serve in the military. Shivers openly supported the use of Nisei in military units. Yoshida and Ching appealed personally by writing letters, circulating petitions, and organizing meetings. They showed how well the Japanese population was behaving and of their willingness to serve as volunteer laborers. In need of more volunteers, the army soon realized they could use the help of the Japanese Americans. Consequently in February 1942, with the help of Ching and Yoshida, a noncombat labor battalion of 169 Nisei volunteers was formed. It was called the "Varsity

Victory Volunteers" (VVV) because it was composed mainly of Nisei college students who had formerly served with the HTG. Despite some opposition, the army decided to bring together the Nisei from the various units, including the 298th and 299th battalions and the VVV, a total of 1,432 men, and formed the 100th Infantry Battalion. The 100th Battalion became an all-Nisei combat unit—no longer were the Nisei in labor battalions. The 100th Battalion was promptly sent to Camp McCoy in Wisconsin for basic training.

Sensing the need for more volunteers, the army sent out a call in the beginning of January 1943 and, to the surprise of everyone, 9,807 volunteered in Hawai'i. This was an amazing 38 percent of all the eligible male Japanese in Hawai'i. At first, the army wanted to have three thousand volunteers—fifteen hundred from the mainland and fifteen hundred from Hawai'i. But the response on the mainland wasn't enthusiastic, which wasn't surprising since the mainland Nisei were suffering the indignities of being confined in internment camps. The army decided to increase the quota from Hawai'i to 2,500, and the mainland contingent was set at one thousand. Hence, a new combat unit composed of all-Nisei volunteers from Hawai'i and the mainland was formed, becoming the 442nd Regimental Combat Team.

On March 28, 1943, it was an impressive sight when a large detachment of 442nd volunteers in khaki uniform and wearing paper leis marched up King Street and assembled on the grounds of the 'Iolani Palace. It was the send-off ceremony, as the unit prepared to leave the islands for training at Camp Shelby, Mississippi. I was moved witnessing this awesome patriotic event.

442nd send-off ceremony at 'Iolani Palace.
Courtesy of Nisei Veterans Legacy.

Hung Wai Ching was one of the few allowed on the pier when the
SS *Lurline* departed in early April 1943 with the 442nd unit aboard, and
he was there in San Francisco to greet the unit when the ship arrived six
days later. Furthermore, he was at Camp Shelby when the train arrived.
For his devotion and support, Ching was elected as an honorary member
of the 442nd Veterans Club. The Hawai'i Nisei veterans also honored
Shigeo Yoshida. Ted Tsukiyama, member of VVV, 442nd, and Military
Intelligence Service (MIS), wrote: "It is for his long, faithful and dedicated
wartime service to his community and to his country that Shigeo Yoshida
will be best remembered...there was no one in the Japanese community in
Hawai'i who was held in higher esteem, confidence and trust by the military and civil leaders, who controlled the destiny of wartime Hawai'i, than
was Shigeo Yoshida."[43]

---

[43] Edward Yamasaki, ed., *And Then There were Eight* (Honolulu: Item Chapter, 442nd Veterans Club, 2003),
23, 32-34.

The 100th Battalion preceded the 442nd and was already in combat when units of the 442nd arrived in Italy. In early fighting in Italy, the 100th Battalion received some nine hundred Purple Hearts and was nicknamed "Purple Heart Battalion." Purple Heart medals are awarded to those killed or wounded in action. The 100th became one of the battalions of the 442nd, but instead of being the first battalion, it was allowed to retain its unique designation. The 100th and 442nd took part in seven campaigns in Italy and southern France, with some units entering southern Germany and participating in the liberation of the concentration camp at Dachau. Probably the most noted exploit of the 442nd was the rescue of the trapped battalion of the 36th Infantry Division from Texas, the so-called "Lost Battalion." In this horrid battle of the Vosges Forest, the 442nd suffered eight hundred casualties in just five days, losing more men than the soldiers they rescued. The 442nd, in terms of its size and length of service, emerged as the most decorated army unit in American military history.[44]

President Truman presenting the Presidential Unit Citation to 442nd.
Courtesy of Nisei Veterans Legacy.

---

[44] It was unusual to have only one Medal of Honor recipient, a small number considering the brutal campaigns in Italy and France and the heavy casualties taken by the 100th and 442nd. Legislation sponsored by Sen. Daniel Akaka was passed, asking the army to review the combat records of Asian Americans in World War II to determine if any deserving service member had been passed over for the Medal of Honor. Indeed, the review found some extraordinary actions had not received the honor they clearly deserved. On June 21, 2000, in a ceremony at the White House, President Clinton presented the Medal of Honor to twenty Nisei; among the recipients was Sen. Daniel Inouye. A major oversight by the army was corrected.

Returning veterans rarely spoke about their war experiences. My brother-in-law, nicknamed "Bozo," was with the 442nd and was wounded in Italy, but seldom talked about the war. He gave me a bunch of shoulder patches, insignia of units the 442nd fought with or were under their command. Occasionally, he would make anecdotal remarks—the unique sounds of the German machine guns due to their rapid rate of fire. The American machine gun would go "rat-tat-tat," a staccato sound, whereas the German machine gun would go "brrrr-up," the sound of a burst of fire. Also, he would comment on the viciousness of the German 88 mm, which was originally meant to be an antiaircraft weapon but was used against the infantry. But unless pressed, he like many veterans were reluctant to talk about their combat experiences.

Sometimes humorous incidents would come out. Bozo once cooked rabbit stew in his helmet. He put lots of onions and other vegetables in it and told his buddy it was chicken stew. His buddy ate it and liked it, but afterward he became sick when he learned it was rabbit. He also remembered Bozo washing his socks in his helmet! Bozo claimed he scrubbed the helmet clean before using it. Over the years, enough stories have emerged, and we have abundant information about the 100th and 442nd. Their exploits have been written in books, documentaries have been produced, and even a couple of movies have been made. The recently opened National Museum of the United States Army in Fort Belvoir, Virginia explores in detail the story of the 100th and 442nd.[45]

Because of all the accolades given to the 100th and the 442nd, another group of Nisei who distinguished themselves in the Pacific War have not been sufficiently recognized. These were Nisei who served as Japanese language interpreters and translators with the Military Intelligence Service (MIS). When the war started, the military desperately needed individuals with Japanese language skills. On December 1942, sixty Hawai'i Nisei were transferred from the 100th Battalion to MIS and were sent to MIS Language School at Camp Savage, Minnesota. Soon the school was

---

[45] For a recent book with stories of individual 442nd veterans and their families, see: Daniel James Brown, *Facing the Mountain: A True Story of Japanese American Heroes in World War II* (New York: Viking, 2021).

outgrown, so it was moved to Fort Snelling, Minnesota. Eventually, over six thousand Nisei attended the school. After graduation, they were sent all over the Pacific, from the Aleutian Islands to Australia, and they also served in the China, Burma, and India Theater. They were assigned as individuals or as small teams to army, navy, Marine Corps, and allied combat units.

These Nisei linguists studied captured enemy documents, deciphered enemy codes, and interrogated prisoners. Since most of their work was clandestine and classified and was done in small groups on temporary assignments, they were unrecorded. It wasn't until the mid-1970s, when the secrecy was lifted, that we learned of the feats of the Nisei linguists. Major General Charles A. Willoughby, chief of intelligence on General MacArthur's staff, credited the Nisei MIS for shortening the Pacific War by two years and saving millions of lives.[46] This was an exaggeration but many have acknowledged the contributions of the Nisei. After the war, Nisei continued to serve as interpreters and translators in the American occupation of Japan and helped in establishing a cordial relationship with the Japanese populace. For all its accomplishments, the MIS Nisei linguists were awarded the Presidential Unit Citation in 2000 and in 2010 were awarded the Congressional Gold Medal, along with the 100th and the 442nd.

The military accomplishments of the Nisei convincingly proved the loyalty of the Japanese. Some argued the war was the only way the *Nikkei* were able to be totally trusted by the American public and in the long run, the war hastened the assimilation of the Japanese. But racist policies were dominant in the military. The 100th and 442nd were segregated units led most often by Caucasian officers. Such was not the case with the MIS, where Nisei were integrated into existing units. However, during the war, few Nisei linguists were commissioned as officers, although Caucasian graduates of the navy and army Japanese language schools with less language skills were given commissions. Policies based on racial lines were only

---

[46] Robinson, *Tragedy of Democracy*, 210. For information on MIS and individual exploits, see: http://www. misveteranshawaii.com/. See also Joseph D. Harrington, *Yankee Samurai: The Secret Role of Nisei in America's Pacific Victory* (Detroit: Pettigrew Enterprise, 1979).

eliminated after the war. Acceptance of the Nisei came after blood had been shed in combat, but it didn't eliminate racism.

WARTIME CONDITIONS

Except for a few individuals, the vast majority of Hawai'i Japanese didn't suffer the trauma of being deported to a strange and desolate place enclosed with barbed wire. Consequently, the impression of the Hawai'i Japanese of the war years is quite different from those of the mainland Japanese. The immediate concern of the Japanese in Hawai'i was the threat of another Japanese attack and possible invasion, and how the people of Japanese ancestry would be treated by the rest of the population. These were real concerns of the *Nikkei* adults, but as a teenager, I didn't think the Japanese would attack again, nor was I worried about reprisal attacks. I was more concerned about the severe inconvenience posed by the many regulations and restrictions.

Panic and confusion ensued after the Pearl Harbor attack as rumor of a possible Japanese attack and invasion circulated, causing all kinds of preparations to be undertaken. The Aloha Tower siren would go off at six o'clock in the evening, announcing the start of curfew, and all windows had to be blacked out so lights wouldn't show. Bomb shelters had to be built. We had a shelter in our front yard, but the ground was hard, as a result, the shelter wasn't deep. It was L-shaped and big enough to accommodate the entire family, but it was never used and soon cobwebs took over. Gas masks were issued to everyone over seven, and we had to bring them to school, where we practiced putting them on. The fear of an invasion was pervasive—many beaches were fenced off with barbed wire, and government buildings were surrounded with sandbags and barbed wire. An antiaircraft battery compound, enclosed with barbed wire, was stationed right in our neighborhood. It seemed excessive to me to have an antiaircraft battery in a residential neighborhood. Several of the defensive measures, including the carrying of gas masks, were rescinded after the American victory in the Battle of Midway.

Since I was too young to drive, gas rationing was of little concern, but the shortage of certain food was disconcerting. Overall, there was an adequate supply of food, but certain types of food were in short supply. The only meat readily available was SPAM, the canned meat product. Now, it is turned down by food elites and rejected by health-conscious consumers. During the war, we ate it regularly and surprisingly got to like it. Today, it is popular in Hawai'i and is considered a comfort food, and in South Korea and the Philippines, it is treated like an expensive delicacy. Prof. Robert Ji-Song Ku calls it "dubious" food, but he loves it, for he grew up eating SPAM in Hawai'i.[47] It didn't take long for a Nisei to come up with SPAM *musubi*, which is SPAM on a rice ball, wrapped in *nori* (dried seaweed). Barbara Funamura from the island of Kaua'i is the creator of SPAM *musubi*; she was surprised by its popularity.

Author's SPAM *musubi*, the comfort food of Hawai'i Japanese.

---

[47] Robert Ji-Song Ku, *Dubious Gastronomy: The Cultural Politics of Eating Asian in the USA* (Honolulu: University of Hawai'i Press, 2014) 190-223. The word spam (in lowercase letters) is used to refer to unsolicited and unwanted email and is said to have originated from critics of this "disgusting luncheon meat." But the popularity of SPAM in Hawai'i continues unabated. Twenty thousand people turn out every April to celebrate a daylong SPAM Jam in Honolulu. According to Hormel Foods Corporation, Hawai'i consumes 6.7 million cans annually, which means each Hawai'i resident consumes 5.5 cans per year.

Schooling was affected by the war. Public schools were closed for two months. When schools reopened, a four-day-week schedule was followed, allowing middle and high school students to work one day in the pineapple fields. There was a severe labor shortage in the islands when the men went to war, so the authorities, ignoring child-labor laws, had students working in the fields. We had to be at Central Intermediate School by five a.m. when it was still dark. We were then loaded onto trucks and were taken in a convoy to the pineapple fields. At first, we picked pineapples and carried them in a sack swung over our shoulders out to the end of the row, where the pineapples were placed in crates. But the pineapples proved to be too heavy, so we were used to pick "slips." A slip is a plantlet found at the base of the pineapple plant and is a faster way to grow pineapples than planting the crown. After working all day, we returned covered with reddish-brown dust. The soil of the pineapple field is reddish-brown due to iron oxide.

Valuable class time was lost, but at that time, I thought it was adventuresome to be away from school. Activities supporting the war effort significantly cut into instructional time—other diversions were saving stamp drives, conservation drives, and various recycling programs of scrap metal, rubber, and paper. Science class became a time to learn how to grow vegetables at the school's "victory garden." It was said that by working on the garden, we were learning about botany and agricultural science. Actually, it did help the school and the war effort, for the vegetables were used in the school cafeteria.

Schools played a major role in drumming up patriotism. We were taken up with all kinds of patriotic activities at school. This spirit of patriotism spilled over and permeated the entire community. I remember two popular songs we sang as students that were written in response to the attack on Pearl Harbor and frequently heard over the radio.

Let's remember Pearl Harbor
As we go to meet the foe.
Let's remember Pearl Harbor
As we did the Alamo.

We will always remember
How they died for liberty.
Let's remember Pearl Harbor
And go on to victory.[48]

Praise the Lord and pass the ammunition.
Praise the Lord and pass the ammunition.
Praise the Lord and pass the ammunition.
And we'll all stay free.[49]

None of the wartime shortages were life-threatening. As a teenager, I viewed the shortages and rationing as being inconvenient. There was a shortage of comic books, and, to my way of thinking, this was terrible. I remember standing in line early in the morning before Rainbow Sweetshop opened, and as soon as the door opened, I would rush in with the crowd and scoop all my favorite comic books. If it's important, you would stand in line.

A more serious shortage was workers. Businesses had a difficult time finding employees. My father's plumbing business had many calls, but he couldn't service all because of the lack of employees. My two older brothers worked for my father as plumbers, but they were drafted into the army. Satoshi, my oldest brother, served with an engineering battalion at Schofield Barracks, and Mamoru was with MIS on the mainland. Only an elderly Issei was left, and although he was a conscientious employee, he couldn't handle the volume of work. There were other employees, but none of them lasted long. Everywhere labor conditions were tight, and the military regulations didn't help matters.

Although my family wasn't interned, the war transformed our lives. My brothers were in the army and our schooling was disrupted. Daily life was affected by numerous and onerous regulations, but as the war progressed and allied victories mounted, regulations were eased but were never fully rescinded. Everything was geared toward the war effort—shortages,

---

[48]https://www.lyricsondemand.com.

[49]http://www.songlyrics.com.

rationing, civil defense measures, war bond and saving stamp drives, labor restrictions, and diversion of school time.

Total war effort even included "Wolf," our German shepherd mutt. The army needed dogs for sentry and other military purposes, so Wolf was conscripted. After the war, the army returned Wolf with a certificate of commendation from the commanding officer. Wolf was the only one in the immediate family to receive a government commendation. The only scar on Wolf was a cut on the right ear. Too bad he couldn't tell us his war stories.

KOTONKS AND BUDDHAHEADS

The war brought together the Hawai'i and mainland Nisei at two junctures—they were assigned to the same army unit (442nd) and, in a few instances, were in the same internment camp. Although the Hawai'i and mainland Nisei had the same ancestry and shared the same heritage, culture, and language, their thinking and outlook were different. But this wasn't a problem for the Issei in Hawai'i and on the mainland because they had similar attitudes and mindset. There were, however, profound differences in the attitude and outlook of the Hawai'i and mainland Nisei, which became a problem for the Nisei.

A story developed in the early days of World War II when Hawai'i Nisei were training with mainland Nisei as members of the 442nd. It seems a fight started, and a mainlander was knocked down. When his head struck the ground, the sound "kotonk" was heard. It sounded like an empty container hitting the ground, the implication being mainlanders' heads are hollow. The mainland Nisei retaliated and called the islanders "buddhaheads," probably referring to the shaven, bald-headed Buddhist priests. This is said to be the origin of the terms "kotonk" and "buddhahead." Although there are other accounts of how the words originated, this story is most intriguing. At the beginning, the terms had a pejorative connotation but later the words became a friendly way to differentiate the mainland Nisei from the Hawai'i Nisei.

Fanciful and amusing as the story seems, it does point out a truism; that there are differences between mainland and local Nisei. The assimilation process experienced by the Hawai'i Nisei differed from that of the mainland Nisei. Historical, geographical, and environmental factors played roles in developing different behavioral and attitudinal traits, resulting in divergent values, outlooks, and lifestyles. The contrast in milieus and the impact of the wide spatial distribution of the mainland emigrants versus the localized plantation system of Hawai'i have been previously discussed. Offered here is another reason for the difference—it is the differential impact of the war on the Hawai'i and mainland Nisei. The total number of *Nikkei* from Hawai'i sent to internment camps was a little over two thousand; the initial group of 712 detainees, mostly Issei, were immediately arrested and sent to Department of Justice camps and about 1,450, mostly Nisei, were subsequently removed to mainland internment camps or to Honouliuli. The Hawai'i Nisei experienced "selective expulsion," with only a limited number of individuals sent to camps. In contrast, 120,000 mainlanders suffered "mass expulsion."

Entire families were forcibly removed whereas in Hawai'i only the head of the family was taken. The mainlanders loss their homes, properties, businesses, and other assets, while the islanders didn't suffer the loss of assets. Therefore, the degree of difference in the number involved and, in the trauma and suffering endured, made for disparate attitudinal and behavioral responses of the Nisei. The traumatic experience of the "kotonks" are examined in the following three chapters and the specific ways in which these attitudinal and behavioral traits are expressed are discussed in chapter 10.

PART TWO

INTERRUPTION

CHAPTER FIVE

GILA RIVER AND POSTON

If a population census of Arizona was taken in January 1943, the breakdown would have been as follows: Phoenix would be the largest city with 65,400, followed by Tucson with 38,800, Poston with 18,000, and Gila River with 13,400.[50] Poston and Gila River? What are they? Are these cities?

The US government euphemistically called Poston and Gila River "relocation centers" and its inhabitants as "evacuees." Critics, scholars, and Japanese Americans, in general, preferred the term "concentration camps." "Concentration camps" may sound harsh, but these camps were surrounded by barbed wire, had guard towers, and armed soldiers. To be sure, they weren't the concentration camps of World War II, the Nazi death camps where millions of inmates were put to death. In these American camps, the inmates weren't tortured or brutalized, and the administration of the camp was humane. The term "prisons" is occasionally used, but the camps weren't designed as penal colonies, for the inmates had committed no crimes. Another term used is "incarceration camps," which sounds formal and legalistic, and is akin to imprisonment. Again, no crimes had been committed.

"Detention camps" is used and has the meaning of temporary custody and holding pattern, but it is too benign a term. I have used this term for the smaller camps administered by the Justice Department and the US Army and were camps only for men detainees and not for families. For the larger

---

[50] Dillon S. Myer, *Uprooted Americans: The Japanese Americans and the War Relocation Authority During World War II* (Tucson, AZ: University of Arizona Press, 1971), 315. About a year later, over two thousand internees were transferred from Jerome Internment Camp in Arkansas to Gila River, thereby increasing its total population to 16,655.

camps, I have no qualms in using "concentration camps" and have used it in my writings, but in this book, I have largely used the term "internment camps," which denotes confinement to a specific area with certain limitations and occurring during wartime conditions. What these camps are called is important, for semantics does matter because it reflects the overall view taken and how the subject is approached. Better public relations with a softer image was sought by the government when it used "relocation centers," as it wanted to show how "evacuees" were moved for their own protection, and the "relocation centers" were places to prepare for assimilation into the larger society so the "evacuees" would have better opportunities. A positive spin was given to the camps. On the other hand, the critics portrayed the "concentration camps" as places where inmates underwent stress and anguish, and where the fabric of family life was destroyed. Considerable inconvenience was endured and, more importantly, psychological and emotional damage was done. The nuances of words need to be understood and appreciated. Words, therefore, do matter.[51]

In the aftermath of the Pearl Harbor attack, anti-Japanese feelings erupted on the West Coast. There had been a long history of discrimination against the Japanese, especially in California, which had the largest number of *Nikkei*. With hatred of the Japanese boiling to the surface, all kinds of rumors circulated, even of a threatened Japanese attack in the coastal areas, and as a result, there was considerable anxiety. Fear of Japanese engaging in sabotage and espionage, and possibly supporting the invaders should they land, caused West Coast whites to demand immediate removal of all *Nikkei*. The media added to the spread of rumors, thereby heightening fear and causing war hysteria. Walter Lippmann, the syndicated columnist writing in the *Washington Post*, warned of an imminent attack and urged all Japanese Americans be moved inland. Furthermore, he charged Japanese Americans were signaling Japanese ships from the shoreline. This was patently false, but the damage was done and panic set in. When racism and fear are combined,

---

[51] Robinson, *Tragedy of Democracy*, vii-viii; Bill Staples, Jr., *Kenichi Zenimura: Japanese American Baseball Pioneer* (Jefferson, NC: McFarland & Company, 2011), 9-10.

a volatile situation is created. Local and state leaders, including California Governor Culbert Olson, State Attorney General Earl Warren, and the entire state congressional delegation, ignoring the constitutional rights of Japanese American citizens, joined in the cry for immediate removal and detention of all people of Japanese ancestry.

There were those who cautioned against taking drastic actions against the Japanese Americans. The Justice Department under Francis Biddle opposed the move. Investigative reports by the Office of Naval Intelligence, Federal Bureau of Investigation, Federal Communications Commission, and the State Department concluded most *Nikkei* were loyal and there was no need to fear any subversive activity. Nevertheless, those advocating forceful removal of the Japanese won out. Most of the policymakers urging mass removal were from the War Department and the State Department and were buttressed by the recommendations of a few military leaders. "Military necessity" was given as the decisive factor in the removal of the *Nikkei,* but it was later found that this wasn't the defining reason. The Commission on the Wartime Relocation and Internment of Civilians (CWRIC) concluded in 1982 that the eviction and detention of the *Nikkei* was based on "race prejudice, war hysteria and a failure of political leadership."[52] To this list of reasons, greed on the part of West Coast whites could be added, for they wanted to eliminate economic competition, while some wanted the properties of the *Nikkei.* A white farmer admitted:

We're charged with wanting to get rid of the Japs for selfish reasons. We might as well be honest. We do. It's a question of whether the white man lives on the Pacific Coast or the brown man. They came into this valley to work, and they stayed to take over....[53]

---

[52] Commission on Wartime Relocation and Internment of Civilians, *Personal Justice Denied: Report of the Commission on Wartime Relocation and Internment of Civilians* (Seattle: University of Washington Press and Washington, DC: Civil Liberties Public Education Fund, 1997), 18.

[53] Yamamoto et al., 98.

Immediately after the declaration of war against Japan, the FBI, using a previously complied list, rounded up Issei and a few Nisei who were prominent in the Japanese community or had strong ties with Japan. The pattern of arrest was the same as in Hawai'i. These were individuals, usually single men, who were perceived to be a high security risk. In all, about 1,300 Nikkei were arrested and by February, the number had grown to some 2,300, of whom about half were from the West Coast. The Nikkei were taken to detention camps run by the Immigration and Naturalization Service of the Justice Department and by the US Army. The eight camps under the Justice Department were as follows: Crystal City (TX), Kenedy (TX), Kooskia (ID), Fort Lincoln (ND), Fort Missoula (MO), Fort Stanton (NM), Santa Fe (NM), and Seagoville (TX). In addition, fourteen US Army facilities were used to house the Japanese.

Two of the camps were in Hawai'i—the previously discussed detention camps at Sand Island and Honouliuli. As much as possible, preexisting facilities were sought since immediate housing was needed. Most of the camps held only Issei men, but Seagoville in Texas had single women and families. Crystal City in Texas was unique in housing mostly families and had German American and Italian American internees and a sizable contingent of six hundred Japanese from Peru. Precise figures aren't available, but over seven thousand Nikkei were interned in these facilities. When the relocation centers were ready to be occupied, about six hundred Issei were allowed to join their families in the relocation centers. The rest stayed at the detention camps for the duration of the war.

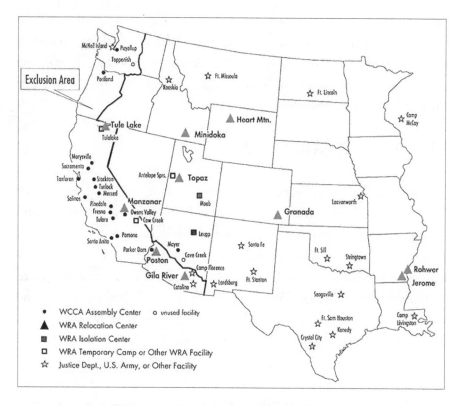

Location of Relocation Centers, Assembly Centers and other camps
Courtesy of the National Park Service.

President Roosevelt signed Executive Order 9066 on February 19, 1942 and the military command under Lieutenant General John L. DeWitt carried out this order for the forced removal from the West Coast of all *Nikkei*. A total of about 112,000 *Nikkei* were removed; roughly two-thirds were Nisei American citizens, and the remaining one-third were Issei who were, of course, aliens. The army was responsible for moving the Japanese from their homes to the army-operated temporary assembly centers. To coordinate and manage the evacuation and detention of the Japanese, the War Department formed the Wartime Civilian Control Administration (WCCA) and its director was Colonel Karl Bendetsen. The WCCA was responsible for finding suitable sites for the temporary assembly centers, and for more permanent relocation centers in the interior, and to administer the assembly center program. Once the process of closing the assembly centers was implemented, the WCCA was replaced by the War Relocation Authority (WRA), which was created by Executive Order 9102 on March 18, 1942. It took over the task of finalizing the locations of the relocation centers. Milton Eisenhower, older brother of Dwight Eisenhower, was the first director.

REMOVAL TO ARIZONA

By the beginning of February 1942, risky individuals, mostly prominent Issei who had strong connections with Japan, had been removed to detention camps operated by the US Army and the Justice Department, and the initial phase was completed. The next phase was the mass removal of entire families from the coastline—but how far inland? Federal authorities decided to declare the western halves of Washington, Oregon, and California: that is the area west of the Cascade Range and the Sierra Nevada to be Military Area 1. The southern part of Arizona, south of Baseline Road below Phoenix, was included in Military Area 1. All *Nikkei* were to be excluded from this area. Once the excluded zone was declared, Army Department and Department of Justice officials encouraged the *Nikkei* to relocate voluntarily—it would be less stressful and burdensome than being forced. Some ten thousand voluntarily took the difficult and painful steps of moving out. A little less than half were wise enough to leave the Pacific Coast entirely, but the rest moved to the eastern part of California. They were told they wouldn't have to move again. They believed the authorities, but this turned out to be a big mistake.

The army found voluntary evacuation to be slow and difficult to manage. Mountain state officials protested the arrival of the Japanese, and residents strongly objected to having these "dangerous" Japanese Americans. It led to General DeWitt succumbing to the pressure and halting the departures by *Nikkei* from the exclusion zone. Moreover, he designated the rest of California to be Military Area 2, thus creating another exclusion zone. But now some five thousand mainland Japanese were caught in an excluded area and had to move again. This time they had no choice—they were forced into an internment camp in Arizona.

The time had come for the majority who didn't voluntarily evacuate to be moved. This uprooting from their homes was the first in a series of traumatic experiences faced by the mainland Japanese. Families were given about one week, in some cases as little as forty-eight hours, to move out. Many affairs had to be settled in a short time frame, such as disposing of homes, businesses, farms, cars, fishing boats, appliances, furniture, and just about all their possessions. A few had friends to keep or store their belongings or someone to temporarily manage their affairs, but for most, they either lost or sold their possessions at a fraction of their value. "Fire sales" were common—selling of goods at ridiculously low prices. They were allowed to bring only what they could carry, usually two suitcases. It was suggested they bring their own silverware, dinnerware, and toiletries. Imagine, the dilemma of deciding what to take.

The government's plan for moving this mass of people was to initially use assembly centers while the permanent internment camps were being built. The assembly centers, therefore, were meant to be temporary quarters, but even with expedited construction, some mainland Japanese were in the assembly centers for as long as seven months. There was a total of sixteen assembly centers. Two were in the Northwest —Puyallup in Washington and Portland in Oregon. Twelve assembly centers were in California—Maryville, Sacramento, Tanforan, Stockton, Turlock, Merced, Pinedale, Salinas, Fresno, Tulare, Santa Anita, and Pomona. Two of the assembly centers were in Arizona—Poston and Mayer. Poston is near the town of Parker, along the Colorado River, which was soon upgraded into an internment camp. Mayer is about seventy-five miles northwest of Phoenix and was a former Civilian Conservation Corps camp. Mayer held only 245 detainees, all from southern Arizona, and was the smallest assembly center. Because of its limited capacity, it was closed after only a month and all detainees were transferred to Poston.

After the shock of being uprooted from their homes, the assembly centers were the second traumatic experience for the Japanese Americans. The chosen sites were racetracks and fairgrounds because they had ample acreage, especially large parking lots, essential utilities, and other infrastructures. Preexisting facilities lessened the construction load; nevertheless, extensive construction was still necessary. Military-type barracks were put up within a month by a massive number of workers under the supervision of the Army Corps of Engineers. The assembly centers were fenced in by barbed wire and had sentry towers with armed guards.

The following description of one assembly center should suffice: On March 27, 1942, the famous Santa Anita Racetrack in Southern California was taken over and opened as the first assembly center. It lasted for seven months, the longest occupied assembly center, and it was the largest, housing 18,719 detainees. A total of 589 military-type barracks were hastily built, but this massive number was surprisingly not enough because of the great influx of internees. Consequently, horse stable buildings had to be used. Sixty-four stable buildings, with its partitioned stalls, were renovated to accommodate about 8,500 detainees. Families were housed in these partitioned stalls, and although attempts were made to clean them out, the smells of animals and dung persisted, while the horse fleas were also a problem.[54] Living in a horse stable was not something you could easily forget.

**Santa Anita Assembly Center—barracks are in the background.
Courtesy of the Library of Congress.**

---

[54] Jeffrey F. Burton et al., *Confinement and Ethnicity: An Overview of World War II Japanese American Relocation Sites* (Tucson, AZ: Western Archeological and Conservation Center,1999), 35-36, 369.

Arrival at the Santa Anita Assembly Center.
Courtesy of the National Archives.

The military barracks and stable buildings were divided into seven districts—basically, it was like a mini-city. In all, there were six recreation buildings, six shower buildings with communal lavatories, six mess halls, a hospital, and a laundry building. Each mess hall could seat about 850 people and serve almost 3,000 people daily. It was crowded and noisy, and the kitchen lacked equipment. Sanitary facilities were overcrowded. For about three months, there were only 150 showers available for over eighteen thousand detainees. It improved over time, but it was never adequate. Medical care was inadequate and medical supplies were lacking. The lines were long for any kind of services and standing in line became necessary for just about everything —from eating at the mess halls, taking showers, and using the communal lavatories.

Boredom was a problem, but some detainees kept busy by working for low wages in the mess hall, helping with maintenance work, teaching, or working in the hospital. There was a camouflage net factory run by a private company under contract with the WRA. The work of attaching earth color fabric to nettings in this dusty factory was done mostly by camp women.

Though lacking funds and equipment, the internees occupied their time by organizing recreational and club activities. There was even a camp newspaper, the *Santa Anita Pacemaker*. It was published twice weekly in mimeographed format, and fifty issues were printed before the paper closed; it was the longest run of any assembly center paper. The detainees tried to make the camp a bit hospitable, but most felt miserable and were eager to get out of the chaotic assembly center and move to their assigned internment camp. But the assembly center did psychologically prepare the Japanese Americans for the internment camp. They experienced crowded and noisy communal living with absolutely no privacy. They learned to stand in line and what it was like to fight boredom. These were challenges they would soon face again. Assembly centers were an introduction to what life would be like in the internment camps.

The third traumatic experience was their removal to the internment camps. There were ten internment camps, what the government called relocation centers. They were Manzanar and Tule Lake in California; Granada, also known as Amache, in Colorado; Heart Mountain in Wyoming; Minidoka in Idaho; Topaz in Utah; Jerome and Rohwer in Arkansas; and Gila River and Poston in Arizona. Gila River Relocation Center and Poston Relocation Center are the subjects of this chapter.

In selecting the sites, the WRA considered its isolation and distance away from major population centers. Gila River is fifty miles south of Phoenix while Poston is twelve miles south of Parker, near the Colorado River. Both are on Indian Reservation land in desolate desert locations. Other factors considered by the WRA were the ease in appropriating the land and the availability of sufficient water resources to supply the camp and to grow crops. The tribal councils of the Gila River Indian Reservation and the Colorado River Indian Reservation (Poston) opposed the use of their land, but the Army Department, the Bureau of Indian Affairs, and the WRA overruled the tribal councils. The federal government simply took over the land and could not be stopped.[55] Finally, the site had to be near a railhead or a major highway, enabling the internees to be brought to the camp by either train, bus, or both.

---

[55] Karen J. Leong and Myla Vicenti Carpio, "Carceral Subjugations: Gila River Community and Incarceration of Japanese Americans on Its Lands," *Amerasia Journal* 42, no.1 (2016) 111-12.

Majority of the internees of Santa Anita Assembly Center were sent to Jerome, Rohwer, Heart Mountain, and Granada, but Poston received 1,503 and Gila River 1,271 detainees. Most of the Poston's internees came from the Salinas Assembly Center, which was near the coastline in central California. Gila River received internees from the Central Valley assembly centers of Stockton, Turlock, Merced, Pinedale, Fresno, and Tulare.[56] Three thousand Japanese Americans went directly from the San Joaquin Valley and Imperial Valley to the Gila River Relocation Center, never entering any assembly center.[57] These *Nikkei* weren't required to go to an assembly center because they were from farming communities where they were needed for harvesting and last-minute farming operations. *Nikkei* from southern Arizona were few and weren't assigned to any assembly center but went directly to a relocation center. Henry "Hank" Oyama, with his mother and sister, went directly from Tucson to Poston. "I don't know why I was sent to Poston. I can't speak Japanese and don't know anything about Japan. I was brought up in the barrio," said Oyama, a fifteen-year-old teenager.[58] Being of Japanese ancestry was enough to be interned. The majority of internees came from the assembly centers in California, but there were Japanese Americans who were moved long distances. About two thousand internees were transferred to the Arizona camps when the Jerome Relocation Center in Arkansas closed in June 1944. Furthermore, 155 Hawai'i Japanese were sent directly from Sand Island Internment Camp in Honolulu to Gila River.

As the mainland Japanese were being sent to the internment camps, there was no organized resistance. There were some cases of refusal to report, but these were isolated incidents. From the beginning, when they were evicted from their homes, there was no wholesale protest. Certainly, the mainland Japanese were angry, but most of them were simply stunned and numbed by the sudden evacuation to the assembly center. They silently, without

---

[56] Burton, *Confinement and Ethnicity*, 36.

[57] Burton, 61.

[58] Conversation with Henry Oyama. His mother was born in Japan but grew up in Mexico. His father, of Japanese descent, died before Henry was born. Oyama was involved in the case challenging the miscegenation law of Arizona and helped break the ban on interracial marriages. He was a veteran, a teacher, an administrator, and a pioneer in bilingual education. A school in Tucson is named after him.

showing much emotion, boarded the train or bus. They had been subdued psychologically and had resigned themselves to their fate. They internalized their suffering.

Although they didn't openly express their feelings, the Japanese Americans did have ambivalent feelings as they reflected on their predicament. Should we show our loyalty by quietly obeying the orders or should we show our resentment? What were their thoughts as they were being shipped to the internment camps? Hatsumi Yamada wrote a letter expressing his thoughts on the train ride to Poston. Hatsumi was born and raised in Santa Ana, California but was sent back to Hiroshima for his education and was a *Kibei*. When he returned in 1927, he attended Santa Ana High School and after graduation worked on his family's truck farm. When war broke out, he and his family were moved to Santa Anita Assembly Center in May 1942. Then, on August 26, they were sent to Poston with the first contingent. As the train left California and entered Arizona, Yamada wrote:

> The concept of American democracy I learned at the public schools and gained from social environment in the community was about to fade away when the evacuation order was issued. Somehow, I managed to hold on to my emotions, and I want my neighbors to know that I did not lose my faith in the American way of life...
>
> I sold everything under the roof of my house for two days while the rest of the family packed. On the third morning everything was in readiness to board the special train destined to a relocation center somewhere in the Arizona desert. I slept on the hard floor with just a newspaper spread without the luxury of mattress or bed coverings on the last night in California. I didn't even bother to take off my clothing or change into a nightgown...

Finally, military police called out the family number which was assigned to every family on the evacuation order, and lined up the group in the order of the family number to board the train. The whole group of 'exiles-to-be' was divided into seven groups of about 60 persons each, including old and young as well as citizens and aliens alike. Two cars were loaded with baggage and one car was loaded with box lunches to be served twice en route to the destination. Evacuees were loaded on the seven coaches in orderly fashion and promptly on the [sic] schedule.

About at noon, the train was rolling past some black sunbaked heaps of lava in scenery surrounded by nothing but the sand, sagebrush, and tumbling weeds. While the train cut through the open country, most passengers were growing tired. Some elders were sleeping and some were reading. Most children were wide awake and occupying every vacant seat for their play. One little girl about 8 years old looking out the window suddenly turned to her mother and said, 'Mother, this place doesn't look like America, it's different.' Mother looked rather surprised at the little girl's statement and did not say a word. 'Where are we going, mother? Are we going to another country?'

The train crossed the river and I knew I was no longer in California. I felt as if I was leaving America, which I loved so much. I was being deprived of my right to enjoy the American way of life. It reminded me of what I learned in American history about the frontier days of colonial pioneers who were dispossessed [sic] their settlement. They kept their faith and toiled. I want my neighbors to know I still love my America.[59]

---

[59] Excerpts from letter by Hatsumi Yamada.

On May 8, 1942, Poston Relocation Center was opened; it followed Manzanar Relocation Center in California as the second internment camp. Poston got an early start because it was originally an assembly center but was converted to an internment camp. It became the largest internment camp with a peak population of eighteen thousand. Gila River opened two months later on July 20, 1942, and it was to have a total population of 16,655. Since these two camps were huge, they were both subdivided. Poston consisted of three units separated by three miles intervals and were known officially as Poston I, Poston II, and Poston III. Gila River had two separate units located three and a half miles apart—Canal Camp on the eastern side and Butte Camp on the western side. Canal Camp was so-named because there was an irrigation canal running alongside, and Butte Camp had a mountain butte on one end.

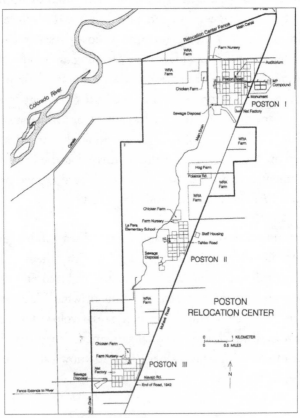

Poston Relocation Center.
Courtesy of the National Park Service.

Barracks at Poston.
Courtesy of the Poston Preservation.

Figure 4.1. Gila River Relocation Center.

Gila River Relocation Center.
Courtesy of the National Park Service.

105

Barracks at Gila River.
Courtesy of azcentral.

The two internment camps sprung up quickly in the space of about six months, and the rapidity of the construction was amazing. Del Webb was the contractor for Poston and for a portion of the barracks at Gila River. The company was pulled from a project in California to work on Poston. The initial phase was hectic; Poston I was completed in less than three weeks, employing five thousand workers. Even though the facilities weren't ready, internees were arriving and before long, the barracks were filled with seven thousand internees. WRA wanted to clear out the assembly centers as soon as possible, since they were intended to be temporary quarters. But facing wartime labor and building materials shortages, it was impossible to complete the projects sooner. At Gila River, construction began on May 1, 1942, and the same thing happened. Internees were moving in before construction was completed, and by the end of the month, over eight thousand had arrived. All the construction at Gila River wasn't completed until December 1, 1942.

Layout of a typical residential block.

The layout and architecture of the buildings at Poston and Gila River were similar. The same military-type buildings, called barracks, was selected for all the internment camps. Each barrack was 20' x 100' and accommodated four to six families. They were symmetrically laid out in grid fashion, arranged in two columns with each column having seven barracks. At the end of one column was the mess hall and at the end of the other column was the recreation hall. The mess hall was a larger-size building with dimensions of 40' x 100'. In the middle, between the two columns of barracks, were the men's and women's lavatory buildings with communal toilets and showers, a laundry building, and an ironing building. The ironing building was instead used for storage purposes.

Altogether the residential barracks, lavatories, laundry, and ironing buildings constituted a "block," which was the basic administrative unit of the internment community. Each block elected a "block manager" and sent a representative to the community council. A block typically housed about 250 to 300 internees. Each camp usually consisted of eighteen residential blocks, but Poston I and Butte Camp were larger and had thirty-six blocks. Apart from the residential blocks, there was a non-residential area, which held administrative offices, schools, warehouses, factories, and the hospital.[60] Barbed wire fences encircled the entire camp with guard towers manned by armed soldiers. Outside, on the perimeter of the camp, were the housing for the WRA staff and the military police.

The rows of homogeneous housing with black tar paper exterior walls made for a drab scene and the overall picture was depressing. Of all the internment camps, Gila River probably looked the best. It had distinctive red roofs and double roof construction to act as added insulation against the high desert temperature; Gila River consistently had higher temperatures than Poston. Another unusual feature of Gila River was the lack of barbed wire on its fences, and it only had a single guard tower. The terrain and the existence of an irrigation canal was said to be enough of a barrier. With its distinguishing red roof and relative lack of security, Gila River offered a softer image and was the place to take official visitors. When Eleanor Roosevelt asked to visit an internment camp, it was no surprise she was taken to Gila River. The WRA was conscious about the image of the internment camps and wanted to favorably impress the First Lady.

Eleanor Roosevelt and Dillon Myer visiting Gila River.
Courtesy of the National Archives.

---

[60] Burton, *Confinement and Ethnicity*, 40-43; Edwin H. Spicer et al., *Impounded People: Japanese-Americans in the Relocation Centers* (Tucson, AZ: University of Arizona Press, 1969), 65-66, 68-70. The recreation halls were used for the following purposes: sewing schools, churches, service organizations, beauty and barber shops, cooperative stores, canteens, and offices for internal police.

CHAPTER SIX

CAMP COMMUNITY

Internees were transported by train to the town of Parker, which was the closest railhead to Poston. They were then shuttled a distance of seventeen miles by bus to the camp. For the internees of Gila River, the railhead was Casa Grande; then it was a half hour drive by bus.[61] Embarking from the bus, internees were confronted by a barren and bleak scene, devoid of grass, shrubberies, and trees. In the process of camp construction, the land was bulldozed and cleared of all vegetation. It was like a moonscape; the starkness was overwhelming. Immediately, the heat was felt with temperatures near triple-digits. Complaints quickly arose about the dust.

Since the land was stripped of vegetation and the earth loosened, any amount of wind kicked up the soil. Even today, dust storms are common and a serious problem in this area. There are electronic signs on Interstate 10, in the vicinity of Gila River, warning drivers of the impending danger. In such a storm, visibility is extremely poor and limited to a few yards. The new arrivals found the swirling dust covering everything, even turning their hair gray. The walls, floorboards, and window frames had cracks, and the fine spaces between the boards allowed the dust to seep through. Newspapers were used to plug the gaps and even the lids of tin cans were nailed to the walls.

---

[61] Burton, *Confinement and Ethnicity*, 41.

Arrival at Poston by bus from railhead.
Courtesy of azcentral.

Controlling the dust.
Courtesy of the National Archives.

The barracks were a big disappointment. Several barracks weren't completed and were lacking doors or windows. Barracks were constructed with fresh-sawn lumber and with the heat, these green pine lumber shrank, creating fine cracks in the wall. The exterior wall was covered with black tarpaper, whereas the interior had no insulation or wallboards.

I have lived in barracks while training at Fort Lewis in Tacoma, Washington, and while serving with the 32nd Infantry Regiment near the demilitarized zone (DMZ) and at Pusan (now known as Busan) in South Korea. Therefore, I know what it is like. Some barracks are just one big room with no partitions while others have partitions. You soon realize it is communal living designed to accommodate a large number of people, and even with the partitions, there is little privacy. The barracks I'm acquainted with were furnished with army cots, blankets, and mattresses and had foot or wall lockers to store clothing and personal items. There were wall electrical outlets.

The internment barracks were worse. The partitions did not go up to the ceiling, and each partitioned section was bare, with nothing provided except army cots with blankets and mattresses that had to be stuffed with straw and light bulbs hanging from the ceiling. The barracks I have lived in had the bathroom adjoining the living quarters, but the internment barracks had no adjoining bathroom. Its lavatory with communal toilets and showers was in a separate building, and sometimes a good distance away. It was inconvenient, especially at night. Since the internment barracks had absolutely no furniture, the men kept busy in the early days of camp by building furniture, tables, and shelves from scrap lumber left by the construction. They made their barracks at least livable.[62]

---

[62] Spicer, *Impounded People*, 72.

Filling straw mattresses.
Courtesy of the National Archives.

Later on, the men began to work on the areas outside the barracks, making them attractive by planting gardens and trees and by building fish ponds. The vegetation provided needed shade and reduced the dust. Camp life was improved by major projects undertaken by the internees, including the construction of an outdoor stage, auditorium, science laboratory, home economics building, plant nurseries, and athletic fields.

Landscape featuring a large pond.
Courtesy of the *Los Angeles Times*.

The biggest complaint was the lack of privacy. Parents used sheets to partition off the allotted family space, but even within the family, there was a lack of personal space. For example, how do you block off one's personal space in a family of four assigned a 20' x 24' space? It was almost impossible to be by yourself. Furthermore, there was no escaping the sounds from adjoining families. Sheets were put up but offered no barrier to sounds. More serious was the lack of privacy in the lavatories. There were no partitions between the toilets, and the shower room was one big area with a series of shower heads. Women were especially embarrassed, and some purposely went to the lavatory late at night.

Family space inside the barrack.
Photo by George Watson, *Los Angeles Times*.

Added to the list of complaints were the chronic water shortages. However, the sewage system was modern and efficient. This caused neighboring communities to complain about the camps having a better sewage system than their outhouses and septic tanks. Therefore, a positive feature of the camps brought on complaints—this time from outside sources. The camp administration was accused of "coddling" the Japanese Americans.[63]

Complaints were filed by the internees, but the administration took little action. Internees decided not to wait and took the initiative to repair and build what they desperately needed. But there were some things they couldn't do. By the fall of 1942, heating stoves were still lacking. In the desert, nighttime temperature drops precipitously, and the barracks can get bitterly cold. Heaters were finally installed, but such late delivery added to the discontent of the internees.

The stress of overcrowding affected all families. The problem was most pronounced in the communal mess halls, which were crowded and noisy.

---

[63] Burton, *Confinement and Ethnicity*, 41.

Traditionally, Japanese families ate together, but in the mess hall, it was difficult for the families to sit together. This became an excuse for the young people to eat with their preferred peer group and for fathers to eat with other men. Soon family members were eating with their age or gender group rather than with their family. Youngsters even went to different mess halls to eat with their friends. In American families, members are on the go and tend to eat separately, but in Japanese families, family dining was a strong tradition. By not eating together as a family, an important familial bond was broken.

People under confinement and isolation suffered psychological consequences from boredom, lethargy, and stress. Internees needed something to look forward to and relieve their anxiety and worry by participating with others in entertaining activities. Two activities played pivotal roles and had lasting impact even after the camps were closed—baseball and big band music.

BASEBALL

Kenichi Zenimura, renowned baseball player and manager, and the most influential figure in Nisei baseball, was forcefully sent with his wife and two sons to the Fresno Assembly Center. In the short time he was there, he built a baseball field and organized a league.[64] The Zenimura family was originally supposed to be transferred from the assembly center to the Jerome Relocation Center in Arkansas, but because Kenichi's wife suffered from tuberculosis, the WRA decided the dry climate of Arizona would be better suited for her health. When Zenimura arrived at Gila River, he was despondent and listless, but before long, he had a vision of building a baseball field. This began an endeavor that was to have a profound impact on internment camp life. At first, it was Kenichi and his sons building the baseball field as people gathered to watch the development. It didn't take long before many joined in building the field.

The field at Gila River was completed in March 1943 and was named "Zenimura Field." It had a small grandstand, two dugouts, and an outfield

---

[64] Staples, Jr., *Kenichi Zenimura*, 115-16.

"fence" made of a hedgerow of trees and shrubs. It was Kenichi's "field of dreams—if you build it, they will come."[65] And they did come—on opening game day, nearly three thousand fans came. He helped to construct two more baseball fields in Butte Camp and Canal Camp. The one in Butte seated six thousand spectators and became the "home" field of Zenimura's coached teams. Eventually, every camp had at least one baseball field. But most of the action took place at Gila River, which had a thirty-two-team baseball league. A small admission was charged, which helped defray expenses for purchasing baseball equipment.

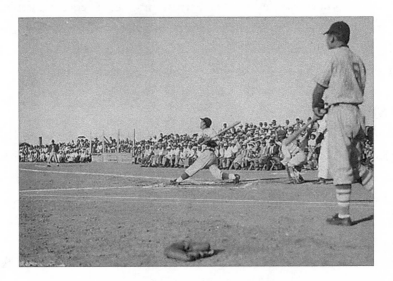

Baseball at internment camp.
Courtesy of *The Japan Times.*

Zenimura's teams, the Butte High School Eagles and Butte All-Stars, played games against top high school, college, and semiprofessional teams from surrounding communities, and in these games, his team was highly competitive. Exchange games were played with internment teams from Granada, Colorado and Heart Mountain, Wyoming. Games with visiting teams promoted better understanding between Japanese Americans in the camps and

---

[65] Staples, Jr., 119-20. Quote is from the film, *Field of Dreams* (1989).

the players from outside baseball teams. However, there was one racial incident, not involving the visiting team but the officials of the outside community. Tucson High School's baseball team visited Gila River and played a game against Butte High School, with Butte High emerging victorious in a close game. A return game was scheduled, but at the last minute, the game was cancelled. Tucson officials didn't want a team of "Japs" coming into town.

Zenimura's letter to Coach Hank Slagle of Tucson High expressed his disappointment over the incident:

> It was a great disappointment to myself and the members of the Butte baseball team when we learned of the cancellation of our return game. We know the circumstances which necessitated the cancellation and understand your position in the decision you had to take. This war has created many unpleasant incidents and I am sorry to have put you and yours in this spot in your district. I can only hope that in due time the difference in opinion can be overcome and that we may be able to resume our athletic rivalry.[66]

Coach Slagle responded:

> As for the possibility of canceling our game—we had never given it a minute's thought—till we arrived home and started hearing from some of these so-called 100% Americans. I sincerely hope it won't be too long till we are all thinking straight again and can live together in a true Democracy that we Americans of all races have created.[67]

Baseball could potentially bring together different races, but even more important for the internees was that baseball was a morale builder for players, spectators, and everyone concerned. The players loved playing

---

[66] Staples, Jr., *Kenichi Zenimura*, 171.

[67] Staples, Jr., 171.

and the fans enjoyed watching the game. It is said some of the best wartime baseball in Arizona was played at Zenimura Field in Gila River. Kenzo, Zenimura's son, said, "Baseball was the only thing that kept us going. If we didn't play baseball, (camp life) would've been unbearable. Even when we didn't play, we were out there watching."[68] Pat Morita, who starred in the *Karate Kid* movies and was a former Gila River internee, commented, "Kenichi Zenimura showed that with effort and persistence, you can overcome the harshness of adversity...Zenimura and others created a fraternal community in the desert—and baseball was the glue."[69] The contributions of Kenichi Zenimura in ameliorating camp life was truly remarkable. He deserves to be called the "Father of Japanese American Baseball."

BIG BAND MUSIC

As baseball lifted the spirit of the internees, dance bands soothed wounded feelings and took the youngsters' minds away from the drabness of camp life. Music uplifted the spirit and spoke to the soul, bringing the young people together. Individuals with musical talent and a yearning to perform with others spontaneously organized dance bands—soon they proliferated in the internment camps. Poston had three dance bands, while Gila River had two bands. From the beginning, dance bands existed on sheer enthusiasm and did the best with whatever instruments and equipment obtainable.

Music Makers, the dance band of Poston I, was a remarkable eleven-piece ensemble. Its theme song was Glenn Miller's *Moonlight Serenade*. The band was organized and led by Hideo Kawano, a precocious seventeen-year-old musician. He was multitalented, an expert in jazz and swing music, played the trumpet in the band and was an excellent drummer.[70] Another member was George Yoshida, a saxophonist who became a well-known musicologist of the Japanese American role in jazz, dance, and

---

[68] Staples, Jr., 182.

[69] Staples, Jr., 182.

[70] George Yoshida, *Reminiscing in Swingtime: Japanese Americans in America Popular Music: 1925-1960* (San Francisco: National Japanese American Historical Society, 1997), 131-32.

popular music. He was later drafted into the Military Intelligence Service (MIS). The Music Makers' branch band at Butte Camp had James Araki playing clarinet and saxophone. Araki was also drafted into the MIS, and while serving with the American occupation of Japan as an interpreter, he spent off-duty hours playing in Japanese dance bands and became a major influence in the development of jazz in Japan.[71]

Music Makers, the big band ensemble.
Courtesy of George Yoshida.

George Yoshida, member of Music Makers and renown musicologist.
Courtesy of Densho.

---

[71] Yoshida, *Reminiscing*, 112-14, 148, 207. While in Japan, Araki became interested in Japanese literature, and he later received his doctorate and taught Japanese literature at UCLA and retired after teaching at the University of Hawai'i at Manoa.

The bands played the popular music of the 1940s, such as *Sentimental Journey* and *Tuxedo Junction*. The repertoire of the Music Makers ranged from fast-tempo tunes, including Woody Herman's *Blues on Parade* for jitterbugs, to slow music, such as *Dream* for the romantically inclined. Band members looked professional, wearing sports coats and ties. It was volunteer work. No one received payment—they did it for pleasure, playing the music they loved and receiving the appreciative responses of the dancers and audience. Assuredly, the music wasn't always of high quality, but the musicians did exceedingly well, given the circumstances—the music was sweet.

The beginning lyrics of the song *Buddhahead Blues*, written by Ernest Michio Masunaga, while at the Santa Anita Assembly Center, expresses the feelings of the young Nisei:

> Going to sprout my wings and fly right over that fence,
> Going to sprout my wings and fly right over that fence,
> 'Cause staying in here don't make no sense.
> Buddhahead boy, what makes you so yellow?
> Buddhahead boy, what makes you so yellow?
> You seem like an ordinary fellow...
> Oh, I don't know why I want to cry,
> I want to die. I'd sure get tight
> If there were gin in sight for me.[72]

Big band music was the diversion young people needed. It was their weekend entertainment—a time to get away from the boredom and despair of camp life. There were several late-night mess hall sessions. The familiar "May I have this dance?" was frequently heard. The Issei were shocked to see the young Nisei girls wearing bobby socks and boys in their zoot suits, doing the boogie-woogie on the dance floor. From the big band music of Glenn Miller, Tommy Dorsey, Benny Goodman, Count Basie, Lionel Hampton, and Artie Shaw, to the fox-trot and jitterbug, this was as American as apple

---

[72] Yoshida, 120-21.

pie! George Yoshida said, "It was a matter of survival and subconscious affirmation of self—a way to express through music: 'I am an American!'"[73]

RELIGIOUS ACTIVITIES

Religion played an important part in the lives of many internees, giving them a sense of purpose and replacing the feeling of futility and despair with that of hope. Tai Shigaki, former Poston internee, wrote:

> The presence of God was very real during this time, and I felt constantly sustained, experiencing a wealth of strength and energy from a source unknown to me. I didn't know where it came from, but I did feel God had a purpose for me, and so I responded without much resistance. I felt cared for.[74]

Each camp had Protestant and Catholic churches and Buddhist temples. However, Buddhist temples were slow in developing because camp authorities were hesitant about Buddhism, believing it interfered with the Americanization process. The Buddhists made their religion more compatible with the administration's view by referring to their temples as "churches." Protestant denominations got together for combined worship services and for Sunday schools, but each church published its own weekly bulletin to publicize their activities. Church services and other activities were held in the recreation building or mess hall until the chapels were built.

An internee of Poston, Donald Iwahashi, described his experience:

> After months of readjusting to communal mess halls, latrines, showers, and wash rooms, life became more

---

[73] Yoshida, 125.

[74] Victor N. Okada, ed., *Triumphs of Faith: Stories of Japanese American Christians During World War II* (Los Angeles: Japanese American Internment Project, 1998). Quote is from the back cover.

tolerable, and I began to turn my thoughts from the visible to the invisible. What is the meaning and purpose of life? Through the influence of young Nisei Christian leaders, we felt the assurance of God's presence in this concentration camp with all its cruelty and injustice. Though I had been baptized a year or so earlier, my search for faith in Christ became more profound and meaningful. I participated in prayer meetings, Bible studies, Sunday school, and other functions of the church with renewed vigor.

By the grace of God, this experience in camp established the foundation of my Christian faith. It has transformed me to accept life's vicissitudes with grace and thanksgiving, undergirded by His presence. Knowing that I am God's child and redeemed by His grace has been a source of real joy.[75]

Most of the Christian activities were centered in Poston I, which was blessed with a core group of strong leaders. Reverend Jitsuo Morikawa, a Baptist minister, led the Issei, and Paul Nagano worked with the Nisei. They were assisted by a few seminary students.[76] This group founded three churches, expanded the number of Bible studies and prayer meetings, and conducted special events, including religious rallies, vacation Bible school, New Year's convention, and evangelistic meetings. When the blind evangelist Kanichi Niizato spoke, more than six hundred heard him. An outdoor Christmas program was presented by a two-hundred-voice choir, singing Handel's *Hallelujah Chorus*. Before long, their ministry stretched out into Poston II and III. All told, in the three Poston camps, there were

---

[75] Okada, ed., *Triumphs of Faith*, 36.

[76] Okada, ed., 5-7, 9-11, 67-68, 77-80, 85-87, 145-47, 153-54, 155-56, 169-71. Seminary students at that time were: Masumi Toyotome, Paul Nagano, and Lloyd Wake. After the war, several Poston internees went on to seminary and became pastors. They were: Sadaichi Asai, Harry Baba, Kei Kokubun, Arthur Tsuneishi, Yasushi Wada, and Carl Yoshimine. Besides the testimonies given by the above internees, this book includes the testimonies of four other Poston internees.

twenty-four ministers, including Presbyterian, Baptist, Free Methodist, Methodist, Holiness, Disciples of Christ, and Congregational ministers. Of the ten internment camps, Poston had the largest number of ministers. Gila River, while not blessed with a large number of clergymen, still had nine ministers.[77] Potentially more important was the development of young Nisei church leaders. Their experience working in camp churches proved to be valuable in developing pastoral and teaching skills; it prepared them for full-time Christian ministry. Indeed, several became pastors of Japanese churches in the postwar period.

Most camp pastors were volunteers. A few received the $19.00 per month pay offered by WRA and some were supported by outside sources, but they were very few in number. Outside help came by way of visits by Christian leaders, providing support and spiritual guidance. Dr. Ralph L. Mayberry of American Baptists and Rev. Herbert Nicholson, a Quaker missionary who was fluent in Japanese, were frequent visitors. E. Stanley Jones, a famous Christian missionary and evangelist, was also a visitor. These visitors brought with them donations from outside churches, such things as hymnals, books, teaching materials, and paper supplies.

In summarizing the experiences of the internees, Dr. Victor N. Okada, editor of a volume of internment testimonies writes, "At times of greatest urgency and despair, only the assurance that God watches over us can bring peace, hope, and wholeness."[78] A significant number of Nisei can trace their commitment and growth in faith to the internment experience. In their recollections of camp life, Japanese Christians said their faith in God helped them to persevere, and they found their faith and commitment strengthened in the midst of indignation and deprivation. The things that matter are not the physical and mental degradations but the personal and spiritual relationship with God, which gave them dignity and purpose. Such was the power of faith.

---

[77] Tsukasa Sugimura, *A History of the OMS Holiness Church of North America* (Los Angeles: Education and Publication Committee of the OMS Holiness Church of North America, 1993), 59, 63.

[78] Okada, ed., *Triumphs of Faith*, 173.

OTHER ACTIVITIES

Women found leisure time to participate in social and artistic activities when they were relieved from preparing dinners and housework. Classes held in the recreation hall revealed the diversity of interest, including classes in flower arrangement, sewing, and tea ceremonies. For men, their free time was spent on woodworking, gardening, and hobbies. Men participated in the traditional Japanese sport of judo and sumo (wrestling). Sumo tournaments were held on specially constructed *dohyo* (sumo ring) with all the traditional trappings. Kabuki (traditional popular drama) and popular stage plays were held at the outdoor stages built by the internees at Gila River and Poston. The Poston Kabuki stage was unique. Photographs reveal the extraordinary effort made to have the setting as authentic as possible. Authenticity was also sought in the required musical accompaniment and in the costumes.

Sumo at Gila River.
Courtesy of the National Archives.

It is interesting to note that although the camp authorities didn't promote it, they allowed traditional Japanese musical instruments to be taught and played and for participation in Japanese sports. Experienced players taught the samisen (Japanese banjo), *shakuhachi* (bamboo flute), and koto (zither-type, long-string instrument), and young men were taught and practiced judo and sumo. Even surprising was the allowance of the performance of Kabuki, an art form steeped in Japanese history and tradition. Therefore, traditional Japanese culture was being preserved and passed to the younger generation—even in the midst of concerted Americanization.

There were activities for the entire family, such as viewing movies. The young people were kept occupied by several group activities, ranging from community-wide Boy Scouts and Girl Scouts to activities sponsored by the schools. Individual and group games were just as popular. For men, there was Go (checker-like board game) and poker, the American card game. Another popular card game played by all the internees was *hanafuda* (flower cards). Children played their own games; some as simple as marbles, or group games like "rooster" and "sink the battleship" or they just made up games as they went along.[79] Youngsters had fun creating their own toys. Edwin Fujinaka, a teenager when he and his family were interned at Poston, recalled those days as "a fun time, playing games, hanging around with friends, and exploring the camp."[80] When Nisei were interviewed about their recollections of internment, many like Fujinaka who were teens said it was a fun time, but they acknowledged they didn't say that to the whites outside the camp, for they knew how strongly their parents resented camp conditions and the loss of their freedom and rights.

All these activities and programs mitigated the loneliness, anxiety, and feeling of futility. They helped to pass the time. Nevertheless, the activities and entertainment didn't always heal psychological wounds. There were occasional suicides. It could have been worse, but the internees undertook

---

[79] Kenneth A. Tashiro, *Wase Time! A Teen's Memoir at Gila River Internment Camp* (Bloomington, IN: AuthorHouse, 2005), 62-63.

[80] Conversation with Edwin Fujinaka. Fujinaka visited Poston many years later, and it affected him. He got emotional remembering the harshness of the scene and the hardships faced by the family. It is a reaction many others have felt.

and participated in activities that relieved the monotonous and stifling aspects of camp life. To a large degree, it was the internees themselves who took the initiative and volunteered their talents, skills, and energy to lift their spirits.

CHAPTER SEVEN

POLICIES AND PROGRAMS

The previous chapter discussed the initiatives taken by the Japanese Americans to relieve boredom and the feeling of constraint. However, the psychological needs had to be met—the internees had to have some purpose in their lives. The WRA's solution was to provide employment for the internees and an opportunity for the Nisei of college age to continue their education outside of the camp.

The employment was of two basic types: (1) jobs outside the camp, which could be seasonal or permanent; and (2) jobs within the camp, which were permanent. The initial job opportunities came from outside farms needing immediate help in harvesting the cotton crop. Under the seasonal employment program of the WRA, internees were allowed to live and work outside the camp and return after the harvesting season was over. The pay was meager and was nowhere comparable to what the Caucasian workers were paid for the same work. The monthly pay was $8.00 for unskilled labor; it was later raised to $12.00.[81]

In contrast to this seasonal employment, most of the employment opportunities were of a more permanent nature—either working within the camp or requiring resettlement outside the camp. When Dillon Myer took over as WRA director in June 1942, he viewed the relocation centers as a temporary stop, and the goal was to resettle the internees as far away as possible from the West Coast. It was a broad program designed to send

---

[81] Burton, *Confinement and Ethnicity*, 37.

vetted Japanese Americans, who had passed the loyalty examination and were cleared by a military board, into the hinterland; thereby reducing the camps' population and helping to assimilate Japanese Americans into American society. The program was officially known as "leave permit" and went into effect on July 20, 1942. Initially, only qualified Nisei were accepted, but after October 1942, all *Nikkei* could apply. Applicants had to find an employer outside the excluded areas (Military Area 1 and 2), who were willing to be the sponsor. Once an employer was found, the internee received a $25.00 allowance and a train ticket to their destination, plus a meal per diem of $3.00 a day.

The leave permits were issued to students who were accepted into a college or vocational program. As it turned out, students experienced better opportunities and results than those taking outside jobs. They faced less racial prejudice and had a more advantageous career start than those seeking outside employment, which usually meant low-level positions, such as housekeeping, factory, or office jobs. The students had the additional support of the National Japanese American Student Relocation Council, a volunteer agency. It raised private funds for scholarships to enable Nisei students to enroll in colleges away from the West Coast and helped in supervising the enrollment process.[82]

It seemed the leave permit was an excellent opportunity for qualified individuals to escape the confines of the camp and to prepare for an adventuresome career. Yet for all its appeal, there were few takers at the beginning. Less than 15 percent of the Nisei applied and were granted leave permits. Two factors discouraged many potential applicants. First, many didn't want to be separated from their families. Second, there was apprehension about moving to a new and possibly hostile environment. Over a period of time, however, a sizable number of young people applied for leave permits, a total of 3,713 students, enrolling in colleges, nursing and vocational schools. Parents encouraged their children to continue their education outside, for they valued education and wanted the best for their

---

[82] Robinson, *Tragedy*, 181-82.

children. They were willing to sacrifice—to be separated from their children even though the future was unpredictable. The leave permit program for students had consequences for the camps. When nearly four thousand young people left, it drained the camps of the talent, skill, and energy of the young men and women and caused disruptions within families and within the communities.[83]

For those not wanting to leave the camp permanently, the alternative was to find employment within the camp. Basically, this meant working for the WRA as helpers in the mess hall, doing maintenance and janitorial work, working in the warehouse, or doing staff support work in the office. The majority of these positions were at the low end of the pay scale of $8.00 per month, which was later boosted to $12.00. But the largest number of hires was in farming, the cultivation of vegetables, melons, and other crops; it extended over a large area, to the outside land adjacent to Canal Camp. At its peak, the Gila River Relocation Center employed nearly one thousand men and women to work on its farm and this was not surprising, for many of them came from farming background and had valuable skills. Gila River was blessed with soil already worked on by the Native Americans, but the key to successful farming was the irrigation system. The Japanese Americans vastly improved the existing irrigation system. So much food was produced that it not only met the needs of the Gila River and Poston camps, but there was enough to ship to all the internment camps. Twenty percent of all the food consumed by the ten internment camps were grown at Gila River. This was an impressive operation. Moreover, a sizable number of internees worked on the extensive livestock program with cattle, pigs, and herds of dairy cows, as well as on a thriving poultry farm.[84]

---

[83] Robinson, 186-87.

[84] Burton, *Confinement and Ethnicity*, 68.

**Workers holding *daikon* (Japanese radish) at Gila River farm.
Courtesy of the National Archives.**

Although private enterprises weren't allowed, business projects aiding
the war effort and communal factories producing food and building materials for local use were permitted. To help the war effort and to provide
employment, the WRA assisted in organizing camouflage net factories in
Gila River and Poston. The factories were run by a privately-owned outside company, but all employees, mostly women, were from the camps. The
factories didn't last long and ceased operations in May 1943 when their
contracts with the WRA ended. There was a garment factory in Poston
III, which similarly hired women but was run by the government. In addition, there was a model warship factory at Poston I. It produced small-scale
wooden model warships, which were used by the US Navy for identification
purposes.[85] I picked up a collection of these model Japanese warships after
the war; they were accurately made and were all in battleship-gray color.

---

[85] Burton, 44.

But not all factories were for the war effort. An example of a communal factory was a food preparation facility in Poston I, producing *tofu* (soybean curd). *Tofu* is an important Japanese staple food and is an ingredient in many dishes; it is an excellent plant-based protein. There was another factory that made adobe bricks, a much needed building material. The factory was wholly conceived and managed by the internees. Instead of the difficult to obtain lumber, adobe bricks were a natural and practical alternative. They were made from clay and straw readily available in the desert environment.[86]

Camouflage net factory.
Courtesy of Santa Clara University Digital Collections.

Professional jobs paid the best, initially at $16.00 monthly, which was later increased to $19.00, but by all measures, the professionals were grossly underpaid. There was a constant shortage of professional workers and long working hours became routine. The recruitment of teachers was a challenge. Caucasian teachers were recruited from California, surrounding communities and Indian reservation schools. There weren't enough qualified Japanese

---

[86] Myer, *Uprooted Americans*, 49, 51-52.

American teachers; hence, seventy-five internees with at least two years of college were employed as teaching assistants. Teachers from outside were, of course, paid more.

At first, the school population was large but the enrollment pressure lessened with time. Poston had 5,200 students at the beginning, but by the third year, enrollment was down to about 3,600 due to the leave permit settlement program. Other challenges confronted the school system. There was a shortage of school buildings, so internees themselves built school buildings with adobe, which was supplied by the adobe-making factory. The furnishings of the school rooms, such as chairs, desks, tables, and blackboards, were built by the internees. Textbooks were lacking, but donations came from outside sources. Conditions got better with time, but the lack of basic supplies persisted. Even with these limitations, schools operated like a typical American school. Each day began with the reciting of the Pledge of Allegiance. Assemblies were held from time to time, and the school year ended with graduation ceremonies. The curriculum was the same as that of an outside school district. There was little need to teach American values, for the children were already Americanized. Lucille Franchi, a first-grade teacher at Poston relates, "I hung up a small American flag in my room. Then from the back of the room, one of the children began to sing 'God Bless America.' I sighed. I stood there with tears streaming from my eyes."[87]

Two services that hired individuals with specialized skills were the hospitals and the newspapers. Each camp had a two-hundred-bed hospital built by the WRA. They were staffed with Japanese American physicians who had lost their practices in California by the forced removal. Considering the large population they had to serve, each hospital was understaffed, and doctors were forced to work long hours. Furthermore, Caucasian women nurses were recruited because there weren't enough Nisei women nurses. Supervisory control was retained by the WRA, with the chief supervisor being a Caucasian doctor. Given the limited personnel and facilities, and

---

[87] Chizu Iiyama, "Memories of Schools at Poston, Arizona," in *Nikkei Heritage*, 10, no. 1 (Winter 1998) 15.

the occasional shortage of hospital beds and medical supplies, the staff was hard put to provide adequate medical care.[88]

Each camp had a daily newspaper, and they were staffed by a small group of workers with previous experience working for prewar Japanese language newspapers. *Gila News-Courier* and the *Poston Chronicle* were the two newspapers, and both came out in mimeograph form. They were the main channels of information for the communities. It was possible to subscribe to an outside newspaper but few bothered. Camp administration didn't impose censorship and sometimes criticisms of the WRA were expressed, but it was usually muted. It was a situation of self-censorship. The administration controlled through its supervisory role and by the hiring of employees.[89]

The employment policy of the WRA offered benefits and advantages, especially to those who wanted to try something new outside the camp or wanted to escape the regimentation of camp life. But the administration didn't pursue the employment policy only for the altruistic purpose of helping the internees; it had its own agenda. Employment advanced the Americanization process, made the camps more self-sufficient, and even helped the war effort. The pay scale was purposely kept low so there would be no compliant about coddling the Japanese Americans, and it could be argued to even exploit the cheap labor. Although the WRA gave the internees wide latitude in regards to employment, the administration kept control by their supervisory role, as seen in the hospitals and the press, and by its administrative control of farming operations. The Japanese Americans never felt they had control over their lives; instead, they felt demeaned.

While the employment policy of the WRA was its way of handling the boredom, apathy, and disillusionment of the internees, what were the principles and practices by which it managed the camps? At the beginning, Poston developed differently from Gila River. John Collier, who headed the Bureau of Indian Affairs (BIA), agreed in March 1942 to let the WRA, at that time led by Milton Eisenhower, to build an internment camp on the

---

[88] Robinson, *Tragedy*, 158; Myer, *Uprooted Americans*, 52-53.

[89] Robinson, 169-70.

Colorado River Indian Reservation, which was under the jurisdiction of the BIA. But Collier was adamant about how Poston was to be developed. He wanted a model community complete with farm cooperatives, using Japanese American farmers to help develop the local farm economy as well as the cooperatives and to build for the long run. When the war ended, the camp was to continue as a model community. He brought in Wade Head as director and a staff of social scientists to conduct studies, and to employ social science techniques to resolve problems. Artists were invited to enrich camp life. For example, the renowned sculptor Isamu Noguchi volunteered. To advance his program, Collier gave several talks and made promises. Many internees took him seriously.

Dillon Myer, who succeeded Eisenhower as director of WRA, had a different philosophy. Myer was bureaucratic, didn't believe in a humanitarian approach, and wasn't interested in community planning or creating a model community. He believed it would lead to administrative problems and a dependence on government aid and an entitlement mentality. He shunned social science approaches; however, he did adopt the use of "community analysts." Myer believed the internment camps were to be temporary and wanted to Americanize and resettle the Japanese Americans into communities in the Midwest and the East Coast as quickly as possible. All camps were to be run uniformly and with little experimentation.

Myer won the struggle with Collier and finally ended the agreement with the BIA. The WRA took formal control over Poston in mid-1943. As a result, the promises made by Collier were dropped, causing confusion and creating an atmosphere of distrust between the administration and internees.[90] Many Japanese Americans began to have doubts about the administration's pronouncements. The government simply could not be trusted.

As the initial shock of settling in wore off, the stress of communal living became evident. First, there was increasing tension between the administration and the internees, particularly with the Issei. The administrative staff favored the Nisei over the Issei. The Nisei, after all, were American citizens,

---

[90] Robinson, 154-55.

spoke English, and were the initial volunteers who helped the administration in preparing the camp before the massive arrival of internees. The administration preferred the Nisei in the block and council leadership positions, which turned out to be a major mistake. When the WRA announced the new policy barring Issei from leadership positions in the barracks and in the council, Issei vehemently expressed their anger at being left out. Back in California, Issei were the pillars of their communities and held key positions; now they were stripped of their traditional roles. They didn't feel confident the Nisei, whose average age was twenty-five, had the ability to lead. Moreover, the Issei were suspicious of the Nisei and accused them of collaborating with the administration at the expense of all the internees.

Next, there was a generational problem. The Issei felt the Nisei were getting too Americanized and losing their cultural heritage. The Nisei weren't respecting their elders and had a different mode of thinking, resulting in a widening gap between the Issei and Nisei. Finally, there was the problem of the Nisei and the *Kibei*, those Japanese Americans educated in Japan. The *Kibei* tended to be pro-Japan, and they used the term *inu* (dog), not in the sense of a pet but as a pejorative, to characterize Nisei informants who had sided with the administration. Tempers soon flared up and fighting erupted between pro-Japan *Kibei* and pro-administration Nisei, with gangs formed by *Kibei* targeting members of the Japanese American Citizens League (JACL), who were known to promote Americanization and to be supporters of the WRA.

At Poston, Saburo Kido, president of JACL, became a target of the *Kibei*. Kido was a Hawai'i Nisei who moved to San Francisco after law school. He was assaulted twice, in September of 1942 and in January of 1943. The second beating was severe and required hospitalization. To prevent further attacks, Kido and his family were relocated to Salt Lake City. Also caught in the infighting was the aforementioned Hatsumi Yamada. Although Yamada was a *Kibei*, he decided to side with the administration. For his stance, he and his family were assaulted one night by hooded men, leaving them bloodied and bruised. Yamada was taken out of the camp under the guise of having measles to protect his family from further attacks.[91]

Tensions came to a climax at Poston I on the night of November 14, 1942. Kay Nishimura, a thirty-year-old Kibei, was badly beaten by a hooded mob. Fifty suspects associated with the judo club were initially taken into custody but later released. The following night, another beating took place. FBI agents arrested two judo leaders, but this action only provoked anger. Three days later, WRA director Myer made a surprise visit. He tried to lessen the tension by announcing Poston would be a temporary camp and everyone would soon be let out, but this caused confusion since BIA director Collier had previously promised to make Poston a future model community. The following morning, November 18, about a thousand internees from Poston I demanded the release of the two judo club leaders. A general strike was called, and it spread to Poston II and III. Crowds gathered around bonfires at nights, listening and talking about the strike. Fortunately, the community analysts Edward Spicer and Alexander Leighton were able to persuade the camp administration not to summon the armed troops. It was a critical decision, avoiding a violent confrontation.

Such was not the case a month later, when a similar riot erupted in Manzanar camp, resulting from the beating of a prominent JACL member. Military police were called, and in the ensuing tussle, gas and then shots were fired, killing one internee and wounding eight others, one of whom later died. Spicer and Leighton avoided armed conflict, but they were unable to calm the strikers. Finally, an agreement was reached through negotiations, where the Issei were given a voice in camp affairs, and one suspect was released while the other was to be tried by a camp court. Meanwhile, the promise was made to the administration that further attacks on suspected informers would end. The strike lasted for a week.[92] The Poston strike revealed the stress of communal life, the hardship and neglect felt

---

[91] Correspondence from Austin K. Yamada, April 12, 2018.

[92] Paul Bailey, *City in the Sun: The Japanese Concentration Camp at Poston, Arizona* (Los Angeles: Westernlore Press, 1971), 119-25, 127-29, 131-33. See Spicer, *Impounded People*, 129-35. See also Alexander H. Leighton, *The Governing of Men* (Princeton: Princeton University Press, 1945), 162-244.

by the internees, and the internal conflict between Issei, Nisei, and Kibei. Adding to the grievances were the broken promises of the WRA, including the lateness in the payment of wages and delays in the delivery of clothing and supplies.

A more troubling event soon arose. The WRA allowed an army recruiting station to open at Poston I. The young Nisei welcomed this, as some wished to demonstrate their loyalty by volunteering. But what followed was a huge blunder. In February 1943, the army used a loyalty questionnaire for screening purposes to determine the loyalty of Nisei wishing to enlist. WRA officials thought the loyalty questionnaire was a good idea and would be helpful in clearing applicants for its leave permit program. Moreover, they were under congressional pressure to isolate disloyal individuals, and a questionnaire would be a good way to achieve this objective. They quickly developed a questionnaire and boldly applied it, requiring everyone over the age of seventeen, including women and Issei, to participate. Unfortunately, it was poorly worded and hastily administered.

Most of the questions were straightforward and easily answered, but the last two questions, the crux of the questionnaire, caused anxiety and confusion. They were as follows:

Question 27: Are you willing to serve in the armed forces of the United States on combat duty, wherever ordered?

Question 28: Will you swear unqualified allegiance to the United States of America and faithfully defend the United States from any or all attacks by foreign or domestic forces and forswear any form of allegiance or obedience to the Japanese emperor, or any other foreign government, power, or organization?

On question 27, Nisei men feared by answering "yes," they would be trapped into joining the army. Issei didn't know what to do with the question, for as aliens they couldn't serve in the army. Also, the women didn't know how to answer this question. It was later revised to handle the gender problem by asking: "If this opportunity presents itself and you are found qualified, would you be willing to volunteer for the Army Nurse Corp or the WAAC?" Of greater concern was question 28. Since the Issei were ineligible for citizenship, by renouncing their allegiance to Japan, they would become stateless. It was later changed to ask if they would "abide by the laws of the United States" and not interfere with the war effort. But the damage was done. Many *Nikkei* felt insulted at being asked to swear allegiance to a government that was denying their constitutional rights.

The loyalty questions caused disruptions and divisions among friends and within families. Confusion and frustration prevailed throughout the camps. A majority of internees answered "yes" to the loyalty questions; however, those that answered "no" to questions 27 and 28 were labeled as "no-no boys." Thirteen percent at Gila River answered "no" to both questions, and the results at Poston were about the same. The government decided to isolate these "no-no boys" from all the internment camps and transfer them to the Tule Lake Segregation Center in Northern California, which was established to house those considered disloyal and their families.[93] Some Nisei who were pro-American decided to follow their parents who had answered "no" in order to be together as a family. They felt compelled to give up their US citizenship. These were moments of anguish. There were some who asked to be repatriated to Japan. In the midst of the war when transportation became available aboard the Swedish exchange ship *MS Gripsholm*, a contingent of those requesting repatriation were sent back to Japan. After the war, the rest were repatriated. The deep division within the internment community was dramatically evident one morning when a bus with young men departed from Poston for an army induction center and, at the same time, another bus headed to Tule Lake with those who were disloyal.[94]

As noted earlier, Dillon Myer considered the internment camps to be temporary, and his primary objective was to resettle the internees as soon as possible into communities far away from the exclusion areas. Meanwhile,

---

[93] Richard Drinnon, *Keeper of Concentration Camps: Dillon S. Myer and American Racism* (Berkeley: University of California Press, 1987), 80.

[94] Bailey, *City in the Sun*, 150-58, 196.

Americanization of the internees was to continue. Not everyone agreed with Myer's policies. Secretary of War Henry Stimson rejected Myer's plan to phase out the camp. Pressure came from Congress, and in April 1943, a congressional subcommittee investigated the WRA and recommended tighter surveillance of the internees and to segregate the disloyal. As we have seen, this added congressional pressure forced the WRA to hurriedly apply the loyalty questionnaire, resulting in great confusion and anguish.[95]

The resettlement program didn't fully materialize as Myer had envisioned. From the beginning, some WRA members weren't enthusiastic about the program and had doubts about its effectiveness. The internees themselves were hesitant; they were unsure and feared moving into an unknown community and possibly facing hostility. Already, reports and letters were coming in telling of discrimination faced by those settling. Students, on the other hand, didn't face such hostility and were welcomed on the campuses and in the small college towns. Their stay, however, was temporary and after schooling was over, they had to decide where to relocate with their families. Even though the WRA promoted resettlement in the eastern hinterland, the younger Japanese Americans, and even the older internees, preferred to return to California while the younger internees definitely preferred the urban centers.

Military service, though not a part of the resettlement program, could be considered a form of resettlement since it was one way male Nisei could leave camp. But most men entered military service for patriotic reasons. They wanted to prove they were loyal citizens; moreover, they felt their actions could have the added benefit of leading to the release of all Japanese Americans from the camps and the restoration of their constitutional rights.

On January 28, 1943, Secretary of War Stimson announced the creation of an all-Nisei unit, the 442nd Regimental Combat Team. The government believed the unit would present a good public image and boost the morale of Japanese Americans. Army recruiters toured the Gila River and Poston camps, but few Nisei men volunteered because they were

---

[95] Bailey, 149-50.

experiencing the harshness and uncertainty of camp life, and because they were angry about the government's denial of their rights.[96] As a result, only eighty-four Nisei from Gila River volunteered for the 442nd.[97] To increase enlistment, WRA and JACL leaders lobbied for the military draft to be reopened to Nisei. The government agreed and opened the draft to Nisei on January 1944. This time, many Nisei men entered the army as draftees. Most of them served with the 442nd and distinguished themselves in the European theater, winning many decorations. A smaller number of Nisei served with the MIS and acted as instructors, interrogators, and interpreters. MIS personnel were deployed in the Pacific theater. A total of 1,110 from Gila River and more than 1,200 from Poston served in the US Armed Forces.[98] Of these, twenty-three from Gila River and twenty-two from Poston made the supreme sacrifice and were killed in action.

Director Myer boldly announced on December 23, 1944 that the camps will be closed in one year's time by December 31, 1945. But the camps closed earlier because the Pacific War ended in August 1945; in fact, the phasing out had begun by early 1945. Poston II and III closed on June 22, 1945. Poston I, being larger, took longer and closed on November 28, 1945, the last camp in Arizona to close. Over at Gila River, Canal Camp closed on September 28, 1945 and Butte Camp on November 10, 1945. The last to leave Butte were 155 Japanese Americans from Hawai'i. Toward the end, the internment camps were made up primarily of Issei and those Nisei with young children. Issei were reluctant to leave and preferred to stay in the camp. They had no place to go and feared going to a strange place and possibly facing discrimination. The government finally had to force them out, thus ending the story of the internment camps in Arizona.

---

[96] Robinson, A Tragedy, 207-8; Donald H. Estes, "A Place Called Poston," in Transforming Barbed Wire: The Incarceration of Japanese Americans in Arizona During World War II, ed. Thomas Nakayama (Phoenix: Arizona Humanities Council, 1997), 6.

[97] Arthur. Hansen, "Gila River Relocation Center," in Transforming Barbed Wire: The Incarceration of Japanese Americans in Arizona During World War II, ed. Thomas Nakayama (Phoenix: Arizona Humanities Council, 1997), 9.

[98] Estes, "A Place Called Poston," 6; Hansen, 'Gila River," 7.

There were two other federal facilities in Arizona that held Nisei in confinement. They were unique in their setting and in their function. Since the number of inmates were small, they were often ignored or forgotten. One was known as an isolation center and the other as an honor camp.

LEUPP CITIZEN ISOLATION CENTER

Early on, the high security risk and potentially disruptive Issei were sent to Department of Justice detention camps. But the WRA also had a problem with certain Nisei who were labeled as "troublemakers." These were Nisei who had led or participated in protest movements, who were uncooperative, and who had caused unrest in their camp. The decision was made to move Nisei "troublemakers" out of the internment camps and send them to an isolation center.

The site chosen was Moab in southeastern Utah, but it was soon found to be unsuitable so the inmates were transferred to Leupp, located in northeast Arizona about eighteen miles northwest of the town of Winslow. Leupp was an abandoned Indian boarding school on Navajo Nation land. The buildings were quite suitable, unlike the barrack buildings of the internment camps. This isolation center was administered like a prison, with living conditions much harsher than in the internment camps. It had high fences topped with barbed wire and guard towers manned by military police. The compound was guarded by 150 military police, an excessive number of guards, considering the prison had only eighty prisoners.[99] Why would you need two guards for every prisoner?

One of those transferred from Moab to Leupp was Harry Y. Ueno, a *Kibei* from Hawai'i who was living in California when the war started. Ueno gained notoriety by organizing a worker's union at Manzanar but got in trouble when he was implicated in the beating of a JACL official. He described his experience of being transported to Leupp. On the morning

---

[99] Drinnon, *Keeper of Concentration Camp*, 62-63; Sue Kunitomi Embrey, Arthur A. Hansen, and Betty Kulberg Mitson, *Manzanar Martyr: An Interview with Harry Y. Ueno* (Fullerton, CA: Fullerton California State University, 1986), 76.

of April 27, 1943, he was put into a wooden box and loaded on the back of a truck. The box was 5' x 6' with a breathing hole on one end. The trip took thirteen hours, and Ueno felt he was in a coffin. He was glad when the truck finally arrived at Leupp, and he was able to get out of the box.[100] Most inmates were brought in with no hearing nor were they charged with any crime. It was said one inmate was sent from Gila River to Leupp because he called a Caucasian nurse an "old maid." The abuses at Leupp came to light when a letter written by Francis S. Frederick, former director of Leupp, was disclosed. Frederick wrote, "How in hell can you Americanize the Japs when Gestapo methods are used in sending them to Leupp—no warrants, no trials, no sentences, separated from their families, and so forth."[101]

Leupp was giving WRA a bad image, and, for that reason, Myer ordered it closed. "I have said from the first that it's illegal, and I still think so. I'm not at all proud of Leupp even though it has been effective," Myer said.[102] On December 4, 1943, Leupp was hastily closed, and inmates were moved to Tule Lake in California.

CATALINA FEDERAL HONOR CAMP

Although Leupp was a small facility holding few Japanese Americans detainees, it didn't fade from the scene in the postwar period because of its bad reputation. However, there were other small detention facilities that few knew about, and it took several years after the war before the general public heard about them. One such facility was discovered at a meeting of the Japan-America Society of Tucson (JAST), an organization promoting Japanese culture, of which I was a founding board member.

At its fall meeting in 1997, a stranger suddenly appeared and inquired, "I want to see the Catalina camp site where I was a prisoner." We were all puzzled and asked, "What are you talking about? What prisoner camp?" This is how we first learned about the Catalina Federal Honor Camp. About

---

[100] Embrey, *Manzanar Martyr*, 74-75.

[101] Drinnon, *Keeper of Concentration Camp*, 102.

[102] Drinnon, 117.

a year later, in late August and early September 1998, articles appeared in the *Arizona Daily Star*, describing the archeological study of the site done by Jeffrey F. Burton and his team at the Western Archeological and Conservation Center in Tucson, a division of the National Park Service. This study was part of an extensive field research of the internment camps. In their research, through documents, they found the Catalina camp held a few Japanese American inmates.

The Catalina Federal Honor Camp was located in the Santa Catalina Mountains, northeast of Tucson, Arizona, on milepost seven of the Catalina Highway. The prison facility was established in 1939 and was under the Federal Bureau of Prisons. The prison was to provide labor to build a highway to Mount Lemmon. During World War II, it took in draft-resisters and conscientious objectors. About forty-five Japanese American draft-resisters were interned. For the government, an isolated prison was the solution to the problem of segregating Nisei who had opposed conscription and who were, therefore, a negative group. Of the transferred Nisei inmates, thirty were from Granada (also known as Amache) Relocation Center in Colorado, and the rest were from Poston and the Topaz Relocation Center in Utah. They were transported to Tucson wearing handcuffs and leg irons. The Nisei inmates eventually worked alongside with more than two hundred other prisoners, including Hopi Indians and Jehovah's Witnesses.[103]

Documents and archaeological field studies provide a picture of the layout and components of the camp. The camp consisted of the following: four barracks, mess hall, laundry building, powerhouse, garage, warehouse, workshop, and a classroom. The administrative staff was housed in a separate area and included an administration building and cottages for prison personnel. In all, there were about fifty buildings. The camp included chicken and turkey farms, a vegetable garden, and a baseball field. The Catalina camp didn't look like a prison, for it had no fence or guard tower, and unlike Poston and Gila River internment camps, security wasn't enforced.[104] Based on comments made by Nisei inmates, the living condi-

---

[103] Burton, *Confinement and Ethnicity*, 409,411.

[104] Burton, 409-11, 414.

tions were much better than those of the internment camps. One inmate asked the favorable comments not be publicized, for he feared he might be sent back to the internment camp. Essentially, the Honor Camp operated as a work camp.

Layout of Catalina Federal Honor Camp.
Courtesy of the National Park Service.

The camp's most famous inmate was Gordon Hirabayashi. At the time of the Pearl Harbor attack, Hirabayashi was a student at the University of Washington, and while at the university, he had become a Quaker and a pacifist. When war was declared, curfew was immediately imposed, and all *Nikkei* were prohibited to be out after curfew. Hirabayashi wondered why as a US citizen he couldn't stay out with his friends. In a calculated act of civil disobedience, he decided to protest the regulation by staying out for several nights. He wasn't arrested. Finally, in frustration, he decided to turn himself in at the FBI office and was promptly arrested for violating the curfew. Moreover, he had missed the last bus taking *Nikkei* out of the exclusion zone, so he was also charged with violating the exclusion order.

Hirabayashi spent several months in jail, as his case worked its way through the judicial system. Surprisingly, the case moved quickly and in May 1943 reached the US Supreme Court. As a national security issue, there was an urgency to expedite the case. The Supreme Court in June 1943 upheld the decisions of the lower courts and found Hirabayashi guilty of violating the curfew. Interestingly, the Supreme Court didn't consider the exclusion violation. Since he had already been in prison for several months, he had only three months remaining in his sentence.

Hirabayashi disliked the jail at Spokane, Washington and asked to be sent to the federal facility in Tucson, which had an opening. The government agreed; however, no funds were available to pay for his transportation to Tucson. He was adamant about going to Tucson and said he'll find a way. He proceeded to hitchhike, and it took him two weeks. When he got to Tucson, camp officials couldn't find his papers; therefore, they would not admit him. He pleaded with them but finally decided, at their suggestion, to wait it out by going to a movie in town. When he returned, they had found his papers, and he was admitted.[105]

Forty years later, Hirabayashi's case was reopened when documents were discovered, showing the government had deliberately withheld and suppressed relevant information and misled the court. A legal team of young Sansei lawyers resorted to the rarely used writ of *coram nobis* (writ of error). In 1987, the Ninth Circuit Court of Appeals overturned the conviction, and the government decided not to appeal. Hirabayashi won, and he became an iconic figure, symbolizing the fight to preserve the rights and personal liberties guaranteed by the Constitution. He was posthumously awarded the Presidential Medal of Freedom, the nation's highest civilian decoration.

The prison camp was demolished in the 1970s, and today only traces can be seen of a few scattered stonewalls, foundations, and masonry work

---

[105] Roger W. Axford, *Too Long Been Silent: Japanese Americans Speak Out* (Lincoln, NE: Media Publishing and Marketing, 1986), 10-11. See also Peter Irons, *Justice at War: The Story of the Japanese American Internment Cases* (Berkeley: University of California Press, 1993), 250. The account is incredulous and amusing, and it was reaffirmed in a conversation with Hirabayashi when he was in Tucson for the dedication of the recreation site.

done by the prisoners. Now, a kiosk explains the history of the camp, the Japanese Americans internment, and about Hirabayashi. The former federal prison camp was dedicated in November 1999 as the "Gordon Hirabayashi Recreation Site" and is part of the US Forest Service, National Park Service. Hirabayashi and a few of his Japanese American inmates returned for the dedication and shared their reminiscences and memories of their work and camp experiences.

Remains of a stairway at Catalina Federal Honor Camp.

AFTERMATH

Approximately 31,400 Japanese Americans were interned in Arizona's two camps during World War II or roughly 26 percent of all Japanese Americans interned in the United States. Generally, what happened in Arizona was similar to what took place in the other eight internment camps. As mentioned, the forced removal of the Japanese Americans resulted in the following traumatic experiences: uprooting from their homes; the move to the assembly centers; the transfer to internment camps; and finally, the resettlement and closure of the camps. Without a doubt, the most consequential phase of the whole episode was the internment camp. The psychological impact, as well as the effect on familial and generational ties, have been discussed. The internees, by their own effort, made camp life a bit tolerable, and their resiliency was surprising. But with all this as past history, what about its remembrance and legacy?

After the closure of the Poston and Gila River internment camps, the physical traces of the camps rapidly disappeared, and for over two decades little attention was paid to the experiences of the internees. The internees, for their part, didn't want to talk about the camp, for the bitter memories were too painful to recall; hence, there was little reminiscing and sharing of information. Conditions changed in the mid-1960s when Sansei began to ask about the wartime uprooting. The political climate impacted by the civil rights movement and the Vietnam War made it conducive for such inquires. Books on the camps began to appear. Historian Roger Daniel's *Concentration Camps USA: Japanese Americans and World War II* appeared in 1971. Not only did research on the internment camps expand, but internees began to openly share their stories and memories in articles and other publications and in recorded oral history. Camp poetry, photographs, and internees' art works were collected and shared. As a result, today, there is an impressive collection of oral, print, and visual records of the wartime internment experience.[106]

As Japanese Americans began to visit the Poston and Gila River sites, a concern arose about maintaining the sites. The Arizona chapter of JACL, with the cooperation of the Gila River Tribal Council, organized a project to clean up the camp site twice a year; a similar effort was undertaken by the Poston Community Alliance. Also, annual pilgrimages were organized, thus securing the remembrance and legacy of the camps.

---

[106] See, for example, Axford, *Too Long Been Silent: Japanese-Americans Speak Out.* Besides the interview with Hirabayashi, there are interviews with four Poston and two Gila River internees. See stories by two Poston internees, including paintings, in Brian Komei Dempster, ed., *Making Home From War: Stories of Japanese American Exile and Resettlement* (Berkeley: Heyday Books, 2011), 1-15, 93-97.

The Poston site is on tribal land, but it is accessible and can be toured. There are a few buildings still standing, and some are used by the Native Americans, but most of the buildings are seriously deteriorated or have been completely demolished. The Poston Community Alliance, in collaboration with the Colorado River Indian Tribal Council, has undertaken the task of restoring or preserving the school auditorium and classrooms of Poston I. Today, the area of what used to be the former residential barracks is used for farming by the tribal communities.

Tribal permission is required to visit the Gila River site, and the tour must be escorted. The camp has been razed and no buildings remain, but there are many signs of the former camp. By taking a tour, it is possible to achieve a feeling for the surroundings and to imagine what it was like. Certainly, I had that feeling. You have to know what to look for, and the site has to be walked. Concrete foundation slabs of the administration buildings, warehouse, high school, and the lavatories can be seen. Footing blocks of the residential barracks and other buildings are clearly visible. There are traces of the landscaping, such as small ponds, and of the irrigation ditches, manholes, and cisterns.

At Poston I, a large memorial monument and kiosk was built in 1992. Both Poston and Gila River have interpretive signs and plaques briefly explaining the history of the camp. A servicemen's honor roll monument, honoring those from Gila River who served in World War II, which was erected by the internees, still stands at Butte Camp. At both internment camps, there are memorial markers honoring the veterans.[107]

Efforts were made at the national level to restore and preserve the internment sites. Congress in 2009 established the Japanese American Confinement Sites (JACS) grant program by appropriating $38 million. Applicants had to match every $2.00 received in federal funds with $1.00 in local money. In 2020, Congress authorized an additional $3.1 million. The grant program included small confinement sites few people knew about. The total number of projects exceeded forty sites. In addition to

---

[107] For information on visiting the relocation centers, see Frank and Joanne Iritani, *Ten Visits: Accounts of Visits to all the Japanese American Relocation Centers* (San Mateo, CA: Asian American Curriculum Project, 1995).

improving and preserving the sites, the program emphasizes the educational purposes—to tell the stories of the internees and to provide instructional materials.

Starting in 1984, Seattle held the first Day of Remembrance commemorating Executive Order 9066. It has become a regular observance in several communities. The format has varied, but usually it is a gathering to discuss and reflect on the internment. Particularly poignant are the sharing of stories, poetry, photographs, drawings—the written and visual testimonies of the camp experiences. Through these activities, the legacy lives on.

The wartime incarceration of Japanese Americans has been described as a "black chapter" in American history. On the Poston Memorial Monument is inscribed the following: "May it serve as a constant reminder of our past so that Americans in the future will never again be denied their constitutional rights and may the remembrance of that experience serve to advance the evolution of the human spirit."[108] A refrain often-quoted after a tragic event had occurred is—"never again"—and it is quoted in the monument.

Today, conditions have changed, but similar forces are still at work undermining our rights and liberties. Instead of war, there is terrorism, and instead of hatred for the Japanese Americans, there is hatred for Muslims and immigrants. The failure of political leadership is clearly evident when political leaders give in to their inner fears and prejudices and take actions against minorities, especially immigrants and marginalized populations, for the sake of national security. During times of adversity, these leaders are willing to compromise the rights and freedoms of others. The warning given is "eternal vigilance is the price of liberty."[109] Vigilance is necessary to protect our constitutional rights and our freedoms. Democracy, after all, is fragile; it can't be taken for granted. Milton Eisenhower wrote, "How could such a tragedy have occurred in a democratic society that prides itself on

---

[108] https://www.hmdb.org > m.asp.

[109] Quotation often attributed to Thomas Jefferson and sometimes to John Philpot Curran, but its authorship is problematic.

individual rights and freedoms?"[110] Unfortunately, it did happen, and the lesson shouldn't be forgotten nor ignored. It is appropriate to evoke the familiar refrain—"never again."

---

[110] Eisenhower's quotation in Leonard J. Arrington, *The Price of Prejudice*, 2nd ed. (Delta, UT: Topaz Museum, 1997), 10.

PART THREE

CONTINUITY

CHAPTER EIGHT

RESETTLEMENT AND POSTWAR DEVELOPMENTS

With the end of the Pacific War and the closing of the internment camps, the process of resettling the internees began. Under the leave permit system, many young Nisei workers and students had already settled in the cities and towns of the Midwest and East Coast. To this could be added about 2,300 young Nisei serving in the army. Of all the internees in the ten camps, about one-fourth were given official permission to leave the camps and settle outside of the West Coast.

There was another group who expressed their desire to be resettled, in this case, to be repatriated to Japan—they wanted to return to their mother country. These repatriates, mostly Issei numbering around two thousand, were returned to Japan aboard the Swedish liner *MS Gripsholm* in a prisoner exchange during the war. They had remained steadfastly loyal to Japan.

More significant were Nisei, known as expatriates or renunciants who voluntarily gave up US citizenship. They renounced their citizenship in order to be with their parents. The loyalty questionnaire created turmoil, and difficult decisions had to be made. But with the end of the war, many Nisei expatriates began to reconsider their decision. They said they were misinformed, deceived, and coerced by pro-Japan groups in the camp to renounce their citizenship. Moreover, the government's questionnaire sowed confusion and caused stress. Finally, they argued that four years of confinement had a demoralizing effect. These factors caused them to make that regrettable decision. At the beginning, these "no-no boys" numbered around two thousand, but they steadily increased, and at its peak, there were around twelve thousand, but this figure included those that refused to answer the loyalty questions or gave ambiguous responses. They were all labeled "disloyal." The expatriates were segregated and sent to Tule Lake Segregation Center and Crystal City in Texas. They were separated so as not to "contaminate" the rest of the camp. In the end, however, because of their decision to reconsider their denial of citizenship, only a total of 5,700 applications were made for renunciation of citizenship.

It was the tireless efforts of the civil rights attorney Wayne M. Collins that forced the government to cancel the renunciations and to stop the deportations. He led the litigation for almost five thousand renunciants, and each case had to be handled individually. Yoshito Wayne Osaki wrote:

> We renunciants of Tule Lake will never forget the invaluable legal assistance provided to us by Attorney Wayne M. Collins, who was one of the few Americans willing to champion the principle of justice on behalf of those imprisoned at Tule Lake. We will never forget the litigation initiated by Mr. Collins on behalf of us—over five thousand renunciants in all—which stopped our forced deportation and enabled me and others to be released from Tule Lake camp six months after the end of the war.[111]

It took longer to regain the renunciants' citizenship. Collins worked on thousands of court cases for twenty-three years. Even some renunciants who were repatriated to Japan were eventually able to return to the United States.[112] In all, only about seven hundred lost their citizenship.

---

[111] Dempster, ed., *Making Home*, 121.

[112] Although Collin's contribution wasn't widely recognized, his contemporaries and internees wrote about their appreciation and indebtedness to Collins. See Michi N. Weglyn's dedication in her *Years of Infamy: The Untold Story of America's Concentration Camps* (New York: Morrow Quill Paperlocks, 1976). Weglyn was an internee at Gila River. Her book is one of the earliest accounts of the internment camps. Additional information on Collins can be found in Charles Wollenberg, *Rebel Lawyer: Wayne Collins and the Defense of Japanese American Rights* (Berkeley: Heyday Books, 2018).

The plight of the Japanese who still desired to be sent to Japan was resolved on December 27, 1945, when the SS *Matsonia* departed from Portland for Japan with 1,659 Issei repatriates and 3,065 Nisei expatriates with their children.[113] Sadly, these *Nikkei* faced formidable problems. Most Nisei had never been to Japan, and now they had to start a new life in a strange, foreign country—a country devastated by the war. They faced shortages of food and other necessities and found it difficult to find housing and employment. They had to grapple with basic survival needs. It was a terrible homecoming.

Aside from those on leave permit with their accompanying families, those in the military, and the repatriates and expatriates, forty-four thousand internees, or about one-third of the original total, remained in the camps; where they would resettle became a major concern. Many of the Issei didn't want to leave. Nearly all of them lost their possessions. No longer the breadwinner of their family, they had little to look forward to. They were too old to start anew and were apprehensive about moving into a possible hostile environment. But they had no choice—they were forced out. The WRA had hoped the *Nikkei* would spread out eastward and avoid clustering in any given area to prevent being viewed as a threat. As we have seen, most of the internees, young and old, decided otherwise and two-thirds of them returned to the West Coast.

Even before the war ended, the Japanese Americans were allowed to return to the West Coast by the Supreme Court ruling in *Ex parte Endo*. The Supreme Court ruled the government had no authority to continually detain, without charges or trial, loyal Japanese Americans. As a result of the court's decision, the army lifted the exclusion orders in January 1945. Then the WRA decided to close the camps, rendering moot the Supreme Court ruling.

The historian Greg Robinson points out that during the war, President Roosevelt and his advisors did make plans to resettle the internees. A key feature of this planning was the dispersing of the Japanese Americans into

---

[113] Roger Daniels, *Prisoners without Trials: Japanese Americans in World War II* (New York: Hill and Wang, 1993), 85.

small groups throughout the rural and underpopulated areas, thus avoiding the establishment of large ethnic communities, which would have surely engendered protest. The plan was called M Project (the M stood for migration), and it was a top-secret anthropological study. Experts were brought in to assess how human migration and resettlement could be carried out, thereby promoting peaceful assimilation and economic growth. It was assumed dispersion and gradual settlement of small groups would avoid protest and would help the local economy. But little was done beyond the planning stage. There was almost no formulation as to how to carry out the dispersion. After FDR's death, President Truman did not follow through and the M Project was forgotten. Perhaps it is fortunate the M Project was never implemented, for later experience shows the dispersion and small grouping of Japanese Americans and the elimination of Japantowns didn't facilitate social harmony and didn't necessarily promote assimilation.[114]

Not much research has been done on the subject of resettlement as compared to studies on camp life. Nevertheless, from the collections of memoirs, stories, and other accounts, we have a good picture of the dispersion pattern and what went into the decision to relocate.[115] Parents joined their children who had settled in Midwestern and Eastern states under the leave permit program. It was usually an urban center, Chicago being a favorite with about 6,500 *Nikkei*, the largest number of former internees for any city outside of the West Coast. Among the states preferred by Japanese American families were Colorado, Utah, and Idaho. Young Nisei preferred the cities for their greater job and social opportunities, and these urban centers were considered to be less hostile than rural areas. Today, many Japanese American families can trace their beginnings in Chicago, Denver, Salt Lake City, and New York City to the resettlement period following the closing of the camps.

---

[114] Greg Robinson, *After Camp: Portraits in Midcentury Japanese American Life and Politics* (Berkeley: University of California Press, 2012), 15, 27-30.

[115] See Dempster, *Making Home.* A collection of twelve memoirs, it tells how the young Nisei students and workers returned to the West Coast with their families.

But the majority of Japanese American families, even some of those under the leave permit program, opted for the West Coast. They were more familiar with the West Coast and thought they could recover part of their possessions or get back to their prewar occupations. It turned out to be a forlorn hope. They could not recover what they had left and, furthermore, soon faced racism with sporadic incidents of intimidation and threats. Statistical data on discrimination is difficult to find, but anecdotal evidence showed a significant number of discriminatory incidents. A few *Nikkei* were fortunate to have kindly neighbors who welcomed them back and had taken care of their possessions, but for the most part, returnees weren't so fortunate.

Uncertainty brought both fear and anxiety as the returnees faced the hardship of day-to-day living. Since they couldn't return to their former occupation or business, they were forced to move into the inner city and take whatever jobs were available. They faced job discrimination, and the few openings available were menial, unskilled, and low-paying, such as gardener or maid. Postwar housing shortage compounded the problem. Some found temporary housing provided by the WRA. However, the housing problem was made even worse by restrictive covenants. Restrictive covenants are promises made by homeowners on their deeds not to sell or rent to members of minority or "colored" groups. The promise is extended to future buyers as a condition of sale. Such restrictions caused many returnees to seek temporary shelter in trailer camps, former army barracks, tent camps put up by local government, or housing provided by churches, temples, and other nonprofit organizations. It is estimated about four thousand Japanese Americans were forced into substandard temporary housing.[116] Housing discrimination made many sections of the city off-limits to *Nikkei*, resulting in their settling in the poorer sections; they didn't have much of a choice.

Later in 1948, when the US Supreme Court declared restrictive covenants unconstitutional because it violated the Fourteenth Amendment, large number of Japanese began to move into suburban enclaves of

---

[116] Robinson, *After Camp*, 63.

Southern California, such as West Los Angeles and Pacoima and especially into Gardena. The federal government didn't want the Japanese Americans to cluster together, but it became unavoidable because of discrimination. Moreover, strong cultural ties existed and community-wide organizations, including Japanese Christian churches, Buddhist temples, and the JACL, wanted the Japanese Americans to coalesce.

Even so, no large Japanese districts were created in the postwar period. The early immigrants had clustered, when possible, into certain districts in the cities because of discrimination, and they found it comforting to be with people of their ethnicity. But now new forces were at work. By the 1970s, younger Japanese Americans had moved out into the suburbs and became part of the growing middle class, while at the same time, urban renewal had demolished the old Japanese districts. Such was the case in Seattle and other big cities where Japantowns, called *Nihonmachi* in Japanese, were eliminated in the process of urban renewal and population shifts. Now, there is only Little Tokyo in Los Angeles, Japantown in San Francisco, and a Japantown in San Jose. Nevertheless, Japantowns in these three cities serve as cultural centers for the Japanese community. The Japanese American National Museum is located in Los Angeles' Little Tokyo and San Jose has the Japanese American Museum. These museums have exhibits, photographs, documents, and numerous paraphernalia that depict the history and culture of the Japanese Americans.

Challenges and the burden of resettlement were borne primarily by the Nisei. They took over leadership in the Japanese community. The Japanese Americans had mixed feelings about the resettlement experience. The younger Nisei considered it an opportunity to undertake something new, while the older Nisei and Issei focused on the ordeal, hardship, and isolation they were facing. Resettlement added to and reinforced the resentment felt by many Japanese Americans about their treatment. They emerged with a chip on their shoulder. They were skeptical of promises made by people in position of authority and lacked confidence in themselves as an important political actor. While belligerent in their attitudes, they were unwilling to take action and lacked assertiveness—they didn't want to make "waves." This mindset becomes noticeable when compared with those of Hawai'i Japanese. The vast majority of Japanese Americans in Hawai'i weren't burdened by a burning resentment; instead, they were optimistic and felt discrimination could be overcome in short order. They were assertive and, in contrast to their mainland counterpart, they were confident they could make a difference.

REDRESS AND *CORAM NOBIS* CASES

In the 1960s, several groups in America began to protest and demand their rights. The civil rights, antiwar, black power, Chicano, and women rights movements organized marches and rallies demanding social justice. Out of this social ferment arose the drive to seek pardons and reparations for Japanese Americans. Speaking to his fellow students, Edison Uno, a Nisei teenager in the Crystal City family internment camp, said:

> This internment is against our constitutional rights. We're American citizens, and as American citizens we should not have been put into camps. If you were in Los Angeles, and you were taken into prison, and they found out that you were not supposed to be in prison, they would let you go and give you a letter of pardon. We need that pardon.[117]

Uno is considered the first Japanese American in an internment camp to ask for reparative justice. He went on to become a leading advocate for reparation by participating in public education and legislative lobbying.

Japanese Americans began to discuss the possibility of seeking an apology and restitution from the government. It is interesting to note the word "reparation" was changed to "redress." Although "reparation" and "redress" have similar meanings, that is, to make amend, correct, or compensate for a wrong or injury, "reparation" is often used to denote the money

---

[117] Jean Jarboe Russell, *The Train to Crystal City: FDR's Secret Prisoner Exchange Program and America's Only Family Internment Camp During World War II* (New York: Scribner, 2015), 145.

given in compensation for damages or losses sustained in war. For example, a defeated nation making payments to a victorious nation. "Redress," however, doesn't involve the transfer of money and is merely a legal satisfaction. Thus, "redress" is a more palatable word.

There were two chapters in the redress movement. The first part was the legal process involving three famous cases; the second was the process of seeking a government apology and individual compensations. These two efforts fully occupied the interest and concern of the Nisei and the Sansei from the 1960s to the end of the 1980s.

Three young Nisei challenged General DeWitt's orders in court cases that reached the Supreme Court. The first challenge came from Gordon Hirabayashi. His background has been previously covered in chapter 7 in the section on the Catalina Federal Honor Camp. Hirabayashi deliberately disobeyed military orders and was charged with violating the curfew and evacuation regulations. He found support from local lawyers who offered their services and friends who helped raise funds. The legal battle ended with Hirabayashi being found guilty on both counts by the district court in Seattle, but the case was appealed to the Ninth Circuit Court of Appeals.

Meanwhile, the second case of Minoru Yasui emerged. Yasui's background was different from that of Hirabayashi. While Gordon was a pacifist, Yasui was an officer in the army reserve. He graduated from the University of Oregon School of Law but had a difficult time finding employment due to discrimination. Finally, he found work with the Japanese Consulate in Chicago. When war broke out, he immediately resigned his consular position and reported for active duty, but the army would not take him. Frustrated, he decided, like Hirabayashi, to do a calculated act of civil disobedience by violating the curfew order. After curfew took place, Yasui walked into the police station and demanded to be arrested.

As it turned out, his case was the first to test the legality of Gen. DeWitt's orders. His act of disobedience didn't mean he was disloyal to America. Even when he spent nine months in solitary confinement, his faith in America remained strong and his loyalty to the United States was never in doubt. The district court judge in Portland held the curfew order was unconstitutional as applied to a US citizen, but because Yasui was employed by the Japanese Consulate before the war, the judge ruled he had indirectly renounced his US citizenship and was, therefore, an alien and liable to the curfew order. He was found guilty as charged. Since this case, like the *Hirabayashi* case, dealt with national security, it was quickly appealed to the Ninth Circuit.

The third young Nisei resister was Fred Korematsu. He differed from Hirabayashi and Yasui in that initially he didn't openly challenge the curfew or exclusion orders. He was a welder by trade and was laid-off when war broke out. Korematsu didn't report to the assembly center as required and tried to avoid arrest by resorting to cosmetic surgery to alter his facial features. He failed and was arrested and charged with disobeying the exclusion order. A local lawyer, Wayne Collier, came to his assistance and offered his services. Collier's work with the renunciants was discussed in the beginning of this chapter. Whereas, the *Hirabayashi* and *Yasui* cases were about the curfew order, the *Korematsu* case dealt primarily with the exclusion order. Korematsu was found guilty by the district court in San Francisco, but no sentence was imposed; hence the case was appealed to the Ninth Circuit.

All three cases coalesced, and since the questions involved were of national security concerns, the appellate court certified the legal questions and sent the three cases to the Supreme Court. On June 21, 1943, the Supreme Court in *Hirabayashi v. United States* ruled Hirabayashi was guilty on both counts. In the *Yasui* case, the Supreme Court on June 2, 1943 unanimously upheld Yasui's conviction on violating the curfew but overturned the lower court decision on Yasui's forfeiture of his US citizenship by working for the Japanese Consulate. The Court only ruled on the curfew and avoided discussing the constitutionality of the exclusion order. After about a year delay, the *Korematsu* case was brought up to the Supreme Court for the second time and paired with the *Endo* case.[118] For political reason, the decision was delayed because of the November election. The Court ruled in December 1944, finding Korematsu guilty of violating the exclusion order. By a six-to-three decision, it legalized the internment camps in wartime at the expense of the civil rights and liberties of American citizens.

If the story of the three cases were to end as described above, it would be a sad commentary on American jurisprudence. But after forty years, the *Korematsu, Hirabayashi,* and *Yasui* cases of the 1940s were reopened in the mid-1980s as *coram nobis* litigation. A *coram nobis* proceeding is a rare and obscure process that enables a person who was convicted long ago of a crime to reopen their case and have the conviction voided if they can prove "fundamental error" or "manifest injustice." The *coram nobis* proceeding is rarely used because it is extremely difficult to prove manifest injustice, since the court does not want to admit it made a major mistake.

Manifest injustice became apparent when new evidence was discovered in 1981 by Aiko Herzig-Yoshinaga, a government archival researcher working at that time for the Commission on Wartime Relocation and Internment of Civilians (CWRIC). She came across the last remaining copy of the original final report of General DeWitt, the general who issued the curfew and exclusion orders. She consulted with Professor Peter Irons, who was doing research for his book *Justice Delayed*. They found War Department officials had altered statements in the final report to make the report supportive of the action to remove *Nikkei* from the West Coast. These officials presented the amended version as the final report and tried to destroy all the original copies. Furthermore, officials at the War Department and Department of Justice suppressed evidence showing the loyalty of Japanese Americans and the absence of acts of espionage. Finally, even though government officials

---

[118] The *Endo* case was another challenge to Gen. DeWitt's orders. Mitsuye Endo differed from her male counterparts, for she wasn't challenging the curfew and exclusion orders but the internment camp itself. She used the civil procedure of a writ of *habeas corpus*—that the government had no authority to detain loyal citizens in an internment camp and had to release persons unlawfully detained. The writ is a legal safeguard to protect from being deprived of one's liberty. The Supreme Court delayed the case to lessen criticism of the government, and when the Court finally made its ruling and ordered the release of Endo, it was a month before the announcement was made that all the camps will be closing.

knew the allegations in the final report were false, they failed to advise the Supreme Court of these misleading claims.

Professor Irons suggested the *coram nobis* approach for all three cases. *Coram nobis* legal teams were formed in San Francisco, Seattle, and Portland. They were comprised principally of Sansei, although Caucasians and Chinese Americans also served on the team. The Korematsu team in San Francisco had twelve members, Hirabayashi team in Seattle had seventeen, and Yasui team in Portland had eleven. Members were graduates of law schools, working in law firms or community agencies. They were noted for being energetic and purpose-driven, working long hours doing research and writing.

In January 1983, identical *coram nobis* petitions were filed in three separate district courts, first by Korematsu, then by Hirabayashi and Yasui. In the petition, the litigants showed how high government officials altered, suppressed, and destroyed information and evidence in order to influence the outcome of the Supreme Court decision. Government officials deliberately omitted relevant evidence and provided misleading information to the Supreme Court. In the following month, these arguments were buttressed by the report of the CWRIC entitled, *Personal Justice Denied*, which provided additional testimonies and documents. To countered these arguments, the government's position in all three cases was essentially the same. The government admitted its mistake in evacuating the Japanese Americans and asked the courts to vacate (nullify) the three men's convictions but moved the *coram nobis* petition be dismissed and for the courts to refrain from ruling on the racism issue and the government misconduct.

In his district court case, Korematsu concluded his statement with, "I would like to see the government admit that they were wrong and do something about it so this will never happen again to any American citizen of any race, creed, or color."[119] The district court judge granted Korematsu's *coram nobis* petition, thus affirming the misconduct of the government and vacating Korematsu's exclusion conviction of December 1944. Korematsu was finally

---

[119] Yamamoto et al., *Race, Rights,* 283.

free from all legal judgments. He continued to fight racial injustices in the ensuing years. In 1999, he was awarded the Presidential Medal of Freedom.

The *Yasui* and *Hirabayashi* cases were more complicated and resulted in delays. In 1984, the US District Court in Portland vacated Yasui's conviction but declined to grant his *coram nobis* petition. Yasui appealed but died November 12, 1986 before the appeal could be decided.

It was June 1985 when the district court in Seattle finally granted Hirabayashi's *coram nobis* petition and vacated his conviction of disobeying the exclusion order. But the court upheld his curfew order conviction. An appeal was made to the Ninth Circuit and a three-judge panel in September 1987 concluded racial prejudice, rather than military necessity, was the basis for the exclusion order, and therefore granted *coram nobis* and vacated the curfew conviction. The government decided not to appeal. Thus ended the *coram nobis* cases; all three were cleared of previous convictions, and the government admitted its mistakes and misdeeds. After forty years, and a process of tortuous judicial maneuvering with several detours, the cases concluded with the vindication of Korematsu, Hirabayashi, and Yasui.

Left to right: **Gordon Hirabayashi, Minoru Yasui,
and Fred Korematsu.
Courtesy of hsiang-court.**

When I took a constitutional law course in the 1960s, the textbook used in the course had a chapter on civil rights and liberties with footnotes referring to *Korematsu v. United States*, *Hirabayashi v. United States*, and *Yasui v. United States*. This is how I was introduced to these cases, from footnotes, and I didn't fully grasp their importance. The *coram nobis* cases grew in importance and became the legal basis for the reparation movement of the 1980s.

Because the *coram nobis* cases were settled at the appellate court level and were not heard in the Supreme Court, the Court's decisions of the 1940s can still be used as precedent. Of the three *coram nobis* cases, the *Korematsu* decision is the most critical. The political branches (Congress and Executive) and the military have used national security as justification for limiting civil liberties and rights of Americans. In cases where military policies and operations are seen as essential for national security purposes and for military exigencies, the Supreme Court has allowed for the limitation on civil liberties. Furthermore, in cases having political considerations, where Congress or the executive branch is involved and military exigencies are not so clear, *Korematsu* may be revisited. In recent years, with the rise of terrorism, Congress has given the president sweeping power to protect national security. The president can view some immigrants as threats to national security. Should their civil liberties be limited? Likewise, certain minority groups are viewed as potential threats—should their civil liberties be limited? At what point should civil liberties be protected at the expense of national security? Where is the balance between protecting our country for reasons of national security and protecting the civil liberties of its citizens?

REPARATIONS AND POLITICS

From the very beginning, the Japanese American redress movement focused on Congress and the Executive branch but used judicial means to achieve its objectives. The *coram nobis* litigation didn't seek monetary compensation, only judicial pronouncements and the correction of injustice.

However, there was a type of legal action that sought monetary relief for property losses and psychological harm suffered during internment.

William Hohri, a community activist from Chicago, founded the National Council for Japanese American Redress in 1979. Its purpose was to lobby for monetary reparations from the government and to raise money to cover court expenses. The strategy of the group was to lobby Congress for reparation legislation and to file class action lawsuits on behalf of internment camp survivors for damages of pain and suffering. The class action suit, *Hohri v. United States,* was filed in March 1983. It listed twenty-one legal injuries suffered by internees and sought damages of $10,000 for each violation per person for a potential reward of about $24 billion. Several documents from the *coram nobis* petitions were included in the class action suit as evidence of the government's complicity.

The Federal District of Columbia Court dismissed the suit because monetary claims were barred by sovereign immunity and statute of limitations. The decision was appealed to the Federal Circuit Court of Appeals, then to the Supreme Court, then was remanded to another court, and finally dismissed in 1988. The use of civil adjudication to request monetary redress was unsuccessful.

The focus on Congress, however, was a success, although it took about a decade before the objectives of the redress movement were achieved. Several young Japanese Americans, including Edison Uno, became active redress advocates. Beginning in the 1970s, JACL led the movement. John Tateishi, leader of the JACL National Committee for Redress, spearheaded the campaign and was the chief lobbyist for redress. The JACL, with the consultation and help of the Japanese American members of Congress, especially the Hawai'i delegation led by Senator Daniel Inouye, fought for passage in Congress. The redress group felt the issue needed attention and the public had to be informed; therefore, it called for the establishment of a government commission to study the facts and circumstances surrounding Executive Order 9066, review wartime orders directing the relocation and detention of American citizens in internment camps, and to recommend appropriate remedies. The relocated Aleut natives of the Aleutian Islands were included to broaden support for the commission.

Some Japanese American activists opposed the idea of a commission. They argued the facts were already known, and prolonged discussion was a waste of time and would dissipate energy and divert the movement from its goals. Nevertheless, the proposal for a review commission won out, and Congress passed the bill creating the Commission on Wartime Relocation and Internment of Civilians (CWRIC); President Jimmy Carter signed the legislation in 1980. A distinguished panel was appointed, including prominent lawyers, former congressmen, a former Supreme Court justice, and well-known religious leaders. Only one Japanese American served on the Commission. One of the Commission's consultants was Aiko Herzig-Yoshinaga, who led a team of researchers in collecting a massive number of documents.

The Commission held public hearings in several major cities and over 750 individuals gave testimonies. Internees told their riveting stories of suffering and the continuing psychological pain they had endured over the years. The Commission found no military necessity for evacuation, relocation, and detention: instead, it found evidence of misconduct on the part of the government. These findings provided the judicial foundation for the *coram nobis* cases. More importantly for accomplishing the redress movement's objectives were the Commission's recommendations in its February 1983 report entitled, *Personal Justice Denied*. Briefly, the recommendations were as follows:

+ A formal apology from the government
+ Pardon for those convicted of violating the curfew and exclusion orders and those who had resisted the draft
+ Reinstate veteran benefits and honorable discharge of those dismissed from the military during the first week of the war
+ Funding a study and educating the public about the internment camps
+ Redress payment of $20,000 to each of the survivors

The Commission played a pivotal role in the redress movement. First, it provided the *coram nobis* cases with documents to substantiate their arguments. Second, it left a legacy of valuable testimonies and documentation of the internment experience that would otherwise be unavailable. Third, it galvanized Japanese Americans who were hesitant or mere spectators to become ardent supporters of the movement—Japanese Americans were overwhelmingly for redress. Finally, the recommendations were compelling and were carried out. It is doubtful redress would have succeeded without the Commission.

The combined actions of congressional lobbying, grass-roots initiatives, investigation and report of the CWRIC, and the legal cases, resulted in the passage of the Civil Liberties Act of 1988. It was signed into law by President Ronald Reagan on August 10, 1988. The Act created the Office of Redress Administration to carry out the redress program. President Reagan made a formal apology, and reparation payments of $20,000 were made to each surviving internee. From 1991 to 1998, reparations along with the presidential letter of apology were delivered. Unfortunately, about 20 percent of internees were deceased by the time the payments were sent.

The 1988 Civil Liberties Act, with its apology and reparations, was a tremendous win for Japanese Americans. Even though the $20,000 compensation covered only a fraction of the loss sustained by internees, they were grateful for what they received. For some, it provided closure; for others, it restored their faith in the American government—few governments in the world would be willing to apologize and make amends for its mistakes. It is not a pretty story, but it is somewhat miraculous to have a government respond in this fashion and is good reason to be proud of America.

The impact of the Japanese American redress movement continues. In the United States and throughout the world, reparation efforts have erupted. In America, African Americans, Native Americans, and Native Hawaiians have made legal damage claims for past injustices. Some of these claims go back several centuries. Internationally, there is the reparation movement in the United Kingdom over the slave trade propagated during the expansion of the British Empire. There is a negative aspect. For those minority groups who have endured discrimination and loss of great magnitude and haven't been compensated, there is the implication that they are less deserving. It is an ongoing debate as to how to handle these issues. The Japanese American redress reparation has become a benchmark.

One case in point is the Rosewood Massacre of January 1923. A white mob attacked a black enclave in Florida, burning homes and killing at least six blacks, though there are estimates that as many as thirty-seven blacks were killed. It was in retaliation for an alleged assault on a white woman by a black man. Seventy years later, in 1994, the Florida state legislature awarded direct cash payment of $2.1 million to the survivors and descendants of the massacre. For the first time, a US state government made compensation for its acknowledged role in racism. The law firm leading the fight for redress referred to the 1988 Civil Liberties Act that awarded reparation for the Japanese American survivors of the internment camps. Similar to the approach used by the Japanese Americans, the African Americans chose the route of the legislature rather than the courts and avoided the use of the term "reparation." But they differed by focusing on the economic principle of the loss of property rights rather than the political principle of civil rights and liberties. The major difference, however, was the African Americans had no comprehensive federal plan; their action was at the state level. This resulted in piece-meal reparation, and the African Americans still lack broad support for reparation at the national level.

PARTY POLITICS IN HAWAI'I

The success of the redress movement in Congress was due, in part, to changes in the Hawaiian political scene. The ascendancy of the Nisei politicians in Hawai'i produced the necessary leadership and clout in Congress to ensure the passage of the redress legislation.

After the first decade of the postwar period, with the election of several Nisei candidates, there was a dramatic shift in the political arena. Up to this point, the Republican Party, representing the haole ruling elites—the Big Five corporations—dominated Hawaiian politics and this dates back to the beginning of the territorial government in the early 1900s. They controlled the legislature and the executive offices. Only a few Asian Americans held political office, and usually it was at the local level. In 1930, two Nisei were elected to the territorial legislature, but this was a rare happening. The Nisei were too young to be a factor in politics. As the opposition, the Democratic Party appealed to Asian Americans, Hawaiians, and part-Hawaiians. The second-generation Chinese were an exception; they were a much smaller group than the Nisei. After leaving the plantations, the Chinese were the first immigrant group to set up retail shops, and they assimilated into American society more rapidly than the Japanese and were able to work with the haoles. They were less prone to vote ethnically. In contrast, the majority of Japanese Americans sided with the Democratic Party. This alignment dates back to plantation days when the Japanese workers confronted the plantation owners.

With the rise of unionism, the complexion of Hawaiian politics changed immediately after the war. The International Longshoremen's and Warehousemen's Union (ILWU) began expanding on the West Coast in late 1930s. By the 1940s, ILWU had extended their organization to include dock and sugar workers in Hawai'i. With the end of the war, the ILWU called a sugar workers strike on September 1, 1946, and twenty-six thousand workers on thirty-three plantations left their jobs; the strike lasted for seventy-nine days. The ILWU surprisingly won a big pay raise for the workers and emerged as a powerful force in Hawaiian politics. Union membership grew rapidly, and the ILWU demonstrated its newly found power by calling a dock strike in 1949. The "Great Hawaiian Dock Strike" began on May 1 and lasted 171 days. It was a struggle between the ILWU and the Big Five, which owned the companies that controlled the shipping industry. The strike was over wage parity; island workers were paid much less than mainland workers for doing the same work.

I remember the bitterness of the strike and how it divided the community. There was a severe shortage of toilet paper and rice because of panic buying and hoarding. The union agreed to unload military cargo, food, medical supplies, perishables, and mail, but since Hawai'i is almost totally dependent on the shipping industry, for as much as 90 percent of goods consumed, it seriously crippled the Hawaiian economy. Many small businesses went bankrupt, unemployment soared as workers were laid off, food shortages developed, and prices rose. The crippling strike finally ended on October 27, 1949 with the workers winning a pay raise, but it fell short of what they wanted.

The strike took place at the time of the "red scare" on the mainland with the rise of McCarthyism. Regrettably, the strike was portrayed as a struggle between capitalism and communism. Union leaders were branded as members of a communist conspiracy. The fear of internal communist subversion was heightened by the Cold War. Meanwhile, the ILWU began to be involved in island politics by providing funds, campaigning, and endorsing candidates. But just at the height of its power in the Democratic Party, the House Un-American Activities Committee was sent to Hawai'i to investigate the strike and the role of the ILWU. The public became alarmed when disaffected ILWU leaders left the union and talked about the communist control. Then, in 1951, Jack Kawano, a long-time Nisei ILWU leader, resigned from the union after he had a falling-out with Jack Hall, the ILWU regional director. He decided to testify before the House Un-American Activities Committee about communist infiltration of the ILWU. As a result of Kawano's testimony, the FBI arrested seven individuals under the Smith Act for conspiring to overthrow the US government by force or violence; of those arrested, four were Nisei. They were found guilty on June 19, 1953 and sentenced to five years in prison and fined $5,000. The convictions were appealed, and the Ninth Circuit Court of Appeals ruled in January of 1958 that the teaching of communism was not a conspiracy to overthrow the government by force or violence, as defined by the Smith Act. The convictions were overturned.

During the turmoil over communism, an opening in the leadership of the Democratic Party occurred as the influence of the ILWU waned. It was an opportunity seized by John A. Burns, a "beat cop" who rose to become a captain in the Honolulu Police Department. His father was in the military, and Burns spent part of his childhood in Hawai'i. The family moved back to the mainland, but Burns decided to return to the islands and became a policeman. He knew his way around Kalihi, a rough district, and was consequently known as a *kamaʻaina* (native). He got to know the local people, and this gave him an advantage when he got into politics. Later, as chairman of the territorial Democratic Party, Burns worked to organize plantation laborers, especially Japanese Americans and Filipino Americans. He realized Japanese Americans formed a large voting bloc and sought the help of Daniel Inouye, a wartime hero and 442nd veteran.[120] At the time of his talk with Burns in 1950, Inouye was completing his studies at the University of Hawaiʻi, taking advantage of the GI Bill of Rights as so many veterans did. He went on for his law degree from George Washington University Law School in 1953. By pursing their education, these veterans prepared for their careers in the professions and for leadership positions in business and in community organizations.[121]

Senator Daniel Inouye.
Official Senate Photo.

---

[120] Ogawa, *Kodomo*, 381.

[121] For accounts of how returning veterans adjusted to life in Hawaiʻi, see: Jayna Omaye, "Soldiering On," *Honolulu Magazine* (December 2019).

The Burns-Inouye coalition was formed, and it lasted for about two decades. It revitalized the Democratic Party and expanded its base by including the 442nd Veterans Club, the ILWU, and other Asian, Hawaiian, and part-Hawaiian groups. Moreover, Issei could become citizens and vote with the passage of the McCarran-Walter Act of 1952. The coalition is sometimes referred to as the "Burns machine" because of its coordinated effect on territorial elections. Party officials expected to pick up a few seats in the first major test in 1954 but were surprised by the results. The election has been called the "Hawai'i Democratic Revolution of 1954" and signified a dramatic shift in power from Republicans to Democrats, from wealthy haole to middle class Asian Americans. People of Asian descent were now the majority—a powerful voting bloc. For the first time, Democrats controlled both houses of the Territorial Legislature. Japanese Americans, the largest subgroup of Asian Americans, occupied nearly half of the newly-won seats, and the political careers of Inouye, Spark Matsunaga, George Ariyoshi, Nelson Doi, and other young Nisei were launched.

Japanese Americans became the largest component of the Hawai'i Democratic Party. The statehood issue brought the Japanese community firmly into the fold of the Democratic Party. Of all ethnic communities, it was the only one in which a majority favored Hawai'i becoming a state. Statehood, which was achieved in 1959, was for many Nikkei a further sign they had been accepted formally into first-class American citizenry. After statehood, young Nisei became the dominant force in the state legislature.

When Burns won the governorship in the election of 1962, the Democratic Party became the paramount party in Hawai'i. Hawai'i essentially became a one-party state. The Democratic Party, on occasions, controlled up to 90 percent of the State House and up to 96 percent of the State Senate. Democrats continually held executive offices and dominated the congressional delegation with its senators, congressmen and congresswomen.

Democratic Party dominance continued, even though it began to face factionalism. The younger Democrats, the progressive wing of the party, became increasingly disenchanted with the establishment, the Burns-Inouye coalition. These progressive Democrats, many of them Sansei and

Yonsei (fourth-generation), held left-of-center views on political and social issues. The leader of the progressive wing, Thomas Gill, challenged Burns, the incumbent governor in 1970. Burns won, but the results were closer than expected, and he only won because of votes from the outside islands. The Burns-Inouye coalition was no longer what it was twenty years ago, as many of the old-timers were gone. The influence of the ILWU weakened and was replaced by the public sector unions, such as the Hawai'i State Teachers Association (HSTA) and the Hawai'i Government Employees Association (HGEA). Both organizations were composed of younger Japanese American members and were particularly important for fund-raising and grass-roots campaigning. The Burns-Inouye coalition faded from the scene after the death of Governor Burns in 1975, thus ended nearly two decades of old guard dominance of the Democratic Party.

The Hawai'i Nisei politicians reached the height of their influence in the period from the 1960s to 1990s. The leading Nisei political leaders of this period were as followed: Daniel Inouye, the first congressman from Hawai'i and senator from 1963 until his death in 2012; Spark Matsunaga, congressman from 1962-1976 and senator from 1977 until his death in 1990; George Ariyoshi, a protege of Burns, elected governor in 1974; and Nelson Doi, lieutenant governor who served under Governor Ariyoshi. To have Nisei occupying the top two executive positions in state government was unprecedented. Ariyoshi, who served with MIS in the occupation of Japan, was the first Asian governor in America and was the longest-serving governor in Hawai'i, in office for three terms or twelve years. Even before the Nisei success at the federal and state levels, Nisei had occupied several local elected positions.

One of the first to hold a high local elective position was Shunichi Kimura, who became mayor of Hawai'i County in January 2, 1965. He was the first Japanese American mayor in the United States. For female leaders, outside of haole women, Japanese American women played a more prominent role in politics than any other women. But it took the Sansei to break away from the traditional nonassertive role assumed by Japanese women. Democrat Patsy Takemoto Mink was the first Asian American woman elected to Congress and served in the US House of Representatives from 1965-1977 and again from 1990-2002. On the Republican side, Pat Saiki served as congresswoman from 1987-1991.[122] In the ensuing decade, a new generation of leaders appeared and the Nisei politicians were replaced by Sansei and Yonsei. The heyday of Nisei political power was over. Nisei and later generations had to learn to live with less political influence. They were still a group to be reckon with but were no longer the dominant force.

When compared with the mainlanders, why was political power so quickly acquired by the Nisei in postwar Hawai'i? The environment was all-important. A large concentration of *Nikkei* in the plantations and urban ghettos enhanced ethnic identification and solidarity. Moreover, the island Japanese intermingled and identified with the mixed-races of Hawaiian society. But identity politics by itself is insufficient. Each ethnic group must see benefits for themselves; it is their shared common interest that makes it possible for members to vote as a bloc. The interest of the Japanese Americans became the interest of other Asians, Hawaiians, and part-Hawaiians. It made it easier to think of this large grouping as a huge voting bloc. The multiracial linkage was based on the ubiquitous "aloha spirit"—a feeling of camaraderie with "locals."

It was obviously a political advantage if you could exploit this trust to galvanize popular support. Consequently, the Hawai'i Nisei had a built-in "community spirit." There was little need for an organization like the Japanese American Citizen League (JACL) to drum up political support. Although the JACL had a chapter in Honolulu, it was not needed; it was superfluous.

---

[122] A prominent Japanese American politician, Senator Mazie K. Hirono, was born in postwar Japan and doesn't fit the definition of Nisei, as used in this book. She has been in the US Senate since 2013 and was Lieutenant Governor of Hawai'i (1994-2002).

MAINLAND POLITICAL AND SOCIAL MOVEMENTS

The picture was different on the mainland. The *Nikkei* were scattered and living in diverse communities, ranging from isolated rural areas to densely populated urban centers. It was difficult to bring these diverse groupings together. Being scattered and seemingly amorphous, they lacked cohesion and consequently lacked political leverage.

An organization was needed to bring together mainland Japanese for political purposes. The JACL was formed in the 1930s. The young Nisei activists struggled to recruit members, and the JACL was not a dominant actor in the prewar Japanese communities. The Issei resented the right-wing political views of the JACL leaders. The young Nisei leaders wanted to fit in with American society and called for Americanization and the cutting of ties with Japan. Of course, these views conflicted with those of their Issei parents who were still the leaders of Japanese communities. The Nisei leaders of JACL were eager to displace the Issei, but they were too young and inexperienced.

But with the outbreak of World War II, the situation changed dramatically. Under the leadership of Mike Masaoka, a young Nisei from Utah, and aided by Saburo Kido, the league president, JACL aggressively campaigned for new members and restricted its membership to US citizens. Their message was Americanism—Japanese Americans are loyal patriots who love America and are willing to cooperate and follow the orders of the government. With this message of Americanism, the JACL, under Masaoka and Kido, swept aside the Issei and took over leadership of the Japanese communities.

Herein laid the problem with the JACL. It was too narrowly focused and inflexible in its support of the government and in its demonstration of patriotism. It went against those in the Japanese community who did not agree with its agenda. JACL collaborated with the government from the beginning of the war. It helped the FBI and military intelligence agencies by identifying disloyal Issei. Suspected Issei were promptly arrested and sent to detention centers. Moreover, JACL failed to protest Executive Order 9066, the incarceration of Japanese Americans. Instead, it advised Japanese Americans to show their patriotism by going peacefully. Within the camps, JACL criticized and denounced the draft-resisters and urged the Nisei to volunteer or be drafted into the military to prove their loyalty and perhaps regain the rights of the internees. Simply put, the aim of the JACL was to cooperate with the camp administration and to avoid confrontation. To do this was patriotic and would help the war effort. Many internees considered these actions and the behavior of the JACL reprehensible. This resentment lingered for many years after the internment and was a source of division within the community.

Outside the camps, JACL assisted in the resettlement of students and workers on the leave permit program. After the war, it continued to aid the Japanese community with civil rights legislation, lawsuits related to race relations, and overturning and amending immigration regulations. It had the following notable achievements in assisting Japanese Americans with specific legislation:

- Lobbied for the Evacuation Claims Act of 1948 that rectified, to a small degree, individual losses and injustices suffered during internment.
- Lobbied for overturning the California Alien Land Law of 1913, which forbade aliens (Issei) from buying or leasing land for more than three years.
- Helped in the passage of the McCarran-Walter Act of 1952, making it possible for Issei to become US citizens.

JACL was ambivalent on some issues. Initially, it opposed the filing of the *coram nobis* cases but later decided to support the litigants. It was also indecisive about the redress movement. There was disagreement among the leaders at first, but eventually they decided to work with Japanese American legislators in Congress and supported the creation of the CWRIC. In the end, JACL lobbying played a key role in the passage of the Civil Liberties Act of 1988.

By the 1970s, with the passing of the Masaoka-Kido leadership, the Sansei and Yonsei generations made amends for the wartime actions of the organization and formally apologized to the Japanese community. Meanwhile, with the changing demographic and political environment, the influence as well as the membership of JACL was waning. JACL had never represented the entire *Nikkei* population, only the Nisei who believed in Americanization. It was an exclusive organization, but it realized it had to be inclusive to survive. Therefore, to accommodate changes in the demographic and political climate, it expanded its mission to protect the rights of Asian and Pacific Islander Americans and mixed-race members. It began engaging with interracial coalition groups covering civil rights issues and working with the National Association for the Advancement of Colored People (NAACP) and with other racial minority organizations. Social issues of interracial marriages and segregation became concerns of JACL. They became involved in public education, youth development projects, and civic projects, such as the maintenance of the internment sites.

Changes in the demographic and political climate not only affected the JACL but the overall political participation of the mainland Japanese. The ascendancy of mainland Nisei in the political arena came much slower and later than in Hawai'i. A few mainland Japanese American politicians began to gain national prominence. Norman Mineta of San Jose, a Nisei, was interned with his family at Heart Mountain Relocation Center. He began his political career as a councilman in 1969 and then became mayor of San Jose. He was the first mainland Japanese congressman, serving in the House for eleven terms (1974-1995), and as President Clinton's Secretary of Commerce (2000-2001), and Secretary of Transportation in President George W. Bush's Cabinet (2001-2006)—one of the longest stints by any cabinet member. A fellow Californian from San Francisco, Robert Matsui, gained political distinction at about the same time. He was a Sansei and was interned with his family at Tule Lake Relocation Center.

Matsui started his political career in 1971 as a councilman in Sacramento. He served as a Democratic congressman for thirteen terms—a quarter century of service. He died in 2005 and was succeeded by his wife, Doris, when she won a special election held in March 2005. Another Sansei Democratic congressman was Mike Honda, who was also a well-known educator. He was a one-year-old when he and his family were sent to Amache Relocation Center in Colorado. Honda represented the Silicon Valley area in California and served eight terms in Congress from 2001 to 2017. The controversial Canadian-born Nisei S. I. Hayakawa is included in this group of prominent Japanese American politicians and educators. He served one term as a US senator (1977-1983). Hayakawa drew the ire of the Japanese community with his opposition to redress and his statement that the internment was beneficial for the Japanese Americans, helping them to integrate into American society. On balance, he contributed little and was a detriment to the advancement of the Japanese Americans.

By the early 2000s, most of the Nisei politicians had either died or retired. Sansei and Yonsei leaders had taken over, but they were fewer in number. Redress had been won, and there were no overarching issues except for the continuing problem of racial discrimination. How do you face the persistent challenge of discrimination when you lack the voter base and political clout? As a small and powerless ethnic group, the Japanese Americans had little chance of meeting the challenge unless they joined in a multiethnic coalition with the NAACP and other ethnic minority groups fighting for racial equality. It was politically advantageous to be allied with the more experienced civil rights groups. The Japanese Americans more closely identified with the African Americans and joined with them in opposing discrimination and fighting for civil rights through lawsuits, lobbying, and public information campaigns. But once legal equality was attained and racial integration had reasonably taken place, there was less need to collaborate and the coalition faded.

There could be differences in how discrimination is viewed within a racial group. Although affirmative action is favored by African Americans and Asian Americans, there are younger Asian Americans who feel they are penalized for their high academic performance when applying for prestigious universities. In a number of court cases, university affirmative action programs have been challenged not only by whites but by Asian Americans. Most controversial has been the *Students for Fair Admissions v. Harvard,* wherein Harvard is alleged to have used racial quotas and other discriminatory practices against Asian American applicants. Therefore, younger Asian Americans have sought to eliminate affirmative action, a program strongly supported by African Americans.

Overall, the younger Japanese Americans, the Sansei, and Yonsei found it easier to work with Asian Americans than with African Americans as they had closer cultural affinity with Asians. These young Japanese American activists tended to have interests and concerns that extended beyond the Japanese community and included all Asians. Assimilation had taken place and perspectives had broadened.

CHAPTER NINE

OASIS IN THE DESERT

A s assimilation takes place, it is assumed ethnic groups lose interest in their culture and customs as they are absorbed into the larger society. However, ethnic groups do retain some of their unique lifestyles and customs. Often, there is an effort to perpetuate a part of the traditional culture through an organization. It could start with individuals forming a society to practice and promote a specific aspect of the Japanese culture. It could be martial arts or Japanese sports, performing arts such as dancing and music, or other forms of artistic expressions. These groups put on their own exhibitions, recitals, and demonstrations. It is all part of cultural development, in this case, the development of Japanese culture.

Yet to have community-wide interest and participation in a wide-range of Japanese cultural activities, an all-embracing organization is required. It is then possible to put on large-scale festivals and art fairs. But here the concern is not with groups formed for socializing purposes. These tend to be formed by Japanese nationals who want to meet new arrivals and to develop friendships. Few Japanese Americans are involved in these social groups, with their informal picnics and potlucks held at parks and beaches or luncheons and dinners at restaurants. Instead, the focus in this chapter is on organizations that promote, teach, and present Japanese cultural arts and traditions. Japanese Americans are heavily involved in this type of organization, and it includes many non-Japanese.

When the ethnic population of a community is large, the attachment to their ethnicity is easier to organize, but in places where the number of ethnics is small, a special effort is needed to create an organization that will encourage involvement. These entities could be large, nation-wide organizations with affiliates, or they could be small and informal societies. Some communities have built-in advantages with universities or colleges offering programs in Japanese studies; a substantial interest in Japan and its culture is a distinct possibility. In cities and surrounding suburbs where there are Japanese business facilities or headquarters, or where there are American companies with ties to Japan, it is reasonable to assume there will be an interest in Japan. But there needs to be more than academic and business concerns to create a community-wide interest—there needs to be individuals who desire to be involved in several areas of Japanese culture and are passionate about it. These individuals enjoy participating in cultural activities and events, are curious to learn, and want to share their enthusiasm for Japanese culture.

It is assumed that what takes place in a community like Tucson, Arizona is found in other American cities with a comparable Japanese population. The emphasis is on the local level organizations because this is where the Nisei were active in community projects in the postwar era up to present day, the twilight years of the Nisei generation. What seems to be mundane, little moments are what keeps Japanese culture at the forefront and assures its maintenance and perpetuity. If the local activities are dismissed, the contributions made at the grassroots by the Nisei would be completely left out. It was largely the passion and devotion of the Nisei and their associates that two organizations emerged in Tucson: the Japan-America Society of Tucson (JAST) and the Southern Arizona Japanese Cultural Coalition (SAJCC). The JAST is covered extensively because of its long history, whereas the coverage of the SAJCC is brief since it is a relatively recent group.

JAPAN-AMERICA SOCIETY OF TUCSON (JAST)

It was a cool desert afternoon in January 1983 when about two hundred Tucson residents gathered at the Japanese Kitchen Steak House on the eastern side of the city, ate traditional Japanese food, and enjoyed the culture demonstrations and dance performances. It turned out to be a highly successful Japanese New Year's celebration, the first of its kind in a city known for its Western and Mexican traditions. Why and how did such an event take place? What kind of an organization is needed to plan and carry out an ethnic holiday celebration?

There was an underlying, strong interest in Japan and its culture in Tucson, and from this basis, an organization promoting Japanese culture and customs arose, the Japan-America Society of Tucson (JAST). The society was established to bring together those of Japanese heritage, to further participation in cultural activities, and to inform Americans about Japan and its culture. JAST was to serve this niche for about twenty-five years.

Society Benefits

- Cultural lectures and demonstrations covering many topics such as art, cuisine, language, religion and educational practices.

- Exhibitions and performing arts programs.

- Opportunity to meet Japanese and American government and business officials.

- Bi-monthly newsletter.

Special Services

- Assistance to tourist industries serving Japanese visitors.

- Assistance with exploring marketing and business opportunities.

- Personal assistance to Japanese visitors or temporary residents.

- Personal assistance to Americans visiting Japan.

- Assistance to school districts in presenting cultural and educational programs.

- Specialized programs, workshops, and seminars for the business community.

- Assistance in promoting Japanese arts and crafts through museums and educational institutions.

JAPAN-AMERICA

SOCIETY of TUCSON

JAST brochure.

I was involved with JAST from its inception as a charter member. The best way to understand the role of JAST and its importance in Tucson is to examine the events, activities, and projects organized or sponsored by the organization. On the individual member level, it is important for the member to appreciate and learn more about Japanese culture and customs and to share this love and interest with others. On the organizational level, the vitality of the organization is affected by the energy and enthusiasm shown by the members working together as a team on various projects. External forces and internal changes do affect an organization, as it waxes and wanes and has its periods of growth and decline. In this chapter, the internal and external factors are discussed as they relate to membership involvement during the life of this unusual ethnic organization that existed from 1981 to 2005.

There has to be an individual, or in some instances a few individuals, to be the spark to set up the organization. This individual must have a vision and a passion to promote Japan and its culture. In Tucson, such an individual was Barbara Bowman Blair. Originally from Salina, Kansas, Barbara lived for many years in Lafayette, Indiana where Byron, her husband, was a professor in the Department of Agronomy at Purdue University. Barbara worked with international students at Purdue and developed an interest in international studies. Then Byron became involved with agricultural research in Japan and, while living there, Barbara took the opportunity to explore facets of Japanese society and in the process fell in love with its culture and customs. In the intervening years, she made several trips to Japan and fully immersed herself in many aspects of the culture. She became a true Japanophiliac, an individual with a profound admiration for Japan and its culture. When Byron retired from Purdue, they decided to spend their retirement years in Tucson.

What convinced me Barbara was a Japanophiliac was when she said she had a *furo* built in her home. A *furo* is a deep, Japanese-style bathtub built of hard wood and sealed as not to leak. You wash yourself outside the tub while sitting on a stool. The water flows out through a drain in the tile floor. You then get into the tub and soak in neck-high hot water—it is very hot and has a sauna-like effect. My parents' house had a *furo*, but I preferred a quick shower. Occasionally, when I had the time and inclination, I would take a *furo* bath, and it was relaxing. Barbara also had a special Japanese room with *tatami* mats. *Tatami* is made from rush straw and is easily damaged, so you walk on it barefoot or with socks or indoor slippers. The special room has a *tokonoma* (alcove), where a hanging scroll of an ink painting or calligraphic writing is displayed and often there is a flower arrangement.

I first met Barbara when she enrolled in my advance class on Japanese society at the University of Arizona. One day, she asked about the possibility of starting an organization promoting Japanese culture. I told her it was a great idea and encouraged her to go ahead. She spoke with my colleague, Professor Chisato Kitagawa, a Japanese linguist, who also encouraged her. Outside of Tucson, she received support from Thomas Kadomoto, Honorary Consul General of Phoenix.

An organizational meeting was convened on January 15, 1981 at the Doubletree Hotel near Reid Park. It was a pleasant surprise to find seventy-five people in attendance, but what was even more surprising was when about fifty paid their charter dues. At a follow-up meeting, an interim slate of officers was selected with Barbara Blair as president, Chisato Kitagawa as vice-president, Patti Toshiro as secretary, and myself as treasurer. The name Japan-America Society of Tucson (*Tsuson Nichibei Kyokai*) was suggested and then adopted.

Barbara was president of the Japan-America Society of Indiana for seven years, an affiliate of the National Association of Japan-America Societies (NAJAS). NAJAS consists of about forty independent Japan-related organizations located in large cities, states, and regional areas. Besides Indiana, affiliates are in Colorado, Dallas/Fort Worth, Houston, Chicago, Washington, DC, Greater Philadelphia, Phoenix, Southern California, Northern California, Hawai'i, and so forth. The majority of these organizations are business-oriented and meant to bring together American and Japanese businessmen. They are excellent for networking and contacting, and while they do assume roles in cultural activities and education, these are ancillary to their main focus on business and economic issues.

Tucson was different—it lacked any significant business ties with Japan. There were only a few Japan-related businesses. Burr-Brown, IBM, and Raytheon (previously known as Hughes) had business connections with Japan, but overall, relations were limited. So JAST was unique for a NAJAS organization. Some businessmen became members, but they joined as individuals, not as representatives of their companies.

JAST didn't have a close relationship with the University of Arizona (UA) or Pima Community College (PCC). JAST supported UA and PCC events by being participants and occasionally co-organizing and cosponsoring events. JAST members, for example, provided entertainment, demonstrations, and displayed cultural items at the Japanese speech contest, where UA and PCC students competed for awards. But, in general, there was a separation of "town" and "gown." There were, however, a few faculty members and students who became members of JAST and participated actively.

The majority of the active members of JAST were Japanese nationals, mostly women married to American servicemen. Many retired veterans, especially Air Force veterans, chose to live in Tucson because of the pleasant climate and the availability of facilities for veterans. Davis-Monthan Air Force Base with its Post Exchange (PX) and a veterans' hospital are nearby. For army veterans, the retirement community is Sierra Vista, where Fort Huachuca is located. Sierra Vista is a reasonable one-hour driving distance from Tucson. These Japanese women formed a sizable generational group. Their marriages took place roughly at the time of the occupation of Japan (1945 to 1952), the Korean War in the early 1950s, the period of the US-Japan Mutual Security Treaty of the 1950s and 1960s, and during the Vietnam War of the 1970s.

It was natural for these women to come together, for they shared similar experiences being married to American servicemen, and it was an opportunity to use their native language. They constituted the core of JAST membership and, when combined with other Japanese nationals residing in Tucson, such as visiting professors and enrolled students, they made up more than half of the membership. In contrast, there were only a few Japanese Americans, mostly Nisei, reflecting their small number in the total population. Sansei and Yonsei were difficult to recruit, and, at this point in time, their priorities were elsewhere. They were not interested in pursuing their heritage. Caucasians made up the rest of the membership.

The relatively small membership and the lack of business ties had its good and bad points. Its smallness made it more intimate and friendly, and the lack of business concerns allowed it to focus on the cultural aspects of Japan. This fitted in with the interest of the majority of the membership who wanted a deeper understanding and appreciation of Japanese customs and traditions. JAST was able to have wide-ranging cultural activities and consequently had a broader appeal than any business-centered organization. This was the strength of JAST, but it was also its weakness. The small membership numbered from sixty to eighty over the years, which was drastically smaller than those of a typical NAJAS affiliate. The society was perpetually strapped for funds, which was derived primarily from the modest annual individual dues of ten dollars and family dues of fifteen dollars. It had only three or four corporate members paying the corporate fee of $100. In almost all NAJAS affiliates, the majority are corporate members, and the income from corporate fees are in the thousands of dollars. In addition, corporations are likely to make donations, adding to the total amount of funds available.

Occasionally, the question of joining NAJAS would arise, but it was never financially feasible; JAST could not even afford the initiation fee. Recognizing its limits, JAST decided to focus primarily on cultural activities and a program that paid for itself, so it moved forward on a shoestring budget. JAST was formally established on September 27, 1981 when an election was held and the board of directors was installed. The officers were: Barbara Blair, president; Chisato Kitagawa, vice president; Grady Loy, secretary; myself, treasurer; and Hiro Ito, program chairman.

CELEBRATIONS AND FESTIVALS

Seasonal celebrations and *matsuri* (festivals) are important traditional community events. The Japanese enjoy celebrating annual observances that are timed with the agricultural cycle of planting and harvesting. The agricultural cycle coincides with the astronomical cycle of the vernal equinox

(March 21-22) and the autumnal equinox (September 22-23). These seasonal considerations became the bases for celebrations.

Rice cultivation, the principal crop of Japan, is labor-intensive, and the transplanting of seedlings in spring and harvesting in fall are especially busy times. It is more efficient for families to work together, moving from one paddy field to another. Moreover, extensive irrigation systems required villagers to come together. Group consciousness developed out of these cooperative efforts, and the Japanese began to place an emphasis on the group rather than the individual. This collective consciousness led to the Japanese society being characterized by its group orientation and social cohesion, and for a tendency to seek collective action.[123] When the collective work is completed, villagers celebrate with a community-wide festival. It is a time to relax and enjoy themselves after the hard work. The biggest celebration, however, comes before the agricultural cycle, which is called *shinnenkai* (parties for the new year).

In Japan, the New Year holiday is a three-day celebration with government offices, businesses, and industries closing down from 1 January through 3 January. Even for overseas Japanese communities, *shinnenkai* is the most elaborate celebration. It reminds the immigrants and descendants of their heritage and evokes their emotional attachment to Japanese culture and tradition. For Japan-related nonprofit organizations in America, *shinnenkai* is the biggest yearly event and is sometimes a fundraising event, but for JAST it wasn't a fundraiser; it was simply a major celebration. Today, in Tucson, the New Year tradition is carried on by the Southern Arizona Japanese Cultural Coalition (SAJCC), the organization that succeeded JAST. The celebration was originally called *Tucson Mochitsuki* (Tucson Rice Pounding), the ritual associated with the New Year festivities, but the name was changed and the celebration became the *Tucson Japanese Festival*. It is the one and only major event of SAJCC.

Shinnenkai features lots of food, such as *gyoji ryori* (traditional food associated with festivals), and includes singing, dancing, and artistic

---

[123] There are many studies making this conclusion. See, for example, Chie Nakane, *Japanese Society*.

demonstrations as part of the entertainment. But the principal attraction is *mochitsuki*, the pounding of cooked glutinous rice into a dough called *mochi*. Usually, two men alternately pound the *mochi* in an *usu* (large mortar), with the pounding done with a *kine* (wooden mallet). A third person, from time to time, turns over the *mochi* and sprinkles water to keep it moist. The whole process has to be synchronized and in rhythm; otherwise, there will be bruised hands.

This labor-intensive effort is an example of collective action; in this case, to prepare food for the communal group. Now, the Japanese use a *mochi* machine—similar to a bread machine—or simply purchase *mochi* at the supermarket. *Mochitsuki* has become a ritual, a symbol of the New Year's celebration. When a Japanese is asked about *mochi*, he or she immediately thinks about New Year's celebration. *Mochi* has become the traditional food for the New Year holiday.

Mochi can be used for religious, festive, and decorative purposes. Because *mochigome* (*mochi* rice) is much more glutinous (sticky and starchy), the dough can be molded into various desired shapes. One common shape is to make round, flat pieces of different sizes. The largest piece becomes the base and three or more tiers of *mochi* are stacked and topped with a *mikan* (mandarin orange). This arrangement is called *kagamimochi* (mirror *mochi*) and is often used as an offering to the deities and as decoration.

Though *mochi* serves as a religious offering and as a decoration, for the majority of Japanese Americans, *mochi* is a food that is consumed year-round and not merely for use in ceremonial or special occasions. Now, *mochi* comes in many different forms and is used in many different ways—from soups to biscuits to confectioneries. It is even found in Americanized *mochi* ice cream.

In my family, we followed the tradition of cleaning the house a few days before New Year's. Then my mother would place the *kagamimochi* offering at the *butsudan* (Buddhist household altar). She would take it down a few days after New Year's. My mother never prayed before the *butsudan*; she was a nominal Buddhist, but grandmother prayed before it. Symbolism is important. The word *kagami* (mirror) doesn't refer to mirror in the usual sense; rather, it is the symbol of the sun. Historically, Japan is referred to as the "land of the rising sun." The mirror is important in Japanese mythology and is one of the three ancient imperial regalia. Besides *kagamimochi* as a New Year decorative piece, another decoration placed at the front of the house or business is *kadomatsu* (entryway decoration); it is an arrangement of pine and bamboo stalks, symbolizing longevity and is usually found near the entryway. These New Year rituals and decorations were reminders for the *Nikkei* of their cultural tradition. The celebratory customs were not allowed to die.

Shinnenkai attendance varied over the years depending on the venue. The first informal *shinnenkai* was held in 1982 at a private home and limited to members and their guests; it was a private potluck with no entertainment. The following *shinnenkai* was a public event, as described in the beginning of this chapter. It was held at the Japanese Kitchen Steak House with an attendance of about two hundred. Restaurants meant more space and the possibility of entertainment, and members didn't have to bring food to share. For several years from 1989 to 1998, it was held at a house owned by a Japanese businessman who generously allowed JAST to use it year-round rent-free; it was later known as the JAST Center. The capacity was expanded to around one hundred people by including the patio and backyard, but it felt crowded. The event wasn't publicized beyond the society's mailing list. In later years, it was held at public community halls to accommodate larger crowds, but from 2004 on, *shinnenkai* reverted back to a member's private home because of dwindling attendance.

Except for the early celebrations at the Japanese Kitchen Steak House, all the rest of the New Year's events entailed extensive food preparation by the members. Particularly laborious is the preparation of *osechi-ryori* (traditional New Year food). They are elaborate and delicate appetizers arranged attractively in lacquered boxes called *jubako* and are prepared a day before the event. Ironically, Barbara taught the Japanese ladies how to prepare the food; she had learned it while living in Japan. Since the preparation of *osechi-ryori* is time-consuming, most Japanese households don't include it on their New Year's menu. For most ladies, this was the first time they were making *osechi-ryori*. When asked how important it was to make *osechi-ryori*, they said they enjoyed working together and the time spent socializing—after all, it did take an entire day.

Another festive occasion involving a sizable number of members was *Aki-matsuri* (Fall Festival) or sometimes referred to as *Higan-matsuri* (Fall Equinox Festival). It was initially held in 1982 and was observed annually until 1985. The festival took place at the large parking lot behind the Japanese Kitchen Steak House. Crowds in the hundreds attended, and it ran from mid-afternoon until mid-evening. The last festival in 1985 had over one thousand attendees. As many as twenty tables and booths were set up, selling food and art and displaying Japanese crafts and other cultural articles. Entertainment consisted of folk and *buyo* (Japanese classical) dances and martial arts demonstrations. The highlight was the audience participation in *bon'odori* (festival dance) with *taiko* (drum) and music accompaniment. *Bon'odori* had its beginning in Buddhist temple grounds as part of a memorial festival honoring deceased relatives but became popular as it largely lost its religious meaning. As a result of the popularity of the dances, *Aki-matsuri* grew too large and JAST lacked the manpower to handle the crowd. In 1985, the festival was discontinued because the labor and time involved became onerous, and it was also increasingly costly.

On a much smaller scale, the *Hina-matsuri* (Doll Festival) was observed. Every year in March, it took place at a private residence or at the JAST Center and ordinarily drew about sixty people, many of whom were children. Actually, it was a special celebration for girls. On display were court dolls on a multilayered, five-to-seven-tiered stand. In addition, other dolls were displayed with stories about the dolls shared by the owners. Children's songs were sung, and there were dance performances and art demonstrations, including *temari* (thread balls) made from embroidery and origami (art of folding paper).

In short, festivals played a major role in JAST. Although *shinnenkai* were open to the public, publicity was minimal with no advertisements, so it could be said it was mainly for members, friends, and acquaintances. *Akimatsuri*, on the other hand, were publicized and geared for the public. The festivals provided an opportunity to meet people and socialize, especially bringing together members and their friends. But the most important contribution of the festivals was the continuation of the traditions and customs. Nisei were reminded of their heritage and given the opportunity to participate in the celebration. For the Sansei and Yonsei, it was an exposure to new facets of Japanese culture, and the hope was that it would be a lasting and favorable impression. In the long run, however, other considerations undermined the future of the festivals. The large crowds necessitated more time and labor, which in turn exhausted the members and eventually played a part in the demise of JAST.

CULTURAL PRESENTATIONS

Cultural programs were always a critical part of JAST's mission to promote awareness and appreciation of Japanese culture. This was a concern of the leadership from the beginning. A few months after its founding, JAST undertook a major project. It cosponsored, with the East Asian Center of the University of Arizona, a concert by the Okinawan court dancers and musicians. The concert was held at Centennial Hall of the University of Arizona on October 14, 1981. In those days, interest in Asia was widespread, and funding was readily available for cultural performances. Grants from the Asia Society, the Japan Foundation, and other organizations insured adequate financial support, but there was concern over attendance—this type of concert had limited appeal. Few Americans were acquainted with Okinawan dances and music, and even among the Japanese, this type of music and dance engendered little interest. However, to the surprise of everyone, this esoteric dance concert attracted an audience of about eight hundred people. The JAST members' hustle to sell tickets made a difference.

Okinawan Court Dance Concert.

Far more challenging was the Theater of Yugen from San Francisco. This small theater group performed on March 30, 1984 at the Tucson High School Auditorium. JAST members sold about three hundred tickets, and this effort, plus the low expenses, enabled the society to escape a deficit—it broke even. Yugen combined the Japanese classic drama form of *kyogen* (Noh comedy) and Noh (dance-drama). Noh was developed in the fourteenth century and is one of the oldest art forms. This abstruse, highly-stylized dance-drama was definitely of limited appeal and not geared for the younger generation.

But not all concerts were risky. There were talented individuals, such as students skilled in playing *koto*, a Japanese zither-type, long-string instrument, as well as dancers and drummers who were willing to perform for free or for a nominal fee. The role of the society's members was to support the recital or concert by helping to publicize the event, sell tickets if needed, and attend the performances. Since some of the performers were JAST members, there was already a strong built-in personal interest. The society hosted Japanese dance recitals by the Azuma School, led by Suzuyuki Azuma, the professional name of Mari Kaneta, the founder and *sensei* (teacher). A close relationship developed between JAST and Suzuyuki-kai, Mari Kaneta's dance group, and it continued for over fifteen years. Recitals were held in school auditoriums to keep the cost down, and occasionally Suzuyuki-kai performed at the society's bimonthly meetings.

A major step in the development of local talent in Japanese drumming and dance began when a non-Japanese person, Stanley Morgan, moved to Tucson in the mid-1990s. Morgan was never a member of JAST, but he independently began to teach *taiko* (Japanese drum) drumming to Mari Kaneta's dancers and to two Tucsonan, Karen Falkenstrom and Rome Hamner, who had developed an interest in the *taiko*. Kaneta's dancers formed the Japanese drumming ensemble, the Suzuyuki-kai Taikoza, which combined drumming with dance. At about the same time, in 2002, Falkenstrom and Hamner founded the drumming ensemble, known as Odaiko Sonora. In 2007, Morgan's group, MoGan Daiko, merged with Suzuyuki-kai Taikoza and became Suzuyuki-kai MoGan Daiko. The ensemble took this name to honor Morgan, who had retired because of illness. Henceforth, interest in Japanese ensemble drumming expanded, and the number of performances grew steadily in Tucson.

Besides dance and *taiko* performances, presentations and demonstrations were given at the bimonthly meetings held at the JAST Center or in private homes on a variety of subjects, including ikebana (flower arrangement), origami, calligraphy, doll-making, and sword-collecting. But there was a demand for arts and crafts to be presented on a larger stage, therefore, an arts and crafts festival was organized and held during spring, an ideal time for an outdoor event. Displays were set up and information disseminated on *cha-noyu* (tea ceremony) equipment, koi (carp) breeding, and bonsai (growing of dwarfed plants or trees). These subjects may seem unusual, but in Tucson, as in many other cities, there are established cultural interest groups. For koi enthusiasts, there is the Southern Arizona Koi Association, and at the national level there is the Associated Koi Club of America (AKCA). For bonsai devotees, there is the Tucson Bonsai Society and at the national level, the American Bonsai Society (ABS). Both the koi and bonsai organizations hold regular meetings and periodically put on their own shows. *Chanoyu* is more individualized, and there are different schools of tea ceremony. In Tucson, for example, one school of tea ceremony is held at the Yume Japanese Gardens of Tucson. Taken together, interest in Japanese cultural traditions is wider than commonly envisioned and explains why a large crowd was drawn to the Spring Arts and Crafts Festival.

There were other aspects of Japanese culture that were displayed and demonstrated at the Spring Arts and Crafts Festival. They included the following: origami, *sumie* (ink painting), ikebana, *shodo* (calligraphy), dolls, Japanese swords, and textiles. The crowd was entertained with *min'yo* (folk music), *buyo* dances, and the demonstration of martial arts. The Spring Arts and Crafts Festival was introduced during the early years of JAST and drew hundreds of people to afternoon and early evening programs. Even though the festival was enthusiastically received and turnout was excellent, it was discontinued after a few years. The festival required extensive planning and coordination, and having limited manpower and resources, the society found the Spring Arts and Crafts Festival to be too burdensome. It may seem puzzling why an organization would abandon a successful project, but for a nonprofit organization without a paid executive director and staff, it must rely on dedicated volunteers willing to continue each year. Some organizations can sustain their projects without exhausting the members, but many in JAST became tired and were unwilling to carry a heavy load.

Another way in which a culture is presented is through its ethnic food. Food is the easiest and the most delightful way to learn about a culture. The cultural power of food is profound. Cooking demonstrations of Japanese food were always popular. They took place in private homes, larger venues like the YMCA, and the backyard of the JAST Center. An *okonomiyaki* (Japanese savory pancake) cooking class and tasting party was held at the JAST Center in the summer of 1997. Members got to make and taste their version of *okonomiyaki*. Because of its popularity, it was repeated the next year at the Pan Asian Center. These events proved to be an attraction, a good way to bring in new people and expose them to the Japanese culture.

Japanese food business began after the Japanese moved away from the plantations. Entrepreneurs started *tofu*, confectionery, *okazuya* (delicatessen), and other small businesses. *Okazuya* sells side dishes of traditional Japanese food that goes with rice. It served the needs of the Japanese for prepared side dishes, but after World War II, its popularity expanded beyond the Japanese population. *Okazuya* developed the plate lunch where you select the side dishes from those on display. I grew up going to these *okazuya* and have fond, nostalgic memories of the wide varieties of comfort food. The plate lunch began with only Japanese dishes, but the food was modified to reflect local taste and later included other ethnic food. The plate lunch has become a unique, local multicultural food. The side dishes can also be used in *bento* (lunch boxes). A variation of the plate lunch is *poke*, which began in Hawai'i in the 1970s and has become a local specialty. It is cubed raw seafood served over sushi rice in a bowl with a variety of toppings. It illustrates how Japanese and Hawaiian-style food combined to form a popular island dish.

But it is more than knowing about the prepared food—it is the total ambience surrounding the serving of food, the visual appeal, that is important to fully understand the Japanese people and culture. The receptacles (bowls and dishes) and the arrangement of the food reflects harmony, balance, and a sense of space—the essence of Japanese aesthetic. The meticulous and refined presentation of Japanese cuisine is an art form in itself. Food is not slopped together: rather, it is arranged by color, shape, and texture, hence food presentation becomes a form of Japanese artistic expression. This is why several years of apprenticeship is required to become a master sushi chef and why a highly skilled sushi chef is an "artist."

Professor Robert Ji-Song Ku, author of *Dubious Gastronomy*, argues that food reflects aspects of ethnic culture and points to the continuity of the ethnic culture, even though the food had undergone many modifications. Japanese restaurants play an important role in maintaining and continuing traditional Japanese cooking. Traditional forms and dishes are preserved in well-established restaurants. Out of business necessity, they have to offer modern or modified Japanese cuisine, but they still serve dishes in the traditional style. Therefore, the restaurants educate Americans about Japanese cuisine, an important part of Japanese culture. But it is more than food, for the Japanese restaurants serve as a place for patrons to socialize and enjoy cultural entertainment. The proliferation of Japanese restaurants reveals, in part, the continuity of Japanese culture in a given community.

There were no Japanese restaurants when I arrived in Tucson in 1977. Then three professors at the university, Chisato Kitagawa, Hiroki Shioji, and myself, discovered the Driftwood Bar and Lounge—a bar located near the entrance to Davis-Monthan Air Force Base—that was also a restaurant and had a dining area. It was owned by Kazuo and Momoko Kakishita. Thursdays happened to be slow days for the restaurant, so Momoko decided to share her passion for Japanese food by offering Japanese cuisine every Thursday. The menu was limited to the standard entree, but Momoko included some exotic dishes only familiar to Japanese customers. Therefore, the menu would change from week to week, and we never knew what would be offered; it all depended on what Momoko decided to cook. But it didn't matter since we were desperate for authentic Japanese food, and the food was good. We went to the Driftwood regularly with our spouses. However, success had its consequences. The Thursday Japanese dinning became popular and increasingly burdensome for the Kakishitas. They decided to forgo it after two years.

There were no Japanese restaurants for a couple of years until the void was filled by the Tokyo Store and Restaurant. The owners were Isidro

Sanchez, a Mexican American, and his native Japanese wife, Michiko. The store carried Asian sundries, fish, and packaged foods, and the restaurant part of the business was confined to a limited space. When it moved to a new location, it changed its name to Tokyo Restaurant and Sushi Bar and became a full-fledged Japanese restaurant. But for those of us Japanese food aficionados, it didn't replace the Driftwood with its exotic dishes.

The Japanese restaurant business in Tucson changed significantly in the early 1980s with the opening of the Japanese Kitchen and Steakhouse, a chain of *teppanyaki* restaurants based in the Western states. *Teppanyaki*-style cooking is done on a hot iron plate, and in a restaurant, the iron plate is a large table with the burner underneath to keep it hot. The table is large enough to accommodate a half dozen customers sitting around three sides. Highlight of *teppanyaki*-style cooking is the preparation and presentation of the food by the chef, who performs with highly stylized culinary skill. It is not unusual to see the chef flip the food in the air with acrobatic skill. Non-Japanese customers love this type of exhibition, but most *Nikkei* would go to the restaurant only if they had out-of-town visitors or for special occasions, for it was considered expensive.

Takeshi Ishihara, the owner of the Japanese Kitchen at Albuquerque, New Mexico, decided to expand into Tucson, once he realized there was a gap in the market for a Japanese restaurant. Ishihara realized the restaurant had to connect with a Japan-oriented organization, hence he established a symbiotic relationship with the Japan-America Society of Tucson. Two dance troupes, Mari Kaneta's and the dance group from Sierra Vista, both closely affiliated with JAST, performed regularly on "Japanese Night" at the restaurant and helped to bring in customers. The Kitchen generously allowed JAST to use the large parking lot in the back for the society's *matsuri* events. The Kitchen participated in the festival itself by having a food booth and even brought a large *taiko* from Albuquerque for the *bon* festival. But once JAST cease having their festivals and moved the New Year's celebration to their own center and other venues, the close relationship ceased.

The Japanese Kitchen reached the height of its popularity in the 1980s, a time when Japanese restaurants grew nationally as Americans acquired a taste for Japanese food, especially sushi. In Tucson, Japanese restaurants began to emerge, and interestingly several of them were owned by Koreans. It was somewhat ironic that a few of the new restaurants were owned or staffed by chefs who had learned their skills and had gained experience working for the Kitchen, who now decided to start their own or work for a new restaurant. These restaurants drew customers away from the Japanese Kitchen, and the Kitchen, having higher overhead, couldn't compete and soon closed. *Teppanyaki* restaurants have a difficult time succeeding in Tucson. The national chain Benihana lasted only a couple of years. It helps if it is embedded in a high-end resort hotel or in a casino where it has built-in customers and many tourists.

Today, there are perhaps twenty-five Japanese restaurants in Tucson. The exact number depends on what you consider a Japanese restaurant. Should ramen noodle, and rice bowl shops be included? What about those on the fringes, serving fusion cuisine, food prepared using techniques and ingredients of two or more ethnic cuisines? There are a couple of restaurants in South Tucson offering "Mexican sushi" with guacamole, jalapeño, and salsa as ingredients. For sushi purists, this is an abomination, and they are not Japanese restaurants.

From time to time, there were institutions and organizations that needed assistance in presenting Japanese culture to their audience. They needed someone to help organize exhibits, demonstrations, and live performances, and to provide background information. In 1989, JAST participated in the Tucson Museum of Art League program "Art in Bloom." Several society members displayed or demonstrated ikebana, origami, Japanese dolls, calligraphy, *hanga* (woodblock print), antique kimono and *obi* (kimono sash) and antique china. Members donated their services, playing the koto and samisen, performing dances, and demonstrating the tea ceremony. Another event JAST assisted with was at the Tucson Children's Museum, which needed help for its Christmas season ethnic display. Society members displayed various cultural objects, even a sword collection, something unusual for a children's museum. Members provided entertainment with Suzuyuki-kai doing dances and Odaiko Sonora performing on the drums. The museum was pleased and the following year asked for a repeat of the exhibit.

An event that received annual support from JAST was the Japanese Speech Contest. The contest began in 1990 under the direction of a JAST member who was Japanese language instructor at the University of Arizona and Pima Community College. Beginning with the Second Annual Japanese Speech Contest in 1991, the society began to provide support, consisting of musical performances, exhibits of Japanese arts and crafts, and providing refreshments. With the passing of years, changes occurred in the format and organization of the contest, and the support of JAST lessened to an annual donation for a monetary prize and the setup at each contest of a few cultural displays.

Beginning in the 1990s, the Tucson Unified School District (TUSD) needed assistance in developing its curriculum on Japan. Society members helped organize the materials and provided consulting services. TUSD received a grant from the Smithsonian Institution, which enabled it to create a traveling exhibit "Artsmobile," with the theme "Japan, Floating World." The theme was a reference to *ukiyo-e* (floating world woodblock print) of the Tokugawa period (1603-1868). Society members assisted by assembling the displays in the "Artsmobile" and preparing instructional materials. In addition, members were asked to evaluate the quality and value of the individual art objects. Starting in 2002, the "Artsmobile" went to various elementary schools, and the project continued for another year.

Inevitably, a number of requests came from the school district for resource people to speak about the culture, customs, and other aspects of Japan. Barbara Blair and I, plus a few other members, served as resource people and gave talks to numerous classes, ranging from elementary to high school. JAST had no strategy in the dissemination of information about Japan. When interest on a topic arose and opportunities opened up, or when inquiries were made, the society responded accordingly. Since this was all volunteer work, the heavy demand became a strain, so much so that members began to reluctantly decline the requests.

To summarize, in the early stages, JAST participated in cultural programs featuring touring groups performing in large halls, which resulted in attendance and financial challenges. Then the society moved into less risky projects. The society was blessed with a talented membership and began to perform in smaller venues, such as private homes and the JAST Center. The Spring Arts and Crafts Festivals were popular but took greater time and energy, and the society, not having enough personnel and resources, soon dropped the festival. Community arts organizations, educational institutions, and the school district began to take notice of JAST and asked if the society would cosponsor or provide exhibits, demonstrations, entertainment, and educational talks. By assisting community organizations and institutions, JAST was able to further expose the public to the arts, music, and culture of Japan. At its bimonthly meetings, talks and panel discussions covered a variety of topics pertaining to Japan and its people, and participants gained an appreciation of Japanese culture and an understanding of contemporary issues.

Cultural presentation at JAST meeting.

HOSTING GROUPS AND DIGNITARIES

The 1980s and early 1990s witnessed the arrival of several Japanese groups to Tucson. The Japanese economy was in a period of high growth, and it was a time of affluence. Money was flowing and groups found it easy to come to the United States. From time to time, they would show up on relatively short notice, and a host had to be found. On occasion, JAST was called upon to act as a host. The groups varied but basically they were of two types: university and city-prefectural delegations.

The Men's Glee Club of Waseda University was touring the country and made a stop in Tucson; JAST was asked to be the host. A dinner party was held at Barbara Blair's home, and a crowd of about seventy packed the house and flowed into the patio and backyard. More challenging were the college athletic teams; they were hungrier. Two Japanese university baseball teams came for training purposes and played exhibition games against the University of Arizona and Pima Community College. The Ryutsu Keizai University team from Ibaraki Prefecture was given a potluck dinner at a Pima College facility, and for the team from Keio University in Tokyo, a luncheon was held at the JAST Center. Members prepared lots of food for the hungry players and their coaches.

Tucson doesn't have a sister city in Japan, whereas Phoenix has Himeji, a city in western Honshu, as a sister city. For many years, JAST pushed for a sister city program with a same size city in Japan, but city officials never got beyond the talking stage. Even without a sister city arrangement, JAST developed a close relationship with individuals and groups in the Gifu region of central Honshu. Why Gifu City and Gifu Prefecture? Barbara had developed contacts with officials of Gifu Prefecture, Gifu City, and Nagoya, the capital city of Aichi Prefecture, which is near Gifu City. She was involved in two major trade expositions in that region and in a project to transport two giant saguaros to a botanical garden in Nagoya. The saguaros, by the way, were transported and transplanted successfully—a remarkable feat. These contacts were developed outside of JAST and were not the society's projects; nevertheless, they help explain the close relationship with the Gifu region.

On November 11, 1989, a twenty-member delegation from Gifu Prefecture arrived for a four-day visit. They came to establish friendly relationships with an American community and to explore trade possibilities. Their visit coincided with the grand opening of the JAST Center. City government officials, headed by Mayor Thomas Volgy, as well as officials from the business and academic worlds were invited. There were over 125 guests. I remember trying to take pictures of the ribbon-cutting ceremony in the living room crammed wall-to-wall with people; it was impossible to take a decent photograph. This was, of course, the most spectacular and important event in the history of JAST. Two years after this monumental event, a second delegation from Gifu arrived, comprised of the usual legislators and business representatives but also included journalists.

But it was not all Gifu—a delegation arrived from Okayama Prefecture. Actually, there were two visits; one in 1996 and the second the following year. The delegations were composed of officials from the cities and towns, the prefectural government, and included educators. The initiative for the Okayama visits came from the prefecture as part of their campaign to initiate trade, tourism, and educational opportunities in the Southwest. JAST acted as host and planned and organized tours, dinner receptions, as well as the customary exchange of gifts. Their gifts had the theme of "peach," since peach is the famous product of the prefecture and Okayama is the "home" of *Momotaro* (Peach Boy), the folktale hero. Our gifts consisted of southwestern products such as bandannas and coffee mugs with local logos.

Apart from the Japanese groups, JAST hosted a number of dignitaries. Consul generals from the Consulate in Los Angeles made periodic visits to Phoenix and included Tucson in their itinerary. For the sake of recognition, these visits were of importance to JAST; after all, Tucson wasn't a major destination and was always overshadowed by Phoenix. It was difficult to get to know the consul generals because their assignment at the Los Angeles Consulate was for only two or three years. It was the policy of the

Gaimusho (Foreign Ministry) to reassign the diplomat after a couple years, leaving little time to get fully acquainted.

Three of the consul generals I got to know were Hiromoto Seki, Shotaro Yachi, and Tsuneo Nishida. Occasionally, the consul generals' wives came along. The usual arrangement was to take them on a tour of the city and surrounding areas and to have a luncheon or dinner reception with about forty to sixty guests at a hotel or the UA Alumni Foundation Building. Consul General Seki visited Tucson more than once after he was reassigned. He was truly a friend of JAST and even made a personal monetary donation to the society. The reception for Consul General Yachi was somewhat unique; a mariachi band greeted him and his wife as they entered the Alumni Foundation Building. What a welcome! Consul General Yachi surprised me. After touring the historic San Xavier del Bac Mission, he walked over with his wife to a fry bread (Native American food) stand and asked to taste the bread. I didn't think it was a good idea since the bread is greasy and the booth was on a dusty road. But he tried it, and he liked it! Consul General Nishida's visit in late February coincided with the Chinese New Year's celebration. Arrangement was made to have him be the main speaker at the Pan-Asian Lunar New Year's banquet at the Doubletree Hotel. An audience of three hundred heard his message.

There was one more visiting dignitary that needs mentioning: the Honorable Yoshio Hatano, Permanent Representative of Japan to the United Nations. I had the responsibility of greeting him at the airport. This was a last-minute, unofficial stopover. Having heard much about Tucson, he just wanted to see the city and did not want the public to be informed. Therefore, I was the only person at the airport. Even though I didn't know what he looked like, I figured it would be easy to find him because there probably wouldn't be any other Japanese passengers. But I missed him at the arrival gate because he didn't look Japanese. It was embarrassing, and I apologized for missing him as he walked by. I never told him I thought he didn't look Japanese.

With dignitaries and delegations, there are all kinds of protocols, and they are especially critical when working with Japanese officials—it was a learning experience. Certainly, these visits required detailed planning and coordination, and the degree of preparation varied with the importance and nature of the visit. The highest Japanese official to visit Tucson was Ambassador Nobuo Matsunaga. A stretch limo was rented for the occasion, an example of the type of arrangement needed to host visiting dignitaries.

BUSINESS PROGRAMS

Affiliates of the National Association of Japan-America Societies have business functions as their raison d'etre, but JAST had cultural and educational functions as its primary focus. However, the society did provide business programs over the years—sponsoring, organizing, and promoting lectures, workshops, seminars, and panel discussions. At times, the events were cosponsored with another organization or JAST served as a contributing participant.

It all began with a "Doing Business with Japan" seminar in September 1982. Barbara served as the moderator, and I participated as a panelist. Over the years, these business seminars featured nationally recognized trade specialists from the private sector and Japanese and US government officials. The topics most frequently discussed were, of course, United States-Japan trade relations and related issues.

The most imposing business program involving JAST occurred in 1988 when the Tucson Metropolitan Chamber of Commerce asked JAST to assist in a series of four business seminars, one a month starting in February for the Tucson World Trade Fair. Further assistance came from Pima Community College and the Sunbelt World Trade Association when they joined as cosponsors.

To understand why these business seminars occurred, it is necessary to look at what was taking place in the United States and Japan at that time. In the 1970s and 1980s, Japan experienced spectacular economic growth and emerged as the second largest economy in the world, second only to the United States. Americans had an ambivalent reaction to Japan's economic dominance, and it expressed itself in terms of two phenomena:

"Japanophilia," admiration and friendly feeling toward Japanese; and "Japanophobia," fear and hatred of Japanese.

In the mid-1970s, Americans responded to the Japanese "economic miracle" with admiration—it could be called "Japanophilia." Many in the academic and business circles considered Japan as a model to be emulated because of its economic success. The mood of the moment was reflected in book titles. In 1979, Harvard sociology professor, Ezra Vogel, published his highly optimistic, laudatory, and provocative book, *Japan As Number One: Lessons for America*. Professor Vogel argued Americans had much to learn from Japan.[124] Another book that was widely read and debated was Professor William Ouchi's *Theory Z: How American Business Can Meet the Japanese Challenge*, published in 1981. It advocated a new Japanese management style—a special way of managing people—and with Japanese productivity the highest in the world, it similarly argued that America can learn a great deal from Japan.[125] Japan was viewed as a model for the development of human resources in education and in the workforce; it was a model to be admired and hyped.

But all this euphoria about Japan had negative consequences. Japan was viewed as a threat to the US economy—it could be called "Japanophobia." Japan was accused of using the close collaboration between government bureaucrats and corporate executives to promote unfair business and trade policies. This close relationship between the Japanese government and the private sector was labeled as "Japan Inc." and was a term widely used in the 1980s to denounce Japanese business practices. Japan's economic growth was said to come at the expense of American job losses. Furthermore, Japanese investors buying famous American commercial and cultural assets, such as Columbia Pictures, Rockefeller Center, Peebles Beach Golf Course, and hotels on Waikiki Beach in Hawai'i, was an attack on the American establishment. Whatever economic woes America was suffering, the layoffs

---

[124] Ezra F. Vogel, *Japan As Number One: Lessons for Americans* (Cambridge, MA: Harvard University Press, 1979).

[125] William G. Ouchi, *Theory Z: How American Business Can Meet the Japanese Challenge* (Reading, MA: Addison-Wesley Publishing Company, 1981).

and economic slowdowns were the fault of the Japanese; Japan became the scapegoat.

Anti-Japanese sentiments peaked in the 1980s and the term "Japan bashing" became popular, only subsiding in the mid-1990s when the Japanese economy began a decade of recessionary decline. "Japan bashing" reached Tucson when a couple of Japanese-owned properties were vandalized. The JAST board discussed the problem, and we decided to remove the "Japan-America Society" sign at the front entrance of the JAST Center. We wanted to avoid any confrontation with anti-Japanese sentiments. It was a concern of Japanese Americans more than it was for Japanese nationals. On June 19, 1982, Vincent Chin, a Chinese American, was beaten to death in Detroit by two unemployed white auto workers. The assailants admitted they thought Chin was a Japanese American. On television, there were scenes of American workers publicly destroying Japanese-made cars. Japanese Americans took these intimidations seriously and had a visceral reaction.

All the attention on Japan led to many discussions in the business world, and it is in this context that a series of business seminars appeared in Tucson. The titles of the seminars give some indication as to what was discussed. The first seminar was "Why Japan Does What It Does," and I participated as a panelist. It was followed by "America's View of Japan Through the Years," then "Business with Rice and Salsa," and ending with "Japan/America—What Next." The panelists were officials from the Japan External Trade Organization (JETRO) and prominent Japanese and American businessmen. The final seminar featured presentations by Ambassador Nobuo Matsunaga and Congressman Jim Kolbe, with Mayor Thomas Volgy acting as moderator. The purpose of this series of seminars was to provide information and materials on trade issues and to discuss potential trade opportunities. The seminar series concluded with a gala black-tie dinner at the Loews Ventana Canyon Resort with Ambassador Matsunaga as one of the speakers.

Left to right: author, Ambassador Matsunaga, Barbara Blair, and Consul General Seki. Tucson World Trade Fair (1988).

At the time of the seminar series, there was little expectation that the Japanese economy would slow down and no one expected the bubble economy to implode in the early 1990s. For Japanese American members of JAST, it was a time of mixed feelings. On the one hand, there was the worry over "Japan bashing," and, on the other hand, there was excitement over Japan's "economic miracle." Both developments proved to be short-lived, with "Japan bashing" and "Japan as number one" disappearing as the Japanese economy declined with the bursting of the bubble economy. Japan's economy had matured, and the possibility of high growth rate became remote. A period of affluence was rapidly followed by deflationary doldrums. For Nisei, such confluence of economic forces would not be experienced again in their lifetimes.

DECLINE AND LEGACY

The founder of JAST, Barbara B. Blair, died on October 2, 2005, almost one year short of the twenty-fifth anniversary. She served as president for six years, from the beginning in 1981 to 1986. I took over the presidency and served for twelve years until 1998 and was succeeded by M (Monwilla) Fumie Craig. After Barbara's death, many of the contacts with Japan were lost because they were personal and not embedded in the organization. For the work to continue successfully, relationships had to be maintained and extended to other leaders; it couldn't be centered around one individual.

As the 1990s came to an end, the interest in Japanese culture diminished nationally, as the heyday of its popularity passed. There was still interest in Japan, but overall, the enthusiasm was not the same. Furthermore, membership changes occurred within JAST. When the society was founded, the majority of active members were native Japanese women married to retired American servicemen. These Japanese women with their spouses became a sizable generational group. By the mid-1990s, this part of the membership declined primarily due to deaths and health issues. They were not replaced, and the Japanese-speaking women remaining in the organization were not married to servicemen and were of a younger generation. The English-speaking segment of the membership, comprised of Japanese Americans, part-Japanese, and Caucasians, took over leadership positions. In addition, JAST lost several young members, who had to leave for employment reasons or changes in their family situation. A gradual decline in membership ensued.

From the beginning, the lack of volunteers to work on projects was a recurring problem. Barbara used to complain about the lack of help, especially on large projects like the festivals. She was often exhausted. This is a challenge found in all organizations—only a small percentage of people, usually the leaders, do most of the work. Decline in membership and enthusiasm meant less volunteers, and ultimately led to less programs, less meetings, and by the early 2000s, only a modicum of meetings were held. It is difficult to pinpoint exactly when JAST ended; the decline was gradual and as the numbers dwindled, the society simply faded away.

But JAST left a legacy. Its mission and forte, was to present and disseminate information about Japanese culture and arts and to perpetuate Japanese customs and traditions. It accomplished this task by presenting a wide-range of programs and events. From the beginning, the focus was on cultural, artistic, and social activities, but it was also noted for its educational role. Although Tucson was relatively weak on economic and business connections with Japan, the society sponsored, organized, or participated in several events concerned with trade and other economic issues.

What I personally gained from my involvement with JAST was learning about facets of Japanese culture I wasn't acquainted with by being introduced to the whole gamut of Japanese culture. It was not only the gaining of knowledge and appreciation but the satisfaction of sharing this wealth with others. JAST was a people-to-people organization. The personal contacts and interactions were short-term, but the mutual understanding gained by working with other Japanese Americans, Japanese nationals, and non-Japanese was priceless. We were brought together by overlapping interests and found working with one another enjoyable and educational. Friendships were formed, and by sharing our knowledge, talents, and skills, we "refreshed" others and, in turn, we ourselves were "refreshed." The Japan-America Society of Tucson was, indeed, a Japanese oasis in the middle of a desert. "A generous man will prosper; he who refreshes others will himself be refreshed" (Prov. 11:25, NIV).

SOUTHERN ARIZONA JAPANESE CULTURAL COALITION (SAJCC)

After the demise of JAST, no community-wide Japanese cultural organization existed in Tucson for several years, although there was still a lingering interest in Japanese culture. But even with an existing interest and a recognized need, it was still necessary to have someone with the passion and vision to bring together the elements of a potential organization. Such was the case with JAST and now with its successor.

I received the following email on October 17, 2011 from Ross Iwamoto, a retired Raytheon engineer. It read, in part, as followed:

> In the next couple of weeks, I will try to come up with a purpose statement to organize a Japanese American Community Council and what the goals might be. I also want to organize an event to promote this. The event would be one specifically for the Japanese (but anyone could attend) and those interested in the Japanese culture. This would be to showcase Japanese culture and activities in Tucson. This is all open thinking right now, but it should give you some thoughts.

Iwamoto sent another email, dated October 19, 2011, which said in part:

> You are receiving this because I am exploring the idea of a unified Japanese community in Tucson. This is not asking you to give up anything. It is not asking to exclude anyone. This is meant to connect all of us so we can share our culture, help each other out, and be able to notify each other of events and any calls for help.

> I would like different organizations and individuals to be represented in meetings so over time we can help each other out at events, health issues, elder care issues, and so forth. We can form a coalition. This coalition could eventually lead to a Japanese Community Center, where organizations could meet, seniors could hang out, classes could be taught, Japanese could feel comfortable spending the day, children could learn about their culture.

In response to these emails, a series of meetings were held from fall 2011 to spring 2012. The purpose of the meetings was to find out what interest there was, who would like to be involved, to share inputs, and to decide on the nature and direction of the organization. The name selected was Southern Arizona Japanese Cultural Coalition (SAJCC), and it was formally established in February 2012.

SAJCC is an informal coalition formed to bring together the following components: Japanese American families and individuals, Japanese nationals and their families, people and organizations promoting Japanese language, arts, and cultural activities, and anyone interested in the Japanese people and its language, arts, and culture. Its purposes are:

* To be able to contact and meet others with common interest and needs
* To learn, share, and promote Japanese language, arts, and culture
* To promote understanding and goodwill

SAJCC is an inclusive organization, and its primary function is to act as a liaison for individuals and organizations within the Japanese community and with those outside who have interest in Japan and its culture. The coalition is loosely organized and is led by a Central Council.[126]

A website was created to provide information and references, and it is managed and maintained by Carolyn Sugiyama Classen. The website lists activities pertaining to Japan and its culture and tradition, including festivals, exhibits, demonstrations, artistic performances, lectures, seminars, workshops, and other activities relating to Japan in Tucson, Phoenix, and surrounding communities. A directory was created to facilitate contacts with individuals and organizations.

---

[126] Charter members who formed the Central Council were: Crystal Akazawa, Carolyn Sugiyama Classen, M. Fumie Craig, Patricia Deridder, Jonathan Holtrop, Yukihiro Ibuki, Ross Iwamoto, Yukari Katayama, Yuko Konishi, Yosei Sugawara, and Minoru and Evelyn Yanagihashi. About a year later, Katayama resigned while Konishi and Sugawara moved. They were replaced by Karen Falkenstrom, Miyako McKay, T.K. Negley, Miki Pimienta, and Ginger and Tom Sugimoto.

It was decided SAJCC would have only one big annual event, and it would be a New Year's celebration, although it would be held after New Year's Day so as not to conflict with family activities. The first New Year's celebration was held on January 4, 2014 at Yume Japanese Gardens and was called *Tucson Mochitsuki*. The featured event was a *mochi* pounding demonstration. Since this ritual is only performed on special occasions, it attracts continual interest. Grilled *mochi* samples were given out, and Japanese drumming entertainment was provided by Odaiko Sonora.

As of 2020, there has been seven annual events.[127] The first three celebrations were called *Tucson Mochitsuki* and were held at different venues—Yume Japanese Gardens, Rhythm Industry Performance Factory, and the downtown campus of Pima Community College. The changes in venue were necessary due to the increase in attendance. The initial event attracted about two hundred people and was considered a success. But each succeeding year saw a greater turnout and by the third year, it was up to six hundred.

The program itself changed. *Mochitsuki*, while still the centerpiece, was supplemented by a wide-ranging program. Besides drumming by Odaiko Sonora, the program came to consist of:

- Instrumental performances: stringed instruments and bamboo flutes
- Dancing by Suzuyuki-kai
- Singing by soloists and groups
- Martial arts demonstrations
- Meditative demonstrations: tea ceremony and yoga
- Artistic demonstrations: flower arrangement, calligraphy, and origami
- Popular culture presentations: anime (animation), manga (comic cartoon), and rock music
- Playing *Go* (Japanese checker game) and other Japanese games

---

[127] The 2021 event was cancelled because of COVID-19, and due to the continuation of the pandemic, the 2022 event was also cancelled.

Mochitsuki at *Tucson Japanese Festival.*

Food service is an important element of the event and always a big attraction with long lines of customers. *Mochi* in different forms are given out as samples with green tea. There has been an increase in the number of food vendors and in the sale of food and art objects by individuals, clubs, and store representatives. As noted earlier, food tends to undergo modifications, so the food served ranged from traditional Japanese fare to other ethnic-styled prepared fares.

The name of the event had to be changed with the expanded program; it was more than the pounding of *mochi*. In 2017, it became the *Tucson Japanese Festival*. The 2017 and 2018 festivals were at the Pima Community College Downtown Campus Center, and the 2019 and 2020 festivals were at the Chinese Cultural Center. Attendance continued to increase, and the 2019 and 2020 festivals had record crowds of over two thousand. The coalition leadership was pleasantly surprised by the steady increase in attendance.

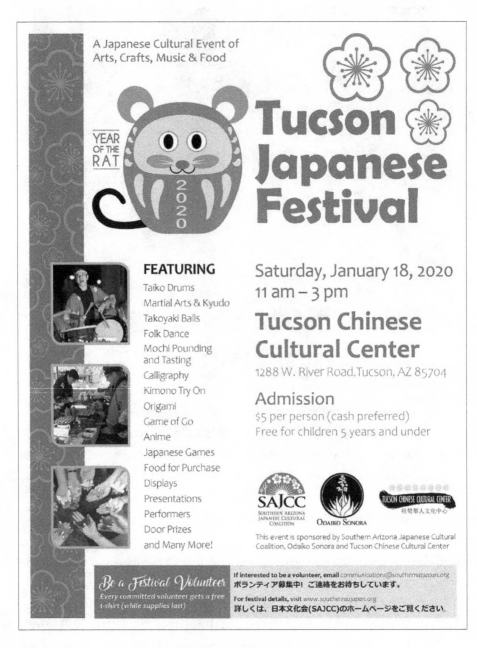

Tucson Japanese Festival poster.

Once attendance reached the thousand level, reserve funds from the festival became adequate to support programs promoting the understanding of Japanese language and culture. The Central Council decided in 2019 to provide scholarships for a Kyoto study abroad summer program by the East Asian Studies Department of the University of Arizona; it also made a donation to the Tucson Japanese Language School. During the COVID-19 pandemic, donations were made to a few select enterprises and cultural organizations to help relieve the financial strain suffered by these entities. They had been supporters of SAJCC in previous years.

On an ad-hoc basis, SAJCC has sponsored lectures and panel discussions on subjects pertaining to Japan and issues associated with Japanese Americans. Besides the two talks mentioned in the preface, the following presentations were given:

* "Japan's Intractable Problems: The Issue of Territorial Disputes"
* "The Japanese Constitution: Alien Document and Peace Constitution"
* "Cowboys and Samurai: Myth and Reality"

The coalition organized a visit to the Gila River Relocation Center site on January 24, 2015. There are only a few Nisei members in SAJCC, but the Sansei and Yonsei wanted to know more about the internment camp. There is no better way to have a feeling of what the camp was like than an actual visit of the site. Then, in 2017, the Tucson Desert Art Museum put on an exhibit and a panel discussion to commemorate the 75th anniversary of Executive Order 9066. On the panel were Carolyn Sugiyama Classen, Kathryn Nakagawa of Arizona State University, and myself. There were displays of photographs, art objects, and literary works. Especially intriguing was the exhibit of then and now photographs of camp survivors by Paul Kitagaki, Jr. Kitagaki placed side-by-side photos of internees as they appeared at the time of their incarceration with his photo portraits as they appear today. The internees' poems and art objects reflected on camp life. This was an opportunity to exhibit and discuss the artwork done by the internees and their descendants—to remind us of the sacrifices along with the suffering experienced by the internees. Their legacy has to be continually remembered.

What is the future of SAJCC? The interest is there, but it depends on the members, whether they are willing to devote time and energy to this endeavor and, at the same time, avoid burning out. The coalition, serving as a communication link and referral center, doesn't carry the heavy burden of managing and coordinating many people over several projects as was the case with JAST. Nevertheless, key leaders are necessary—individuals who are energetic, have a vision, and are willing to make the commitment. It is increasingly difficult to find such leaders. The younger generation see their role as spectators with only occasional commitments to serve in a Japanese American organization. They opt for less involvement because time-consuming ethnic activities are not what they want. Sansei and Yonsei would rather focus on personal identity and are concerned more with identity than cultural activities or group relationships. They tend to be activists and advocates of political and social issues and are apt to include Asian Americans and Pacific Islanders in their thinking rather than specifically concerned about Japanese Americans. Indeed, they feel the Nisei's striving to conform to the expectations of white majority culture to be misguided and didn't help to solve the problem of racism. They feel the emphasis should be on self-identity and asserting the cultural heritage as buttresses against racism toward not only Japanese Americans but all Asian Americans. The Nisei have been criticized by the younger generations for not uniting with other ethnic groups in solidarity against racism. The Sansei and Yonsei are attuned and are more aware of the racial dynamics and shared history of ethnic discrimination.

The SAJCC began as a cultural organization and eschewed taking position on political and social issues. Activist-oriented members could pursue individually their interest in these issues and do it outside of the organization or by joining issue-oriented groups. However, during the COVID-19 pandemic, SAJCC did sign petitions protesting the hate crimes and other forms of discriminatory acts taken against Asian Americans and asked political leaders to stem these attacks. With its broaden concerns, SAJCC can appeal to many younger Japanese Americans and to non-Japanese, thus expanding membership and making it easier to find potential leaders. In all probability, the non-Japanese will have to take on more of the leadership, but this could be a plus in broadening the base of support and could generate a wider interest in Japanese culture. It is evident even in a midsize city like Tucson, with its small Japanese population, that there is continual interest in Japanese culture. A large Japanese population isn't necessary, but for community-wide participation in Japanese cultural activities to occur, an organization is needed. Such was the case with JAST and now with SAJCC. JAST has made its run, and now the torch has been passed to the SAJCC. At times, the flame seems to be flickering, but it is still burning and whether it will burn brightly remains to be seen.

CHAPTER TEN

CONCLUSION

Of the many challenges facing the Japanese Americans, three concerns were dominant—the question of loyalty, the question of cultural continuity, and the question of cultural identity. These were intergenerational problems, but for the Nisei, the first two questions were particularly troublesome.

The loyalty question wasn't burdensome for the Issei. Yes, they didn't like being questioned about their loyalty, but being immigrants, they understood why their loyalty would be questioned from time to time. Most Issei were loyal to the United States, and they expressed this openly. After all, they had lived in the United States for many years, settled down in their occupation or business, and their children were American citizens. Their future was in America, not Japan. With the passage of the McCarran-Walter Act in 1952, the Issei were given the right of citizenship. I asked my father why he didn't apply for US citizenship. "For many years we weren't allowed to become citizens and now it's too late," said my father.

Japan is among a number of countries that forbid dual citizenship. Therefore, if my father became a US citizen, he would have to renounce his Japanese citizenship. Japan was his birthplace, and he had relatives back there. He would have to forsake all ties with Japan, including his property rights, and this was asking too much. Consequently, he decided to keep his Japanese citizenship while asserting his allegiance to America. Like many Issei, he found it difficult to give up his emotional attachment to Japan—it was part of his psyche.

But for the Nisei, it was a different story. Loyalty for the Nisei was vexing and deeply troublesome. They were American citizens, born and raised in the United States, spoke English, could hardly speak Japanese, attended American schools, dressed, ate, and acted as typical Americans. In other words, they were like other Americans in all respects, except for their looks. Herein lies the problem—they physically stood out—they were different from white Americans.

Only a few Americans blatantly espouse anti-foreign, nativist, and white supremacist views; most Americans don't consider themselves racist. But there is latent or subconscious racism. It is embedded in the inner-most psyche and finds expression as a sort of tribalism—"we" versus "they" or "our people" versus "others." "They" and "others" are immigrants, racial minorities, and marginalized groups. Differences are highlighted. Once these individual mindsets are formed, they become racist views, making associations, which leads to assumptions and creates a preexisting disposition. It becomes a subtle form of racism that is not openly practiced. But when there is a crisis, threat, or uncertainty, these sentiments are aroused. "Foreign" elements are perceived to be threatening. In the 1920s and 1930s, it was the "yellow peril," the threat of Japanese imperialism in East Asia with its imposing military power. Then, there was the waves of Asian immigrants coming to the United States and working for low wages, and it was perceived they took jobs away and lowered the living standards of American workers. Now, with demographic changes taking place in America, non-whites will soon be the majority, and this will diminish white power. It is perceived as a threat by right-wing extremists. But it could be more than war, terrorism, economic dislocations, or demographic changes. It could be a health-care crisis like the COVID-19 pandemic.

When the coronavirus first appeared in Wuhan in December 2019, the Chinese government was deliberately slow in making the announcement. The Trump administration said the virus came from a Wuhan lab, and China hid the initial spread of the virus. Whether this assertion was accurate is problematic, but now the public health crisis was politicized. President Donald Trump proceeded to label the coronavirus the "Chinese virus," and this became a political cudgel against China. Immediately latent racism was aroused, causing anti-Asian backlash with Chinese restaurants and Asian retailers losing business, and Asian Americans being harassed and intimidated. According to the April 21, 2021 report of the Pew Research Center, during the pandemic, nearly one-third of Asian Americans feared threats and physical attacks.[128] The organization, Stop AAPI Hate, received 9,081 hate incidents reports against Asian Americans in the period from March 19, 2020 to June 30, 2021.[129] These were racially motivated attacks related to the pandemic. It is believed the actual number of cases is higher because many attacks go unreported.

The president later used the racial slur "kung flu," further stoking the passions of bigots. If the COVID-19 had occurred in Hiroshima rather than in Wuhan, would it be called the "Japanese virus" or "Jap virus?" The World Health Organization has discouraged the use of a location or ethnicity to name a virus pandemic and insist it be called by its scientific name. The Spanish influenza pandemic of 1918 didn't originate in Spain. Everyone agrees this is a misnomer, but labels once used tend to persist. In today's world, misinformation is rapidly disseminated by social media. What we have is a virulent form of racism, resulting from asymmetrical threats—terrorism and disease are difficult to define and control. As a result, there is greater uncertainty, and this has heightened the rise of racism.

When racist thinking emerge, doubt is cast about the loyalty of the Japanese Americans. We saw this type of thinking erupting with the outbreak of war. The often-quoted bigoted statement by General DeWitt that a "Jap is a Jap," clearly illustrates what some American leaders thought about Japanese Americans. DeWitt went on to say:

> The Japanese race is an enemy race and while many second and third generation Japanese born on United States soil, possessed of United States citizenship have become "Americanized," the racial strains are undiluted... it makes

---

[128] https://www.pewresearch.org. April 21, 2021.

[129] https://stopaapihate.org. National Report, Aug. 12, 2021.

no difference whether he is an American citizen, he is still a Japanese. American citizenship does not necessarily determine loyalty...[130]

The Japanese Americans were thought to be capable of subversive activities, and all sorts of rumors spread throughout the West Coast about disloyal Japanese Americans helping the enemy. The loyalty question subsided only after Japanese American servicemen shed their blood in combat, and the threat lessen with allies' victories in the Pacific. Patriotism is demonstrated by sacrifices, and this was surely the case. Even so racism still persisted. Daniel Inouye, back from the war in full uniform, with ribbons and newly won captain's bar, tried to get a haircut and was told, "We don't cut Jap hair."[131] Nisei veteran, Mitsuo Usui, shared this story:

> Coming home, I was boarding a bus on Olympic Boulevard. A lady sitting in the front row of the bus, saw me and said, "Damn Jap." Here I was a proud American soldier, just coming back with my new uniform and new paratrooper boots, with all my campaign medals and awards, proudly displayed on my chest, and this? The bus driver upon hearing this remark, stopped the bus and said, "Lady, apologize to this American soldier or get off my bus"— she got off the bus. Embarrassed by the situation, I turned around to thank the bus driver. He said that's okay, buddy, everything is going to be okay from now on out. Encouraged by his comment, I thanked him and as I was turning away, I noticed a discharge pin on his lapel.[132]

There were Nisei who were disloyal, but they comprised only a small percentage of the Japanese Americans incarcerated. Undoubtedly, they were

---

[130] CWRIC, *Personal Justice*, 65-66.

[131] Daniel Inouye, *Journey to Washington* (Englewood Cliffs, NJ: Prentice-Hall, 1967), 207-8.

[132] CWRIC, *Personal Justice*, 259-60.

an irritation for the WRA, a source of constant unrest, but they were usually unorganized. In addition, there were, as previously noted, die-hard Issei with their families, known as renunciants, who were repatriated to Japan during and after the war. The total number of those repatriated was around 4,700.[133]

The other groups of so-called disloyal Nisei were the draft-resisters and the "no-no-boys." The largest number of draft-resisters were at Heart Mountain. They were organized and vocal in their opposition. Sixty-three resisters were tried and convicted of draft evasion and sentenced to three years in federal prison. When the war ended, many groups began to consider the imprisonment of the draft-resisters as an injustice, for they were protesting in good consciousness about the treatment they had received from the government. In 1947, President Harry Truman pardoned all the draft-resisters—the Heart Mountain resisters and 230 resisters from other camps. It took longer for some *Nikkei* to forgive the resisters. The JACL finally apologized in 1988.

The "no-no-boys," on the other hand, were a large group, numbering around twelve thousand, but they weren't considered a threat and none were criminally charged. They were simply segregated to Tule Lake to keep them from contaminating others with their disloyal views. As noted earlier, the majority of these expatriates recanted and had their citizenship restored. Nevertheless, their anguish and pain, caused by the loyalty questions, weren't easily forgotten and lasted for many years after the internment.

The draft-resisters and expatriates could perhaps be characterized as disloyal by their statements and actions, but none of them engaged in subversive activities. Without subversive activities, how could you legitimately prove disloyalty? The courts have shown how the loyalty question could be handled during wartime or in a crisis.

The *coram nobis* decisions of the lower courts helped in vacating the convictions of the three Japanese Americans who violated curfew and evacuation orders during World War II, but the Supreme Court didn't overrule

---

[133] Spickard, *Japanese Americans*, 126.

or discredit the *Korematsu* (1944) decision. In this decision, the Supreme Court gave deference to the military's conclusion about Japanese American disloyalty. The court accepted the government's argument that certain racial characteristics of Japanese Americans predisposed them to commit espionage and sabotage and to be disloyal. Relying on this argument, the court upheld the military rules restricting the rights of citizens for the sake of national security.

Justice Frank Murphy in his dissent wrote:

> The main reasons relied upon by those responsible for the forced evacuation, therefore, do not prove a reasonable relation between the group characteristics of Japanese Americans and the dangers of invasion, sabotage and espionage. The reasons appear, instead, to be largely an accumulation of much of the misinformation, half-truths and insinuations that for years have been directed against Japanese Americans by people with racial and economic prejudices.[134]

The troubling question is this: Can an entire racial minority pose a security threat and can this prediction of potential disloyalty be made on the basis of certain racial characteristics? It is unclear whether *Korematsu* (1944), which still stands as a legal precedent, would be used in the future to curtail civil liberties of citizens during wartime or during a crisis. Arab Americans came under suspicion, as a racial group, during the Persian Gulf War of 1991 and after the 9/11 terrorist attacks. The loyalty of Arab Americans was questioned. Being born in a foreign country makes you a "foreigner" and even though you are a naturalized citizen, your loyalty can be questioned. It happened to Lt. Col. Alexander Vindman, Ukraine-born immigrant infantry officer, wounded in the Iraq War, and who had served

---

[134] Yamamoto, et al., *Race, Rights*, 148.

in the US army for twenty years, including a stint as national security officer at the White House.

Yet he wasn't immune from racial attacks and the questioning of his loyalty when he gave his testimony during President Trump's impeachment hearing. He had overheard the phone conversation between Trump and the Ukrainian President, wherein Trump sought an investigation of Joe Biden and his son Hunter in exchange for promised military aid.[135] Republican congressmen and the conservative media came to the defense of Trump by attacking Vindman. During times of tension and apprehension, the loyalty of individuals and groups can be questioned, and even the court is not free from this pressure. The Supreme Court has tended to accommodate the government's national security reasoning. *Korematsu* (1944) could be revisited.

Loyalty to your adopted country is assumed to be a prerequisite of the assimilation process, but there is a misunderstanding that it will entail the subversion of the ethnic culture. But assimilation doesn't mean the disappearance or obliteration of Japanese culture and customs. Successful assimilation means the absorption of an emigrant group into the dominant culture, but with elements of the minority culture still visible and vibrant. To use a metaphor, it is like a vegetable salad with all the vegetable ingredients visible; it is not a vegetable soup with ingredients blended and no longer visible. America is really a "salad dish" and not a "blended soup" or a "melting pot," as it is often alluded to. Indeed, the strength of America lies in its distinct diversity, a country where differences should be celebrated, not feared. This diversity didn't result in the diminution of ethnic groups' loyalty, instead, their loyalty intensified.

The other continuing challenge faced by all immigrant communities is cultural continuity. Recent arrivals want to retain their cultural identity; they are outsiders who are not yet accepted into the larger society. These first-generation immigrants are interested in making a decent living and are not openly seeking assimilation. Moreover, many in the larger society

---

[135] https://www.npr.org > 2019/11/08.

consider the recent arrivals incapable of being culturally assimilated and feel they should initially be kept within their culture and should be controlled.

Changes occur slowly, and the first phase of Japanese acculturation began in the last decade of the nineteenth century and extended into the first decade of the twentieth century, with the Issei adapting to American norms while holding on strongly to Japanese values and customs. It gradually picked up momentum till the end of immigration in 1924; then with the Nisei coming of age and reaching adulthood, acculturation began to accelerate and continued unabated until the beginning of the war. By then, even the Issei had been acculturated into the American way of life.

Assimilation became obvious at this point. It is a relentless process depressing the immigrants' culture. The Issei viewed with alarm the Americanization of their children. But for proponents of Americanization, this was exactly what they wanted. They ideally believed almost all traces of Japanese culture would disappear, and there would be cultural homogeneity and uniformity. The Nisei, on their part, sought assimilation; it made it easier to get along with Caucasians and opened the path to social mobility. They accepted change openly and wanted to move out of the lower strata of society occupied by the Issei. The Nisei positioned themselves for assimilation by living in the suburbs and getting jobs where they had more contact with Caucasians and other minorities than with Japanese. They increasingly socialized with non-Japanese.

However, there was a lingering desire by the Nisei to know more about their culture and to advance their heritage. They could achieve this by working with other Japanese Americans. Some Nisei, especially the older ones, got involved with Japanese community organizations, such as the JACL and festival committees. The Cherry Blossom Festival of Honolulu and the Nisei Week of Los Angeles were spearheaded by Nisei. Other Nisei were involved with tours of internment sites and working on cultural exhibits, demonstrations, workshops, and forums.

Yet there were common experiences that enabled the Nisei to symbolically link with the larger ethnic entity and its culture. An example of such symbolic linking is the almost universal internment experience of the mainland Nisei. When two Nisei strangers meet, the conversation could be as follows:

Nisei A: "What was your camp?"
Nisei B: "I was at Poston 1"
Nisei A: "Oh really, I was at Butte camp, Gila River"

The shared experience of the internment brings individuals together in a strong sense of cultural identity, a bond that needs no further explanations. The redress movement is another example of a symbolic link bringing together the Japanese Americans working or supporting the movement or being a recipient of the reparation. This turns out to be the last hurrah bringing together the Japanese community. There are no galvanizing movement today. In Hawai'i, the personal links would be what plantation did you come from? Did you attend McKinley or Farrington? (Honolulu high schools that have many Japanese Americans) Are you from Makiki or Kalihi? (Honolulu districts that are predominantly Japanese Americans). These experiences create a sense of community and give people an awareness of their shared history and culture.

The younger generation lacks the broad cultural links of the Nisei. But they can secure cultural links by being involved with cultural interest groups, such as origami, ikebana, bonsai, judo, aikido, and koi groups. Loosely organized, these associations often have more non-Japanese members. These are personal interest groups, liken to a hobby or recreational activity done for personal enjoyment. This experience is quite different from working on a community-wide activity of an organization or a movement, but in their small ways, these cultural interest groups are links to Japanese culture, and they contribute towards its continuity.

Another factor affecting cultural continuity is the increasing number of intermarriages. Because miscegenation laws existed in many states until the early 1950s, the number of intermarriages was relatively low, and it was not a major factor. But beginning in the 1960s, it began to increase significantly and in the 1980s, about 60 percent of Japanese marriages were interracial, mainly Sansei and Yonsei marrying whites. Intermarriage of Japanese Americans increased faster on the mainland than in Hawai'i. The larger Japanese population in Hawai'i created greater in-group pressure, hindering intermarriages, whereas on the mainland, Japanese did not have such community pressure and had greater exposure and interaction with whites. Intermarriage is considered by many to be the final phase of assimilation—a sign of high degree of assimilation.

Intermarriage was frowned upon by Issei. They encouraged in-group marriage (homogamy). Japanese were to marry within their own group to maintain the family system and to do otherwise was to bring shame. When my sister married a part-Caucasian, part-Hawaiian, my father became angry and disowned her. My mother, although disappointed, kept quiet. It was a bitter moment. But later the rift was healed, everything was forgiven, and my father had drinks with his new son-in-law. I believe this type of reaction was typical in traditional families. It took time to heal, but assimilation affected human relationships and had its consequences; old values and attitudes had to change.

Accompanying intermarriages are the increased number of mixed-race children called *hapa*.[136] *Hapa* are mostly Sansei, Yonsei, and younger generations. Being of mixed blood, they have an identity problem. They are thoroughly Americanized, speak no Japanese, and have a superficial understanding of their heritage. An interest in knowing their part-Japanese heritage can by triggered by participating in *bon* dances at Buddhist temples, local festivals, Japanese American sport leagues, and in Japanese student clubs. Suddenly, they ask themselves, "What does it mean to be Japanese American? Who am I?" What intrigued Nisei earlier about their ancestors is now evoking an interest among the younger generations—they want to know their roots and to know about their ancestors. Sometimes these youngsters find old family pictures, or have talks with grandparents, or stumbled onto *taiko* drumming, anime, manga, Japanese movies, karaoke, or even sushi. Any of these encounters can bring about an interest in things

---

[136] *Hapa* is a Hawaiian word and means "part" or "half" as in part-Japanese; a person of mixed blood. It is similar to the Japanese *hafu*, which means "half" or "multiracial."

Japanese. But the *hapa* have the challenge of deciding which heritage to hold on to, one or both. It seems an increasing number are claiming both parts of their ethnic identity. In the long run, for all the younger generations, new ways have to be found to bring them together with Japanese culture and some galvanizing issues to sustain their interest within an ethnic organization. Otherwise, there will only be sporadic interest groups with little sense of ethnic solidarity.

Demographic changes will affect cultural continuity. The *Nikkei* population has declined percentage-wise, when taken as part of the total Asian population, while other Asian groups have shown significant growth. The largest Asian communities are the Asian Indians and the Vietnamese due mainly to immigration. Meanwhile, the Japanese population has stabilized; according to census reports, the annual increase was 1.2 percent from 2000 to 2010.[137] Reflecting the usual urban pattern, the birth rate of the Nisei has been one of the lowest for any ethnic group, and the size of the nuclear family has shrunken. Moreover, smaller numbers of Japanese are coming to reside in America, and most importantly, intermarriages and a large number of *hapa* has had an impact. Among Asian groups, the Japanese Americans have the highest rate of intermarriages, and it is predicted that soon the majority of Japanese Americans will be multiracial.[138] Given these demographic trends, Gil Asakawa argues the best way for Japanese Americans to have a greater influence is to combine with the Asian Americans and Pacific Islanders (AAPI) organization, which represents the fastest-growing multicultural group in America.[139] However, there are those who say the AAPI is too broad. Such pan-ethnicity organizations find their groups' grievances to be diverse and difficult to manage. The Asian Americans are preoccupied with immigration issues, whereas the Pacific Islanders are focused on decolonization and sovereignty rights. The Pacific Islanders feel their concerns

---

[137] US Census Bureau. *The Asian Population: 2010*. Census Brief, Table 6.

[138] https://www.janm.org > exhibits > visible and invisible.

[139] Gil Asakawa, *Being Japanese American: A JA Sourcebook for Nikkei, Hapa... & Their Friends* (Berkeley: Stone Bridge Press, 2004), 149-51.

are being ignored. Nevertheless, coalition leaders realize the organization has to be inclusive and must have the strength in numbers to affect policies.

ASSIMILATION AND ITS CONSEQUENCES

In his speech before the Democratic National Convention in October 2016, Julian Castro used an appropriate metaphor to describe how immigrants become assimilated. He said the process isn't a sprint or a marathon—it doesn't come about quickly, but it doesn't take generations. It is a relay where the baton, the legacy, is passed on from one generation to another.

Historical circumstances and geographical settings affect the inherent character of the assimilation process—its timing and speed. The whole process began, of course, with the Issei. They didn't hope for assimilation; in fact, they dreaded it, knowing it was inevitable. The Issei managed to retain their ethnic identity with its values, cultural arts, and behavioral patterns; they survived albeit with modifications in a dominant American society. This was accomplished by undergoing acculturation, the process of adopting traits and patterns of other cultures but not succumbing to the larger society. Their ethnic identity was strong enough to maintain group solidarity, although at the same time flexible enough to allow for their culture to adapt to the larger society.

If the challenge of the Issei was acculturation, the challenge of the Nisei was assimilation; the process whereby an immigrant group is absorbed into the broader community and culture. The Nisei witnessed and participated in the blending of Japanese and American traditions. It led to conflicts between the Issei and Nisei. The Nisei became so Americanized, few spoke Japanese, and they had little knowledge of Japan. They found it difficult to understand and relate to what their immigrant ancestors had experienced. Nisei concentrated on blending into the dominant American society by removing the most visible signs of their racial and cultural differences by anglicizing their first names. My parents gave their children Japanese first names, which tied in with their Japanese heritage, but my three sisters officially adopted English names, and their Japanese name became their middle name. They did this on their own initiative, and my parents didn't object. The girls were sensitive to social relationships and wanted to fit in with other groups, especially in the school environment. My two brothers and I didn't feel the need to take such steps and never took on English names. A few families simplified or changed their surname to sound less foreign; for example, Shimabukuro became Shima. In some families, members refused to speak Japanese and even eschewed eating Japanese food; in other words, they totally immersed themselves in American culture.

However, even though assimilation has taken place, there are still examples of continuity. Having lived through the depression and wartime years, the Nisei generation carry certain patterns of thinking, such as orderliness and frugality. These ways of thinking are so ingrained they find expression in family circles and in intimate group settings. The Nisei are constantly reminded to respect the elderly and not bring shame to themselves and their families. Education is highly valued, and the close link between academic achievement and success in life is understood by everyone. Families save their resources and make sacrifices so their children would have the best training.

Common behavioral practices are affected by Japanese values and customs. It affects how you feel and react to circumstances and is often done unconsciously—for example, taking off shoes at the entrance door not only at home but at a Japanese American friend's home. At home, we take our shoes off and walk in barefoot, or with socks, or house slippers. It does have a beneficial effect—it keeps dirt out and keeps the house clean. Nothing is said if our guests walk in without taking off their shoes, but most of our friends know better and do it automatically.

A persistent behavioral pattern is *enryo* (reserve or restraint). My wife reminds me when I'm doing it. Once when I was invited to a party while working at California State University at Los Angeles, the host asked if I wanted the delicious-looking dessert. I politely said no thank you, that I was full and will pass on it. In Hawai'i, in a Japanese American home, the host would ask again and even a third time if I wanted dessert. Practicing *enryo*, you suppress saying "yes" right away—it's brash and you are supposed to be demure and not express your true feelings. The host in Los Angeles never came back. I wanted the dessert and was shocked I wasn't asked again!

An onerous traditional practice is *giri* (reciprocal obligation). It is reciprocal gift-giving, usually a monetary gift, but it could be goods or services and is given for special occasions, such as weddings, funerals, graduations, and birthdays. Reciprocation is between immediate family, relatives, friends, and acquaintances, and things of equal value are exchanged. It could become a widening web of never-ending obligations, highly formalized and demanding exact calculations. A colleague of mine at the University of Michigan, a Japanese national, told me he dreaded going back to Japan after living in the United States for several years because of the system of obligations. He enjoyed the freedom of being away from the web of obligations and didn't want to be involved again. Nisei have moved to lessen the degree of obligations, but it is difficult to escape the social obligation of *giri* if one associates and lives in close proximity with other Japanese.

A behavioral pattern that presents difficulties at times is modesty or self-effacement, called *kenkyo* in Japanese. The Japanese learn to be humble and extremely modest to a fault. It used to annoy me when my parents resorted to *kenkyo*. A friend would compliment me for winning an award, and my parents would say, "Oh, it wasn't much—others could have won it." Such remarks caused friction between Nisei children and their Issei parents. Americans are taught to "toot your own horn." When someone offers a compliment, accept it as given and thank the person for their recognition. Although Americanized, I caught myself occasionally resenting those who openly parade their knowledge, ability, or talent as showing off, and I wasn't about to acknowledge their accomplishments. In essence, I was demanding the same standard of modesty that my parents showed. Traditional values persist.

There are other behavioral patterns; for instance, the avoidance of aggressive and conspicuous behavior—sticking out from the group—that reflects traditional values. Several behavioral traits, such as perseverance, duty, honor, and frugality are traditional ideals that stem from the warrior class of feudal Japan. Non-Japanese have commented on certain personality characteristics of the Japanese—how the Japanese control their emotions and resort to nonverbal communication, wherein there is a long period of silence and a reliance on implicit understanding. The adage is: Saying nothing means something. Unfortunately, it has led to stereotyping. Caucasians criticize the Nisei for being unemotional, but the Japanese are emotional; they're just taught to not display it. Americans find it disconcerting when Nisei use nonverbal communication, since Americans are more direct and assertive. The point is, these behavioral patterns are ingrained and reflect deep-seated values. How rigidly these cultural values are held varies with the individual. The trend is for these traditional behavioral norms to diminish, but traces of these behavioral traits will persist in future generations.

The milieu can affect behavioral and attitudinal traits. The differential effects of the environment are evident when Hawai'i Japanese are compared with mainland Japanese. The disparity in attitude and behavior began with the arrival of the Japanese to Hawai'i and to the mainland. When the Japanese arrived in Hawai'i, they weren't viewed as a threat; in fact, they were desperately needed by the sugar plantations. It was only much later that a small number of upper-class Caucasians opposed the Japanese when their numbers grew rapidly. In contrast, the Japanese arriving on the mainland were viewed as a threat. Mainland Japanese faced blatant discrimination, and political and economic actions were taken against them, primarily by blue-collar workers and farmers. When the Japanese sought agricultural work, white farmers viewed them as unfair competitors. Large numbers of lower-class Caucasians accused the Japanese of working for low wages and taking their jobs.[140] Therefore, the mainland Japanese faced immediate opposition and were definitely not welcomed.

In Hawai'i, the working environment was different. The plantation system was unique and nothing like it existed on the mainland. The Japanese, Chinese, and Filipinos had their respective camps. The close-knit nature of the Japanese camp helped to maintain the group's values and culture and

---

[140] Recent studies reveal immigrants don't take jobs away and don't lower wages of the local workers. See: Adhijit V. Banergee and Esther Duflo, *Good Economics for Hard Times* (New York: Public Affairs, 2019), chap. 2.

promoted group solidarity, but at the same time, they were close to the Chinese and Filipinos camps and were able to intermingle using pidgin English to communicate—so a potential to coalesce existed.

The mainland Japanese had no such exposure to a multicultural environment. They were scattered throughout the West Coast. Many were isolated in communities where they became a small distinct minority. They came to fatalistically accept their powerless position. But in Hawai'i, the Japanese were always a large group and until the end of World War II, they constituted a little over one-third of the total population. Hence, the Hawai'i Japanese didn't view themselves as an isolated minority. To be sure, there was discrimination, but growing up in Hawai'i, I never considered myself an oppressed minority.

Contrasting ways of thinking developed. Even before the war, there was a significant disparity in the attitude and behavior of the Hawai'i Japanese when compared with their mainland counterparts, but the wartime experience exacerbated the differences. Relocation had little impact on the Hawai'i Japanese, but for the mainland Japanese, it had a profound effect on their attitudes. The harsh experience engendered bitterness and a lessening of self-confidence. When I first arrived on the mainland, I was surprised by the bitter resentment of the mainlanders, their feeling of intimidation, their minority consciousness, and their sensitivity toward racial issues. In contrast, Hawai'i Nisei are more confident, gregarious, outspoken, and relaxed about racism. The slogan "go for broke" illustrates our assertiveness and confidence. The disparities extend beyond the ways of thinking. It is evident in our mannerism and most strikingly in our speech with the use of pidgin English with its unusual vocal inflection.

The attitudinal and behavioral differences between the Hawai'i and mainland Japanese Americans accounts to a large degree why acculturation took hold quickly in Hawai'i and enabled the Hawai'i Nisei to breakthrough faster in the political, economic, and social spheres. The Hawai'i Nisei readily adopted the island lifestyle—the men wore aloha shirts (Hawaiian loose shirts) and the women wore *mu'umu'u* (loose-fitting dresses), spoke pidgin, and enjoyed the distinctive local food and entertainment. They embraced the "aloha spirit," the open and friendly attitude toward everyone, even strangers; thereby making them quite distinctive from their mainland counterparts.

Beginning in the 1950s, a myth was popularized that the Hawai'i Japanese is the model Japanese—an oppressed minority group that success-fully overcame racism and achieved socioeconomic and political successes. The myth concluded the Hawai'i Japanese could serve as a model for other minorities to follow. But this model-minority myth is misleading in many ways. According to this myth, the Nisei with their cultural values were able to achieve remarkable success. But it is problematic how strongly these values were held and it varied widely with individuals, and their connection to success is debatable. Moreover, the Hawai'i experience was unusual—the timing, environment, and historical circumstances cannot be duplicated. As previously discussed, the experience of the Hawai'i Japanese was different from that of the mainland Japanese—in their arrival, and in the wartime and resettling events. The Hawai'i experience turns out to be unique. This makes the Hawai'i Japanese sui generis—one of its kind—a remarkable ethnic group.

The Nisei were thoroughly assimilated and had met the challenges of loyalty and cultural continuity. By the late 1970s, majority of Nisei had retired, and the Sansei had taken over leadership. The legacy of the Nisei was firmly set—they had made enormous progress. They impacted the political world, being the dominant ethnic group in Hawaiian politics, and even on the mainland, although progress was slower, Nisei mainlanders began to hold high political positions. In terms of their education, almost all Nisei were high school graduates, and many had attained undergraduate and advanced degrees. With their educational background, they were able to attain mainstream business, occupational, and professional positions. As we have seen, they advanced socially and are now part of the American middle class.

It is a complex journey, for America is a new kind of experience, and it is a dream with great expectations. The Nisei learned to adapt quickly in the prewar period. While absorbing the American cultural traits and blending into the Hawaiian society, they had to maintain their cultural heritage. The war brought on open racism and the questioning of their loyalty. The Nisei demonstrated their patriotism, but it wasn't all ballyhoo patriotism. There was dissent; there were ugly incidents. The Nisei emerged from the war with a greater sense of purpose—to gain wider recognition for the *Nikkei* and to correct past injustices. The other aspiration was to expand the awareness and appreciation of Japanese culture and traditions. These purposes were accomplished by working together and participating in organizations. There were internal challenges. Some older Nisei persisted with a male-dominance, staunchly patriarchal attitude in which women suffered from a subservient role. But such behavior faded away. For all the imperfections, changes were made in rapid fashion, and the Nisei were able to achieve upward mobility for all. And so, even with the interruption of the war, the Nisei accomplished a great deal in a remarkable time of less than a hundred years. The role played by the immediate descendants of immigrant families is immense, and this is true for all ethnic groups, but the experience of the Nisei is extraordinary. There is a frequently used Hawaiian sequence, *no ka ʻoi,* meaning "the best." Assuredly, we can say, Nisei *no ka ʻoi*—Nisei is the best.

GLOSSARY

Hawaiian words are indicated as such in the definition.	
aburage	fried soybean curd
ahina	Hawaiian word meaning denim cloth used in making jackets and pants
aikido	art of self-defense using locks and holds
Aki-matsuri	Fall Festival
anime	animation
bachi ga ataru	you'll be punished
bango	number
bento	boxed lunch with partitions
bon	honoring the dead
bon'odori	festival dance
bonsai	art of growing dwarfed plants or trees
buddhahead	Hawai'i Japanese
burakumin	descendants of outcast groups dating from feudal times

butsudan	Buddhist household altar
buyo	classical dance
chambara	sword-fighting movies
chanoyu	tea ceremony
daikon	Japanese radish
dekasegi	sojourn; temporary stay
dekaseginin	sojourner; temporary resident
dohyo	sumo ring
enryo	reserve, restraint, modesty
eta	pejorative and prohibited term for *burakumin*
furigana	tiny *kana* placed alongside *kanji*, indicating the pronunciation of the *kanji*
furo	deep Japanese-style bathtub
gaman	bear, endure, perseverance
Gannnenmono	first group of Japanese emigrants who arrived in Hawai'i in 1868
giri	reciprocal obligation
Go	checker-like board game
gyoji ryori	traditional food associated with festivals
haji	shame, disgrace
hakama	trouser

hanafuda	flower cards game
Hana-matsuri	Flower Festival
hanga	woodblock print
haole	Hawaiian word for Caucasian or white person
hapa	mixed-race; Hawaiian word meaning "part" or "half"
Higan-matsuri	see *Aki-matsuri*
Hina-matsuri	Doll Festival
hole	Hawaiian word meaning to strip the leaves from the stalk of a sugarcane
holehole bushi	immigrant workers' song
huli bango	pidgin English for no work, no pay
ie	extended household or family
ikebana	art of flower arrangement
imingaisha	Japanese emigration companies
inu	"dog," pejorative term used to refer to Nisei who sided with camp authorities
Issei	first-generation Japanese emigrants who settled in America
jigoku dani	hell valley; Honouliuli Internment Camp
jubako	lacquered boxes used to serve traditional New Year's food

judo	a sport employing throws and holds on an opponent
Kabuki	traditional popular drama
kachi-gumi	win the war group
kadomatsu	New Year's entrance decoration for home or business
kagamimochi	stacked tiers of mochi used for decoration or offering
kama'aina	Hawaiian word for native-born
kana	Japanese syllabary
kanji	Chinese character
Kanyaku Imin	government contract laborers
karaoke	literally means "empty orchestra"; a device with recorded instrumental accompaniment of songs to which the singer sings along; it is a form of entertainment
karate	art of self-defense using hand strikes and kicks
katta-gumi	win the war group
kendo	Japanese fencing
kenjinkai	prefectural associations
kenkyo	modesty, self-effacement
Kibei	Japanese Americans educated in Japan who returned to America

kine	wooden mallet used in *mochi* pounding
koden	money offering to the bereaved
koi	carp
koto	zither-type, long-string instrument
kotonk	mainland Japanese
kyogen	*Noh* comedy
kyudo	archery
luna	Hawaiian word for overseer or foreman
mahele	Hawaiian word for division or to divide
manga	comic; cartoon
miai	arranged marriage meeting
mikado	emperor of Japan
mikan	mandarin orange
min'yo	folk music
mochi	steamed glutinous rice cake
mochigome	type of rice used for making *mochi*
mochitsuki	rice pounding to make rice cake
Momotaro	Peach Boy; folktale hero
mu'umu'u	Hawaiian word for a loose-fitting gown

Naichi	Japanese from Japan proper; used to differentiate from those of distant peripheral islands
nakodo	go-between in arranged marriage
Nihonmachi	Japantown
Nikkei	all persons of Japanese ancestry
Nisei	second-generation Japanese Americans; children of Issei
no ka 'oi	Hawaiian sequence meaning the best
Noh	dance-drama
okazuya	Japanese American delicatessen selling side dishes to go with rice
okonomiyaki	savory pancake
origami	art of folding paper
osechi-ryori	traditional New Year's dishes
samisen	three-stringed Japanese banjo
Sansei	third-generation Japanese Americans; children of Nisei
sensei	teacher; a term of respect
setsubun	last day of winter
shakuhachi	bamboo flute
shashin hanayome	picture bride
shikata ga nai	it can't be helped

shinnenkai	parties for the new year
shodo	calligraphy
Showa-tenno	Emperor Hirohito
shushin	moral and ethical training
soshiki	Japanese funeral
sumie	ink painting
sumo	wrestling
taiko	drum
tanomoshi	mutual financing group
tatami	floor mat made of rush straw
temari	decorative thread ball
Tenchosetsu	emperor's birthday celebration
tofu	soybean curd
tokonoma	alcove decorated with hanging scroll and flower arrangement
tsukemono	pickled vegetables
tsuya	Buddhist wake service
ukiyo-e	floating world woodblock print
usu	large mortar used in *mochi* pounding
yobiyose	wives, children, and close relatives summoned to join emigrants

Yonsei	fourth-generation Japanese Americans
yugen	combination of *kyogen* comedy and *Noh* dance

BIBLIOGRAPHY

Arnold, Bruce Makoto. "The Problem with Persistence: The Rise of Tucson's Japanese Cuisine and the Fall of Its Nikkei Community." Chap. 10 in *Chop Suey and Sushi from Sea to Shining Sea: Chinese and Japanese Restaurants in the United States*. Edited by Bruce Makoto Arnold, Tanfer Emin Tunc, and Raymond Douglas Chong. Fayetteville, AR: University of Arkansas Press, 2018.

Arrington, Leonard J. *The Price of Prejudice*. 2nd ed. Delta, UT: Topaz Museum, 1997.

Asakawa, Gil. *Being Japanese American: A JA Sourcebook for Nikkei, Hapa - & Their Friends*. Berkeley: Stone Bridge Press, 2004.

Asato, Noriko. *Teaching Mikadoism: The Attack on Japanese Language Schools in Hawai'i, California, and Washington, 1919-1927*. Honolulu: University of Hawai'i Press, 2006.

Axford, Roger W. *Too Long Been Silent: Japanese Americans Speak Out*. Lincoln, NE: Media Publishing and Marketing, 1986.

Bailey, Paul. *City in the Sun: The Japanese Concentration Camp at Poston, Arizona*. Los Angeles: Westernlore Press, 1971.

Banerjee, Abhijit V. and Esther Duflo. *Good Economics for Hard Times*. New York: Public Affairs, 2019.

Blair, Chad. *Money, Color and Sex in Hawai'i Politics*. Honolulu: Mutual Publishing, 1998.

Brislin, Tom. "Weep into Silence/Cries of Rage: Bitter Divisions in Hawai'i's Japanese Press." *Journalism and Mass Communication Monographs* 147 (December 1995).

Brokaw, Tom. *The Greatest Generation*. New York: Random House, 1978.

Brown, Daniel James. *Facing the Mountain: A True Story of Japanese American Heroes in World War II*. New York: Viking, 2021.

Burton, Jeffrey F. and Mary M. Farrell. *Jigoku-Dani: An Archaeological Reconnaissance of the Honouliuli Internment Camp, O'ahu, Hawai'i*. Tucson, AZ: Trans-Sierran Archaeological Research, 2008.

Burton, Jeffrey F. and Mary M. Farrell. *World War II Japanese American Internment Sites in Hawai'i*. Tucson, AZ: Trans-Sierran Archaeological Research, 2007.

Burton, Jeffrey F., Mary M. Farrell, Florence B. Lord, and Richard W. Lord. *Confinement and Ethnicity: An Overview of World War II Japanese American Relocation Sites*. Publications in Anthropology 74. Tucson, AZ: Western Archaeological and Conservation Center, 1999.

Commission on Wartime Relocation and Internment of Civilians. *Personal Justice Denied. Report of the Commission on Wartime Relocation and Internment of Civilians*. Seattle: University of Washington Press and Washington, DC: Civil Liberties Public Education Fund, 1997.

Daniels, Roger. *Concentration Camps USA: Japanese Americans and World War II*. New York: Holt, Rinehart and Winston, 1971.

Daniels, Roger. *The Politics of Prejudice*. New York: Atheneum, 1974.

Daniels, Roger. *Prisoners without Trials: Japanese Americans in World War II*. New York: Hill and Wang, 1993.

Daniels, Roger, Sandra C. Taylor, and Harry H. L. Kitano, eds. *Japanese Americans: From Relocation to Redress*. Salt Lake City: University of Utah Press, 1986.

Davies, Roger J. and Osamu Ikeno, eds. *The Japanese Mind: Understanding Contemporary Japanese Culture*. Rutland, VT: Tuttle Publishing, 2002.

Day, Takako. *Show Me the Way to Go Home: The Moral Dilemma of Kibei No No Boys in World War Two Incarceration Camps*. Middlebury, VT: Wren Song Press, 2014.

Dempster, Brian Komei, ed. *Making Home from War: Stories of Japanese American Exile and Resettlement*. Berkeley: Heyday Books, 2010.

Discover Nikkei. *Fred Kinzaburo Makino: A Biography—His Contributions to Society Through the Hawai'i Hochi*. Pts. 1 & 2. Honolulu: Hawai'i Hochi, November 29, 2010.

Drinnon, Richard. *Keeper of Concentration Camps: Dillon S. Myers and American Racism.* Berkeley: University of California Press, 1987.

Duus, Masayo Umezawa. *The Japanese Conspiracy: The O'ahu Sugar Strike of 1920.* Berkeley: University of California Press, 1999.

Dubs, Masayo Umezawa. *Unlikely Liberators: The Men of the 100th and the 442nd.* Honolulu: University of Hawai'i Press, 1987.

Embryo, Sue Kunitomi, Arthur A. Hansen, and Betty Kulberg Mitson. *Manzanar Martyr: An Interview with Harry Y. Ueno.* Fullerton, CA: Fullerton California State University, 1986.

Ericson, Steven J. "Matsukata Fiscal Policy." Vol. 5 of *Kodansha Encyclopedia of Japan.* Tokyo: Kodansha, 1983.

Estes, Donald H. "A Place Called Poston." In *Transforming Barbed Wire: The Incarceration of Japanese Americans in Arizona During World War II.* ed. Thomas Nakayama. Phoenix: Arizona Humanities Council, 1997.

Falgout, Suzanne and Linda Nishigaya, eds. "Breaking the Silence: Lessons of Democracy and Social Justice from the World War II Honouliuli Internment and POW Camp in Hawai'i." *Social Process in Hawai'i* 45 (2014).

Garner, Anthony J. *Hawai'i Under Army Rule.* Stanford: Stanford University Press, 1955.

Geracimos, Helen. *Shaping History: The Role of Newspapers in Hawai'i.* Honolulu: University of Hawai'i Press, 1996.

Hansen, Arthur. "Gila River Relocation Center." In *Transforming Barbed Wire: The Incarceration of Japanese Americans in Arizona During World War II.* ed. Thomas Nakayama. Phoenix: Arizona Humanities Council, 1997.

Harrington, Joseph D. *Yankee Samurai: The Secret Role of Nisei in America's Pacific Victory.* Detroit: Pettigrew Enterprise, 1979.

Hatamiya, Leslie T. *Righting a Wrong: Japanese Americans and the Passage of the Civil Liberties Act of 1988.* Stanford: Stanford University Press, 1993.

Hazama, Dorothy Ochiai and Jane Okamoto Komeiji. *Okage Sama De: The Japanese in Hawai'i 1885-1985.* Honolulu: Bess Press, 1986.

Hosokawa, William K. *Nisei: The Quiet Americans.* New York: William Morrow, 1969.

Iiyama, Chizu. "Memories of Schools at Poston, Arizona." *Nikkei Heritage* 10, no.1 (Winter 1998).

Inada, Lawson Fusao, ed. *Only What We Could Carry: The Japanese American Internment Experience.* Berkeley: Heyday Books, 2000.

Inouye, Daniel. *Journey to Washington.* Englewood Cliffs, NJ: Prentice-Hall, 1967.

Iritani, Frank and Joanne. *Ten Visits: Accounts of Visits to all the Japanese American Relocation Centers.* San Mateo, CA: Asian American Curriculum Project, 1995.

Irons, Peter. *Justice at War: The Story of the Japanese American Internment Cases.* Berkeley: University of California Press, 1993.

Irons, Peter, ed. *Justice Delayed: The Record of the Japanese American Internment Cases.* Middleton, CT: Wesleyan University Press, 1989.

Japanese Cultural Center of Hawai'i. *Family Torn Apart: The Internment Story of the Otokichi Muin Ozaki Family.* Honolulu: Japanese Cultural Center of Hawai'i, 2012.

Japanese Cultural Center of Hawai'i. *Life Behind Barbed Wire: The World War II Internment Memoir of a Hawai'i Issei.* Honolulu: Japanese Cultural Center of Hawai'i, 2008.

Kashima, Tetsuden. *Judgment Without Trial: Japanese American Imprisonment During World War II.* Seattle: University of Washington Press, 2003.

Kimura, Yukiko. *Issei: Japanese Immigrants in Hawai'i.* Honolulu: University of Hawai'i Press, 1988.

Ku, Robert Ji-Song. *Dubious Gastronomy: The Cultural Politics of Eating Asian in the USA.* Honolulu: University of Hawai'i Press, 2014.

Leighton, Alexander H. *The Governing of Men.* Princeton: Princeton University Press, 1945.

Leong, Karen J. and Myla Vicenti Carpio. "Carceral Subjugations: Gila River Community and Incarceration of Japanese Americans on Its Lands." *Amerasia Journal* 42, no. 1 (2016).

Matsuda, Mary Gruenewald. *Looking Like the Enemy: My Story of Imprisonment in Japanese-American Internment Camps.* Troutdale, OR: NewSage Press, 2005.

Matsuo, Dorothy. *Boyhood to War: History and Anecdotes of the 442nd Regimental Combat Team.* Honolulu: Mutual Publishing, 1992.

McCaffrey, James M. *Going for Broke: Japanese American Soldiers in the War Against Nazi Germany*. Norman, OK: University of Oklahoma Press, 2013.

Miyamoto, Kazuo. *Hawai'i: End of the Rainbow*. Rutland, VT: Tuttle Company, 1964.

Morrison, Susan and Peter Knerr. "Forgotten Internees." *Honolulu Magazine* (November 1990).

Myer, Dillon S. *Uprooted Americans: The Japanese Americans and the War Relocation Authority During World War II*. Tucson, AZ: University of Arizona Press, 1971.

Nagata, Donna K., Jacqueline H.J. Kim, and Kaidi Wu. "The Japanese American Wartime Incarceration: Examining the Scope of Racial Trauma." *The American Psychologist* 74, no. 1 (January 2019): 36-48.

Nakane, Chie. *Japanese Society*. Berkeley: University of California Press, 1970.

Nishimoto, Richard S. *Inside an American Concentration Camp: Japanese American Resistance at Poston, Arizona*. ed. Lane Ryo Hirabayashi. Tucson, AZ: University of Arizona Press, 1995.

O'Brien, David J. and Stephen S. Fugita. *The Japanese American Experience*. Bloomington, IN: Indiana University Press, 1991.

Odo, Franklin S. *No Sword to Bury: Japanese Americans in Hawai'i During World War II*. Philadelphia: Temple University Press, 2004.

Odo, Franklin S. *Voices from the Canefields: Folksongs from Japanese Immigrant Workers in Hawai'i*. New York: Oxford University Press, 2013.

Ogawa, Dennis M. *Jan Ken Po: The World of Hawai'i's Japanese Americans*. Honolulu: University of Hawai'i Press, 1978.

Ogawa, Dennis M. *Kodomo No Tame Ni (For the Sake of the Children): The Japanese American Experience in Hawai'i*. Honolulu: University of Hawai'i Press, 1978.

Okada, John. *No-No Boy*. Seattle: University of Washington Press, 1976.

Okada, Victor N., ed. *Triumphs of Faith: Stories of Japanese American Christians During World War II*. Los Angeles: Japanese American Internment Project, 1998.

Okamura, Jonathan Y. *From Race to Ethnicity: Interpreting Japanese American Experiences in Hawai'i*. Honolulu: University of Hawai'i Press, 2014.

Okamura, Jonathan Y. *Raced to Death in 1920s Hawai'i: Injustice and Revenge in the Fukunaga Case.* Urbana, IL: University of Illinois Press, 2019.

Okihiro, Gary Y. *Cane Fires: The Anti-Japanese Movement in Hawai'i, 1865-1945.* Philadelphia: Temple University Press, 1991.

Okihiro, Gary Y. "Japanese Resistance in America's Concentration Camps." *Amerasia Journal* 2 (Fall 1973).

Omaye, Jayna. "Soldiering On." *Honolulu Magazine* (December 2019).

Ouchi, William G. *Theory Z: How American Business Can Meet the Japanese Challenge.* Reading, MA: Addison-Wesley Publishing Company, 1981.

Pukui, Mary Kawena and Samuel H. Elbert. *Hawaiian Dictionary.* Revised and Enlarged Edition. Honolulu: University of Hawai'i Press, 1986.

Reeves, Richard. *Infamy: The Shocking Story of the Japanese American Internment in World War II.* New York: Henry Holt and Company, 2015.

Robinson, Greg. *After Camp: Portraits in Midcentury Japanese American Life and Politics.* Berkeley: University of California Press, 2012.

Robinson, Greg. *By Order of the President: FDR and the Internment of Japanese Americans.* Cambridge, MA: Harvard University Press, 2001.

Robinson, Greg. *The Great Unknown: Japanese American Sketches.* Boulder, CO: University Press of Colorado, 2016.

Robinson, Greg. *A Tragedy of Democracy: Japanese Confinement in North America.* New York: Columbia University Press, 2009.

Rosa, John P. *Local Story: The Massie—Kahahawai Case and the Culture of History.* Honolulu: University of Hawai'i Press, 2014.

Russell, Jean Jarboe. *The Train to Crystal City: FDR's Secret Prisoner Exchange Program and America's Only Family Internment Camp During World War II.* New York: Scribner, 2015.

Sakai, Robert K. and Mitsugu Sakihara. "Okinawa." Vol. 6 of *Kodansha Encyclopedia of Japan.* Tokyo: Kodansha, 1983.

Sato, Claire and Violet Harada. *A Resilient Spirit: The Voice of Hawai'i's Internees.* Honolulu: Japanese Cultural Center of Hawai'i, 2018.

Scheiber, Harry N. and Jane L. Scheiber. *Bayonets in Paradise: Martial Law in Hawai'i During World War II.* Honolulu: University of Hawai'i Press, 2016.

Soga, Yasutaro (Keiho). *Life Behind Barbed Wire: The World War II Internment Memoirs of a Hawai'i Issei*. Translated by Kihei Hirai. Honolulu: University of Hawai'i Press, 2008.

Spicer, Edwin H., Asael T. Hansen, Katherine Luomala, and Marvin K. Opler. *Impounded People: Japanese-Americans in the Relocation Centers*. Tucson, AZ: University of Arizona Press, 1969.

Spickard, Paul R. *Mixed Blood: Intermarriage and Ethnic Identity in Twentieth-Century America*. Madison, WI: University of Wisconsin Press, 1989.

Spickard, Paul R. *Japanese Americans: The Formation and Transformations of an Ethnic Group*. New York: Twayne Publishers, 1996.

Stanley, Jerry. *I Am an American: A True Story of Japanese Internment*. New York: Crown Publishers, 1994.

Stannard, David. *Honor Killing: How the Infamous "Massie Affair" Transformed Hawai'i*. New York: Viking Press, 2005.

Staples, Bill Jr. *Kenichi Zenimura: Japanese American Baseball Pioneer*. Jefferson, NC: McFarland & Company, 2011.

Sugimura, Tsukasa. *A History of the OMS Holiness Church of North America*. Los Angeles: Education and Publication Committee of the OMS Holiness Church of North America, 1993.

Takaki, Ronald. *A Different Mirror: A History of Multicultural America*. Toronto: Little, Brown, 1993.

Takaki, Ronald. *Pau Hana: Plantation Life and Labor in Hawai'i*. Honolulu: University of Hawai'i Press, 1983.

Tamura, Eileen H. *Americanization, Acculturation, and Ethnic Identity: The Nisei Generation in Hawai'i*. Urbana, IL: University of Illinois Press, 1994.

Tamura, Eileen H. "The English-Only Effort, the Anti-Japanese Campaign, and Language Acquisition in the Education of Japanese Americans in Hawai'i, 1915-40." *History of Education Quarterly*, 33, no. 1 (Spring 1993): 37-58.

Tashiro, Kenneth A. *Wase Time! A Teen's Memoir at Gila River Internment Camp*. Bloomington, IN: AuthorHouse, 2005.

Tateishi, John, ed. *And Justice for All: An Oral History of the Japanese American Detention Camps*. New York: Random House, 1984.

Tateishi, John. *Redress: The Inside Story of the Successful Campaign for Japanese American Reparations.* Berkeley: Heyday Books, 2020.

Tenten, Haisho. *An Internment Odyssey.* Honolulu: Japanese Cultural Center of Hawai'i, 2017.

Thomas, Dorothy Swaine, Charles Kikuchi, and James Sakoda. *The Salvage.* Berkeley: University of California Press, 1952.

Thomas, Dorothy Swaine and Richard S. Nishimoto. *The Spoilage: Japanese-American Evacuation and Resettlement During World War II.* Berkeley: University of California Press, 1946.

Vogel, Ezra F. *Japan As Number One: Lessons for Americans.* Cambridge, MA: Harvard University Press, 1979.

Weglyn, Michi Nishiura. *Years of Infamy: The Untold Story of America's Concentration Camps.* New York: William Morrow and Company, 1976.

Wilson, Robert A. and William K. Hosokawa. *East to America: A History of the Japanese in the United States.* New York: William Morrow and Company, 1980.

Wollenberg, Charles. *Rebel Lawyer: Wayne Collins and the Defense of Japanese American Rights.* Berkeley: Heyday Books, 2018.

Yamamoto, Eric K., Margaret Chon, Carol L. Izumi, Jerry Kang, and Frank H. Wu. *Race, Rights and Reparation: Law and the Japanese American Internment.* New York: Aspen Publishers, 2001.

Yamasaki, Edward, ed. *And Then There Were Eight.* Honolulu: Item Chapter, 442nd Veterans Club, 2003.

Yoshida, George. *Reminiscing in Swingtime: Japanese Americans in America Popular Music:1925-1960.* San Francisco: National Japanese American Historical Society, 1997.

ABOUT THE AUTHOR

Minoru Yanagihashi was brought up in the multicultural Hawaiian environment. Early on, he developed an interest in learning about his Japanese heritage and a desire to share this knowledge with others. He holds degrees from the University of Hawaii at Manoa (BA), University of Washington (MLS), University of California, Berkeley (MA), and University of Michigan (PhD). Before embarking on his teaching career, he served as an officer with the 32nd Infantry Regiment, 7th Division, in South Korea and was a reference librarian at California State University at Los Angeles. His teaching experience includes the University of Michigan, University of Colorado, University of Kansas, Canisius College, and University of Arizona. His interest ranges from Japanese electoral politics, in which he did field research in Hyogo Prefecture under a Fulbright-Hays grant, to Japan's foreign policy and relations. In recent years, he has focused on the role of Japanese Americans in Hawai'i and on the mainland. Participation in community-wide ethnic organizations has been a vital part of his background. He is a charter member of Pan-Asian Community Alliance, Japan-America Society of Tucson, and the Southern Arizona Japanese Cultural Coalition.